T0314132

THE PROFESSIONAL LITERARY AGENT IN BRITAIN, 1880–1920

The Professional Literary Agent in Britain, 1880–1920

MARY ANN GILLIES

UNIVERSITY OF TORONTO PRESS
Toronto   Buffalo   London

© University of Toronto Press Incorporated 2007
Toronto Buffalo London
Printed in Canada

ISBN 978-0-8020–9147-5

Printed on acid-free paper

Library and Archives Canada Cataloguing in Publication

Gillies, Mary Ann, 1959–
The professional literary agent in Britain, 1880–1920 / Mary Ann Gillies.

(Studies in book and print culture)
Includes bibliographical references and index.
ISBN 978-0-8020-9147-5

1. Literary agents – Great Britain – History – 19th century. 2. Literary agents –
Great Britain – History – 20th century. 3. Authors and publishers – Great
Britain – History – 19th century. 4. Authors and publishers – Great Britain –
History – 20th century. I. Title. II. Series.

PN163.G45 2007   070.5'20941   C2007-901488-7

University of Toronto Press acknowledges the financial assistance to its publishing
program of the Canada Council for the Arts and the Ontario Arts Council.

This book has been published with the help of a grant from the Canadian Federation for the Humanities and Social Sciences, through the Aid to Scholarly Publications Programme, using funds provided by the Social Sciences and
Humanities Research Council of Canada.

University of Toronto Press acknowledges the financial support for its publishing activities of the Government of Canada through the Book Publishing
Industry Development Program (BPIDP).

For F.W.E.

Contents

Acknowledgments

I wish to acknowledge the following for providing financial support that enabled me to undertake this project. A Canada Research Fellowship, provided by the Social Sciences and Humanities Research Council of Canada, allowed me to begin the research and writing of this book. Generous financial support provided over the years by various fellowships and grants awarded by Simon Fraser University – a President's Research Grant, SFU/SSHRC Small SSHRC Grants, and SSHRC Travel Grants – permitted me to continue the work and to complete the project. The publication of this book was made possible by a grant from the Aid to Scholarly Publications Program, administered by the Canadian Federation for the Humanities and the Social Science Federation of Canada. I am grateful not only for their support of my book, but more importantly, for their ongoing commitment to humanities and social sciences research in Canada.

Contemporary print culture scholarship makes much of the fact that an individual text is the product of many different collaborative functions. In practice, this means that authors incur debts of many kinds at every stage of composition. This book has taken over a decade to reach its final audience and in that space of time I have been sustained by the wisdom, encouragement, and friendship of colleagues, friends, and family. These people have meant the world to me over the last decade and more.

At the University of Toronto Press, I have incurred many debts. Jill McConkey, my editor, has been an unfailing source of encouragement and wisdom. I owe the publication of this book in large measure to her faith in it. I wish also to thank Barbara Porter, Editor, Managing Editorial Department, for seeing the book through the publication process, and Judy Williams, whose insightful and careful interventions at the copy-editing stage were most welcome. I am truly grateful to the Press's anonymous readers for their perceptive comments on the manuscript. The book is a better study of literary agency because they gave so generously of their time and knowledge.

While researching the book, I was fortunate to work in several literary archives. First and foremost, I must thank R. Russell Maylone, Curator of the McCormick Library of Special Collections at Northwestern University, who not only gave me access to the Pinker Papers housed in his collection, but whose enthusiasm in showing a novice how to explore archival material provided a foundation for this project. Mrs Ellen V. Howe, volunteer extraordinaire at the McCormick, inspired me to make sure that this study would be accessible to all interested readers. I am grateful as well to the Curator and staff at the Manuscripts Department, The University of North Carolina at Chapel Hill, where I consulted the A.P. Watt Papers. The Curator and staff of the Manuscripts Room at the library, Trinity College, Dublin, were very helpful when I consulted the papers of Edith Somerville and Violet Martin housed there. I spent significant time at the New York Public Library consulting materials held in the Berg Collection and I am grateful to the assistance provided by successive curators and their staffs. Lynn Copeland, Simon Fraser's University Librarian, and her staff have cheerfully handled every request I have made of them, for which I thank them.

Valerie Pinker and the late Nigel Gowland, J.B. Pinker's grandchildren, very generously shared their family lore with me. Valerie's comments helped to correct some lingering misconceptions about her grandfather's life, for which I am in her debt. I very much regret that Nigel is no longer with us to see this book published.

I have had the pleasure of the company of many colleagues during this project and while I thank them all, a few deserve special mention. I owe a debt to Ronald Bond that I will never be able to repay – without his intervention at a crucial moment in my career, the research for this book would never have been undertaken. I am most grateful to Betty A. Schellenberg and Carole Gerson who not only read the final manuscript, but who also commented on various chapters in draft form. Paul Keen read significant parts of early drafts, for which I thank him. Talia Schaffer and Patricia Lorimer Lundberg were invaluable sources for information on Lucas Malet and I thank them for sharing so freely of their own work. Patricia Thomas Srebrnik, Anne McWhir, David Oakleaf, David Finkelstein, Leith Davis, James L. West III, and Sharon

Shaloo encouraged the work from the beginning of the project, long before it became fashionable to undertake print culture studies. My colleagues in the English Department at Simon Fraser University have graciously listened to my musings on the literary agent and I thank, in particular, Paul Budra, Paul Delany, Sandra Djwa, Tom Grieve, Anne Higgins, and Sheila Roberts.

I have benefited from the assistance of several fine graduate and undergraduate research assistants over the years. I thank Pamela Bedore, Stephen Collis, Britta Duggan, Terry Han, Lee Simons, and Amanda Watson.

Dania Sheldon compiled the index and Christopher Weeks and Rick Bellairs assisted with reading the proofs. I am grateful to them for their help.

My family's love and encouragement make the difference in my life and I wish to acknowledge them here: Ron Gillies, John and Sherry Gillies, Alan Gillies, Carolyn and Terry Gawalko. I am sorry that my mother did not live to see this project finished as I valued her comments and insights over the years and would have loved to present her with a copy of this book. I am most grateful to the following wonderful people who have sustained me in so many ways over the years: Ila Burdette, Gary Maier, Leslie Poole, Joseph McAleer Jr., Janis McCaffrey, Hilary McKay, Louise Doyle, May Chow, Patricia Aarvold, Joan Barker, Robin and Steve Forrest, Mavis Hanneson, and Juanita Tucker. The completion of this book would not have been possible without the wise counsel of Dr Maylynn Woo, for which I will be forever grateful.

Permissions

Every effort has been made to obtain permission from the copyright holders of unpublished material from which I quote in this book. I am grateful to the following for granting me permission to quote.

Excerpts from letters from 'Lucas Malet' are reproduced by permission of Professor Peter Covey-Crump.

Excerpts from letters from George MacDonald are reproduced by permission of Laura Clark Brown, Head of Public Services, Manuscripts Department, The University of North Carolina at Chapel Hill.

Excerpts from letters from Rebecca West are reproduced by permission of PFD (www.pfd.co.uk) on behalf of the Estate of Rebecca West.

Excerpts from letters from A.A. Milne, Copyright © The Estate of C.R. Milne reproduced with permission of Curtis Brown Group Limited, London.

Excerpts from letters written by AP Watt and contracts negotiated by AP Watt are reproduced with permission of AP Watt Ltd on behalf of AP Watt Ltd.

Excerpts from letters written by Edith Somerville and Violet Martin are reproduced with permission of Curtis Brown Group Ltd, London on behalf of the Estate of Somerville and Ross. Copyright © Somerville and Ross.

Excerpt from contract of Wilkie Collins reproduced with the permission of Faith Clarke.

Excerpt from letter from Cassell to A.P. Watt reproduced with the permission of Cassell PLC.

Excerpts from materials held in the Berg Collection of English and American Literature; The New York Public Library; Astor, Lenox and Tilden Foundations are reproduced by permission of Wayne Furman, Office of Special Collections, New York Public Library.

THE PROFESSIONAL LITERARY AGENT IN BRITAIN, 1880–1920

Introduction

This is the age of the middleman. He is generally a parasite. He always flour-
ishes. I have been forced to give him some attention lately in my particular business. In it he calls himself the literary agent.[1]

William Heinemann concluded his remarks on literary agents, made in
the *Athenaeum* in 1893, with this wish: 'I cannot help hoping that [The
Society of Authors] will go a step further and lend its powerful aid to kill
the canker that is eating itself into the very heart of our mutual
interests.'[2] Heinemann's virulently anti-agent comments are among the
first salvos launched in one of the most contentious debates in turn-of-
the-twentieth-century literary culture. Publishers almost uniformly
condemned the literary agent as an unwelcome, opportunistic inter-
loper. Agents were singled out for harsh criticism on all sorts of
grounds, not the least of which was Heinemann's later contention that
'once an author gets into the claws of a typical agent, he is lost to
decency. He generally adopts the moral outlook of the trickster, which
the agent inoculates with all rapidity, and the virus is so poisonous that
the publisher had better disinfect himself and avoid contagion.'[3]

However, the anger manifest in Heinemann's 1893 comments seems
disproportionate to the immediate provocation. In 1894, for example,
there were only six agents registered in the London *Post Office Directory*.[4]
Moreover, the actions performed by agents – negotiating contracts,
advising their clients on how to revise a manuscript for sale or what
price to ask for it – had previously been carried out by men and women
who were not publishers. Indeed, Anne Goldgar points out that in
Holland during the eighteenth century, individuals, whom she calls
agents, performed many of the functions we associate with literary

agents. As she notes, these men went 'to great lengths to find publishers, make terms, and even, on occasion, represent authors in written contracts.'[5] They were not paid for these services, earning their living, instead, as correctors of proofs or in some other capacity related to the book trade. Writing in the *Athenaeum* in 1897, A.B. Bence-Jones remarks that Lord Brougham wrote about the existence of literary agents in revolutionary France. Bence-Jones quotes Brougham's comments from *Albert Lumel*, dating from 1844, but published in 1872. Brougham stated that in late eighteenth- and early nineteenth-century France, there existed

> A middleman between the publisher and the author, like a regrater between the hop-grower and the hop-merchant or the brewer, a *verlager* they call him, [who] would come round to make bargains, buying up the MS. which was ready written, or else setting authors to write. Those who wanted a vent for their written works or sought employment and could not wait till applied to, being unemployed, would go to some *verlager* and make their bargains.[6]

Other middlemen were actively at work in the nineteenth-century publishing world on both sides of the Atlantic.

Charles Johanningsmeier points out that in America from about 1860 onwards, newspaper unions, such as the American Newspaper Union or the Western Newspaper Union, and then newspaper syndicates, such as Irving Batchelor's or S.S. McClure's, acted as literary middlemen. They procured material – fiction and non-fiction – from authors and sold it in various formats to the newspapers that were members of their union or syndicate.[7] As Johanningsmeier says, the syndicates published a wide cross-section of authors, from those 'whose names are unrecognized today' to those 'who have been and are the object of extensive scholarly research.'[8] Such newspaper syndicates had been active in Britain from the 1850s, and Heinemann regularly conducted business with the best-known of them, Tillotson's Newspaper Bureau, which had been founded in Bolton in 1871.[9] In the realm of public lectures, a lucrative sideline for writers, middlemen were also very active. From at least the middle of the nineteenth century, bureaus were set up to arrange for lecture or speaking tours. In America, the most famous of these was James Redpath's Boston Lyceum Bureau, which booked tours for many of the eminent writers of the period – American and British alike.

Back in England, literary middlemen carried out a variety of services. In 1830, Thomas Hailes Lacy established the firm that in the 1850s was to become the Samuel French dramatic agency. His innovation was to license the rights to the texts of popular dramatic works and then publish them so that actors would have a full script to work with; he also began the practice of sub-licensing the performing rights to the plays to amateur and provincial acting companies.[10] In both cases, his firm took a share of the royalties earned by the owner of the dramatic work from these licences. Throughout the century, publishers' readers often acted as *de facto* agents, not only screening manuscripts for their employers, but also proffering advice to the writers who had submitted them. Geraldine Jewsbury and Edward Garnett are two noteworthy publishers' readers who operated in this fashion in the last few decades of the nineteenth century.[11] Finally, as James Hepburn and others have suggested, literary agents 'performed a task that others had been doing as long as authors have had friends.'[12] George Henry Lewes's actions on behalf of George Eliot are well known, as are the services provided by John Forster for Charles Dickens and other writers.[13]

In light of the history and importance of these various middlemen, what was it about the newest middleman – the literary agent – that excited such animosity from Heinemann? There are likely two main reasons. First, he feared the agent's emergence as a powerful figure in the business of publishing; this fear was based on his deep anxiety over the shifts in business practices occurring in the book trade, shifts which he believed were deleterious not only to publishers but to the trade as a whole, and for which he believed the agent bore, at the very least, some responsibility.[14] As Heinemann knew, the emergence of the literary agent threatened to manifestly alter traditional trade practices. Indeed, an agent bought and sold copyrights much as a cotton broker bought and sold cotton: he sought out markets for his clients' products in which he could secure the highest price for the commodities he had to sell.[15] This was not the gentlemanly conduct that Heinemann and others believed was the way the publishing business ought to be conducted. Heinemann's second, and arguably greater, fear was that literary agents would alter the relations between authors and publishers to such an extent that they would no longer be recognizable. He expressed this latter concern forcefully in 1893 when he said that agents would '[eat themselves] into the very heart of [author-publisher] mutual interests.'[16] By inserting himself into the middle of the publisher-author dyad, the agent not only disrupted social relations between individual publishers and authors, but also destabilized the underlying social conventions that had created and supported the dyad in the first place. As the record shows, Heinemann had sound justification for his animosity and fear, for by 1905 agents were becoming fixtures in the publishing world. By 1914 they had thoroughly insinuated themselves into the fabric of publishing and literary culture, and in the process of doing so had contributed to a wholesale change in it.[17]

The central concern of this book is to identify the ways in which the literary agent's interventions in the publishing world challenged existing practices, and to use the information gleaned from identifying these changes to support the contention that literary agents were important players in the transformation of literary culture in the period 1880–1920. However, this study's narrative of the agent's rise to prominence, like any story, is consciously constructed. The dialogues occurring in contemporary print culture studies supply the framework in which this construction takes place.[18] John O. Jordan and Robert L. Patten's *Literature in the Marketplace* has become a touchstone for scholars seeking to develop an approach to what they rightly say is 'a subject still in its formative phase.'[19] Jordan and Patten identify twin impulses to which scholars would be wise to pay heed – the drive to acquire 'the small and intransigent details' that 'form a bedrock of fact' on which we may build our histories of literary production, circulation, and consumption; and the necessary realization that these '"details" differ according to the nature of the story or argument being constructed.'[20] They argue that close attention to both impulses is a basic requirement of contemporary print culture scholarship. By combining the two, a flexible, but rigorous, framework can be fashioned.

The current study's 'small and intransigent details' have been culled from a wide variety of sources. The two most important of these are the archives of literary agents and publishers, which contain letters, diaries, account ledgers, and contracts;[21] and the books and periodicals of the time in which not only were the products of the agents' clients printed, but so too were the debates surrounding the state of literary culture. As subsequent chapters will illustrate, by having access to the daily correspondence agents conducted with their writers, with publishers, and with other members of their own agencies, for example, it has been possible to reconstruct not only the business practices, but also the personal relationships that ensued. As a result, a far more comprehensive account of the agent's role may be developed than heretofore has been accomplished.[22]

The 'nature of the story or argument being constructed' depends on the fundamental assumption underpinning this study, which is that, in Janet Wolff's words, 'Art is a social product.'[23] Although such a statement is so deceptively simple as to appear banal, it nonetheless explicitly or implicitly underpins some of the most interesting and most important scholarship that has been undertaken in recent print culture studies – the work of Roger Chartier, Robert Darnton, Nigel Cross, and Peter Keating, for example.[24] This study examines the literary agent's rise to prominence within the social contexts in which that rise happened. In practice that means examining the ways in which the agent's emergence shaped or reshaped various facets of publishing – from publishing contracts to advertising campaigns for books to public relations for authors, for instance – as well as the social institutions or structures in which these facets existed.

Given the mass of 'small details' accumulated from the archives, it was necessary to impose some limitations on the current study in order to make the story it would tell manageable. Literary agency went through two distinct phases during the period in which it was establishing itself. Selecting one agent from each phase permits a charting of the changes within the agenting profession as a whole. Examining different agents' interactions with other figures and issues in the book trade during these two phases also provides an instructive contrast that illuminates not just the workings within individual literary agencies or the relationships that authors and agents enjoyed but also how the print culture field operated and altered over time. Including A.P. Watt was an easy decision. He is generally regarded as the first professional literary agent; indeed, such was his importance that an article written at Watt's death by W. Robertson Nicoll bore the headline: 'A.P. Watt: The Great Napoleon of the Realms of Print.' Studying him makes a logical starting point. Whom to include from the second wave of agenting, which began in the late 1890s, is more difficult. Two individuals stand out: Albert Curtis Brown and James Brand Pinker. Pinker was selected because, like Watt, he was a pioneer whose actions had significant influence in the broader field of print culture, and more specifically in the professionalization of authorship. The time frame for this book is directly related to the lives of these two men. Watt first began to function as an agent around 1880 and Pinker died in 1922, thus ending the formative era in the history of literary agency. Examining the working lives of the two of them provides a compelling portrait of the emergence and rise of the agent.

Which of the agents' clients to include in the study also provides a substantial challenge, since Watt and Pinker represented a who's who of writers of their era. Two major principles shaped the choices here. Most writers at the time produced material for a wide variety of publication venues. The dynamics of the venues might in general be governed by the literary marketplace's rules, but on an individual level they functioned in variable ways. Here a concept called publishing planes, developed by Henry Seidel Canby, provides a useful way forward. For Canby, the planes of publishing were intimately related to the need to match different books to different audiences. In her work on the Book-of-the-Month Club, Janice Radway notes that Canby and the other Club selectors 'thought of the literary field itself as a universe encompassing all kinds of print productions' and thus 'they categorically differentiated books from each other on the basis of their differential functions and variable appeals to readers.'[25] Radway further elaborates on Canby's notions of planes, concluding that the 'very concept of different planes … constructs a vision of a print universe conceived not as an organic, uniform, hierarchically-ordered space. Rather, the print universe appears as a series of discontinuous, discrete, noncongruent worlds.'[26] David Finkelstein makes this aspect of Radway's argument explicit when he says, 'in many cases, different arenas or planes of textual production, whether it be how-to manuals, atlases, science textbooks, biographies, or novels, quite openly operate on differing planes of meaning, meeting the needs of different audiences with discrete and technically distinct codes, structures, and formats.'[27] Since it would have been impossible to deal fully, or even adequately, with more than one or two publishing planes, the study focuses on one plane.

The fiction plane is an obvious choice, in part because it was the most volatile of publishing planes at the end of the nineteenth century and in part because of its ever-growing domination of the literary marketplace. Simon Eliot notes that in the period from 1814 to 1846, the *Bibliotheca Londinensis* shows fiction, which was grouped with juvenile literature, as making up 16.2 per cent of titles published. This put it in third place, behind religion at 20.3 per cent and geography, travel, history, and biography at 17.3 per cent.[28] By the 1890s, fiction had taken over first place, accounting for 31.5 per cent of titles published, with religion falling to 9.5 per cent and geography, travel, history, and biography to 11.7 per cent.[29] When one considers that the periodical press also published a substantial amount of fiction – by the 1890s a growing amount of it in the form of short stories that might not be republished in book form –

then it becomes clear that fiction likely dominated much more than 30 per cent of the literary marketplace. Eliot is rightly cautious in his presentation of these statistics, noting both 'the statistical problems which inevitably confront any enquiry into the patterns of book publication in the nineteenth century' and the reality that it is difficult, to say the least, to sort out publishing statistics when the material is poorly organized.[30] Nonetheless, fiction clearly did occupy a significant place in the late nineteenth-century marketplace. Because it did, it also occupied a larger portion of agents' time than any other genre of literature.

The second broad principle employed in selecting the authors for study was to balance their genders and status, so as to provide a more comprehensive picture of agents' interactions with their clients. Balancing genders was particularly important. A growing body of scholarship has demonstrated that while women authors were significant players in print culture from at least the eighteenth century, they have not always been accorded the critical attention that their numbers deserve.[31] Examining the interactions of Lucas Malet and of Somerville and Ross with Watt and Pinker respectively provides some insight not only into the business of literary agenting, but also into the working lives of women writers of the period. Balancing status was equally important, given that one of the lingering perceptions about agents is that they were happy to represent commercial authors, but were less happy, or willing, to represent writers for whose work there was no ready market. Thus George MacDonald and Somerville and Ross were selected to represent authors for whom there was a ready commercial market. MacDonald's children's novels and Somerville and Ross's hunting stories are still in print today, attesting to their ongoing popularity.[32] In contrast, although Joseph Conrad and Lucas Malet also achieved commercial success during their lifetimes (and continuing throughout the twentieth century in Conrad's case), their fiction was accorded the kind of critical recognition that was for the most part denied to MacDonald and Somerville and Ross.

Before this introduction is brought to a close, a final word is needed to explain why this study was written, particularly in light of the plethora of books about publishers, authors, and other aspects of print culture that have appeared in the last decade or so. Jordan and Patten identify four principles that they believe ought to form the foundation of a new approach to publishing history. The first of these is 'the principle of mediation,' which requires an examination of the ways in which 'mediating agencies altered the nature, pace, and results of publishing.'[33] Among the 'mediating agencies' they identify is the literary agent. While work on this book predates the publication of Jordan and Patten's remarks, it nonetheless was fuelled by the same belief that the examination of mediating agencies is crucial to a renewed understanding of print culture at the turn of the twentieth century. Indeed, this study originated from the observation that though literary agents were major figures in the print production of this period, they have seldom been accorded the same level of attention as other key figures, such as authors, publishers, or editors. To date there is only one full-length account of literary agency, James Hepburn's *The Author's Empty Purse and the Rise of the Literary Agent*, which was published in 1968. Hepburn's study is an invaluable source of information, but it is preoccupied with making the case for the agent's inclusion in scholarly assessments of publishing history. To make his point, Hepburn traces the agent's emergence and rise to influence in a broad context, at points necessarily sacrificing depth of analysis for breadth. In contrast, this study accepts that Hepburn has made the case for inclusion of agents and thus is more concerned with examining what agents did for their clients and how the actions they took influenced not only the careers of their individual clients but also literary culture as a whole.

Other publications that treat literary agency fall into three broad categories: memoirs written by literary agents, such as Albert Curtis Brown's *Contacts*; studies of publishing houses or individual authors in which attention is paid to the roles played by literary agents, such as Finkelstein's *The House of Blackwood* or Hepburn's edition of the correspondence between Pinker and Arnold Bennett, *Letters to J.B. Pinker*, and more general treatments of several authors or broad thematic accounts in which the agent figures as one of many individuals being examined, such as Victor Bonham-Carter's *Authors by Profession*, John Feather's *A History of British Publishing*, Joyce Wexler's *Who Paid for Modernism?* or Peter McDonald's *British Literary Culture and Publishing Practice 1880–1914*. Memoirs are valuable for the perspectives they provide, given that the authors worked as agents and thus have intimate knowledge of the tasks involved in the profession and of the personalities of agents and clients alike. However, they are of limited value in a more broadly based reconsideration of the agents' influence on the field of print culture because they generally lack the necessary scope that would enable them to look beyond the author's own experiences. Studies such as Finkelstein's that look at the interaction between an agent and a client (whether author or publisher) play a significant, though limited, role in mapping out the agent's position. They are important because they often bring to light specific services agents performed for their clients and they also articulate the roles agents played in the publication of specific texts, yet they are limited because their focus is restricted. In books such as Bonham-Carter's or Feather's, which provide wide-ranging treatments of publishing in Britain, accounts of agents rarely occupy more than a dozen pages. Thus their comments on literary agency lack depth and comprehensiveness. Studies such as McDonald's or Wexler's, in which discussions of an agent's activities for several clients contribute to the broader arguments being formulated, raise the profile of agents and support the general arguments put forward in this study about the central position agents held in print culture. However, since the agent's activities are primarily presented in order to illuminate the larger issues with which these critics are concerned rather than for the purpose of enlightening the reader about agents, we see a limited spectrum of what agents do. Through no fault of the authors, whose interest and subject matter reasonably lie elsewhere, readers are thus left with fragmentary impressions of agents. In marked contrast to previous work, this study takes a much more comprehensive look at agents by contrasting the practices of Watt and Pinker, by drawing on a cross-section of authors, and by extensively deploying 'small details' gleaned from archives in aid of the arguments put forward.

In the process of delineating the role played by the literary agent in the crucial period of 1880–1920, this book heeds Jordan and Patten's call for publishing history to dispense with 'the linear paradigms of production that commence with the writer's idea and proceed straightforwardly to publication and reception' in favour of 'conceptions of the activity of producing and consuming books that decenter the principal elements and make them interactive and interdependent.'[34] By so doing, it takes part in the wider project of contemporary print culture studies, that of knowing 'more about how books were produced and consumed' and understanding 'how that knowledge directs as well as contributes to our interpretations of culture and history.'[35]

1 Why Did the Professional Literary Agent Emerge in the 1880s?

In the late 1870s, A.P. Watt set up shop as a literary agent. His self-proclaimed task was to 'do nothing but sell or lease copyrights,'[1] and to make his living doing so, thereby distinguishing him from 'amateur' literary agents – the friends or relatives of writers – who had preceded him. Before examining Watt's establishment of himself as a literary agent, it is necessary to answer the question: what was it about this time that prompted Watt, and others who followed his lead, to embark on a business that until then had not been thought of as necessary? If we look outside the publishing world to some of the major social and material shifts occurring in Victorian Britain, we may be able to identify a few events, policies, or practices that contributed to the changes occurring within print culture at this time that paved the way for the agent's emergence.

Material Shifts

Chief among the material shifts would be modifications of existing taxation policies and technological innovations that altered how printed matter was produced. The fight for the abolition of the 'tax on knowledge' was revived and led in 1851 by Richard Cobden's Parliamentary select committee.[2] As a result of the committee's work, the penny tax on newspapers was abolished in 1855 and in 1861 the paper duty was eliminated. The publishing world was thus freer from political and economic restrictions than it had been since early in the eighteenth century. One would expect that this economic change would prompt a response in the literary marketplace, likely increasing the amount of printed matter produced and also increasing the incomes of the producers of the material – authors and publishers. There was, indeed, a substantial increase in printed matter. However, the expected increases in income did not materialize in the way envisioned. Competition within the marketplace itself increased dramatically as its current denizens contested their positions not only against their customary opponents, but also against new rivals who sought to take advantage of the opportunities created by the abolition of paper taxes and duties. Some individual authors, editors, or publishers did increase their economic capital, but many found themselves worse off than they had been before the changes in taxation policy. Their shares of the market were smaller than anticipated because of the increased competition, and they had to work harder to maintain the share that they already had.

Similarly, scientific breakthroughs also played significant roles in print culture. Advances in engineering, specifically in terms of steam- or electric-powered machines, had direct impact on printing technology. The widespread use of steam-powered printing machines in the 1840s; the introduction of the high-speed Hoe press from America in the 1860s, used primarily for printing newspapers and mass-circulation periodicals; and the advent of the linotype machine in 1886, which changed the way that type was set, dramatically changed the way that printed matter was produced.[3] As Richard Altick says, 'toward the end of the century ... periodical printing became one of the most highly mechanized of all English mass-production industries.'[4] Yet not all members of the literary world viewed mechanization as a success. Indeed, some commentators at the time saw the mass production of printed material as symptomatic of what Henry James called 'This age of advertisement and newspaperism,'[5] by which he meant the end of literature as a gentleman's pastime and the emergence of a vulgar, commercial literary culture. Thus rather than being an unqualified boost, technological innovation created greater tension in literary culture and, in fact, challenged the rules and norms by which it functioned.

Social Factors

Taxes and technology alone do not account for the great post-1870 boom in the publishing industry, nor do they explain the substantial and sustained change in the print culture field itself. Although a number of important social factors could be cited, two broad elements can be isolated that provide some insights into what led to the boom: the growth in market demand for reading material and the professionalization of authorship that accelerated throughout the nineteenth century.

Reading Demand

In 1957, Richard Altick, in *The English Common Reader,* stated: 'Everyone knows that in the nineteenth century the number of readers, and there-fore the productions of the press, multiplied, spectacularly.' He went on to lament that 'the phenomenon has been taken for granted; the whys and hows have not been inquired into.'[6] Altick, of course, rectified this in his monumental study, in which he catalogued the 'whys and hows,' and in the process charted the growth of literacy in England during the nineteenth century. Jonathan Rose's book *The Intellectual Life of the British Working Classes* (2001) builds on Altick's landmark study. Together these two works admirably document many of the social and material conditions that resulted in widespread literacy among all classes in Britain by the end of the nineteenth century.[7] This widespread literacy is a principal cause of the increased demand for reading mate-rial that helped fuel the post-1870 publishing boom.[8]

Altick and Rose make clear that the growth in literacy was incremen-tal from about 1800 until the late 1860s, with the numbers of readers slowly increasing as the century wore on.[9] Literacy was highest among the upper and middle classes whose money gave them access to private schooling – tutors or governesses were the educational choice of some, while others sent their children (mostly their sons) to public or gram-mar schools. In the absence of state-mandated universal education, less well off families had more restricted choices, since public funding for schools, only available from 1833 onwards, was severely limited. This meant that the literacy rate in these classes was markedly lower than in the more privileged groups. Church-based schools were the predominant suppliers of education for lower-middle-class children. These schools' reliance on poorly trained teachers and student moni-tors often meant that education amounted to little more than rote learning; literacy was measured by the students' ability to read selected biblical passages. Working-class families who could not afford even the modest fees charged by church schools sought education for their children in dame schools and private schools designed for the children of upper-working-class families – tradesmen and master arti-sans.[10] Most children emerged from the dame schools functionally illiterate, and the private day schools were frequently no better.[11] As both Altick and Rose concluded, the quality of education for most of those attending church-based, dame, or working-class private day schools 'was fearfully low.'[12]

Yet the demand for higher-quality basic education grew as the century went on, in part fuelled by the increasing numbers of adult learners who looked to mechanics' institutes and working men's colleges to augment the meagre education that they had received as children. They wanted more for their children and were prepared to agitate for change. Throughout the 1850s and 1860s educational reformers from across the social spectrum produced study after study that illustrated that 'England still was plagued with widespread illiteracy.'[13] Their activities bore fruit with the passage of W.E. Forster's Education Act of 1870, which mandated basic elementary level schooling for all children with the government responsible for ensuring that education was provided in locales where voluntary efforts were insufficient. Altick is right to caution us not to exaggerate the effect of the Act, but he is also right to emphasize that the state's intervention in 1871 was crucial in maintaining the steady growth in literacy noticeable from 1800 onwards.[14] By the end of the century even 'very poor children, living in slums or in remote country regions, were taught to read.'[15]

This slow but steady increase in literacy directly affected print culture in two crucial ways: it created an increase in demand for reading material at all levels of society and it subtly began to alter print culture itself. The former point will be dealt with here, while the latter will be taken up later in the chapter.

For the working classes, the self-improvement movement of the nineteenth century, embodied in the figure of the autodidact, meant that there was a growing hunger for all manner of printed material. Science of all sorts, theology, biography, and history, as well as literature, were staples of the self-improver's diet. Because working-class incomes were usually insufficient to permit purchases of new or expensively made books, most books were purchased second hand, borrowed from neighbours, or, more frequently, borrowed from libraries maintained by miners' or workers' associations. These libraries thus became major forces in the publishing world. Producing material that would interest the members of workers' or miners' libraries became attractive because such material often meant guaranteed sales, thus reducing the risks borne by the publisher. Middle-class demands for reading material also rose throughout the century, as leisure time and disposable income increased. While a greater number of middle-class readers could afford to buy books, many still relied on circulating libraries, such as Mudie's, for a regular supply of printed material. Mudie's, and the other libraries, functioned in an analogous fashion to workers' or miners' libraries and thus exerted a similar influence on publishing decisions, though the kind of materials purchased by these libraries often differed in consequence of the middle class's differing backgrounds and tastes. Upper-class readers' numbers were not manifestly altered by a growth in literacy, though, as will be evident later in the chapter, their reading habits were challenged, and even changed, by the flood of material in new formats that swamped the marketplace in the latter part of the century.

By 1880, the effects of mandatory education were beginning to be felt. The call for material in a variety of subjects, but especially in English poetry, fiction, and drama, expanded the school text market, thus enabling publishers to earn steady streams of income from their backlists and copyright holdings.[16] But perhaps most important, the effect of educating so many more of the nation's citizens was to create an appetite for reading outside the schoolroom that could not be satisfied by existing publishing practices.[17] The proliferation of penny papers of all sorts, including illustrated newspapers; the advent of new weekly, monthly, and quarterly magazines; and the pressure on circulating libraries such as Mudie's to provide more novels at lower costs to readers attest to the growing demand for reading material. Indeed, the eventual demise of Mudie's may well be attributed, in part at least, to public demand for a greater variety of inexpensive books.[18] One obvious result of the increased demand for reading material was an increase in the sheer numbers of books, newspapers, and other printed material that were produced by century's end. As will be noted later in the chapter, a more interesting observation is that the insertion of large numbers of readers from differing classes into the literary marketplace altered it in profound ways.

Professionalization of Authorship

Certainly the increased demand for books and periodicals that resulted from a steadily increasing number of readers meant that writers had to produce more material and, in fact, that more writers were able to earn livings from their pens. Indeed, statistics from the nineteenth century bear witness to the fact that the number of writers increased dramatically over the course of the century.[19] The sheer increase in numbers of writers was bound to have ramifications on how authorship was conceived, by writers and non-writers alike. Undoubtedly, one of the most important motivators for reconceptualizing authorship was the increasing amount of what Pierre Bourdieu has called cultural capital – in this case economic capital (money, property, or other financial gain) and symbolic/cultural capital (markers of social recognition) – that was available to members of the print culture field. Authors' strategies to accumulate a larger share of the newly available capital consisted of two main tactics: a drive to enhance their social status, which would enable them to accumulate symbolic/cultural capital and thereby strengthen their claim to a larger share of the available economic capital; and a campaign to amend copyright law so as to secure greater control over their work and thus share in the increased economic capital that it had begun to generate.

The first step to increasing the social status of authors actually began in the eighteenth century where the professionalization of authorship commences.[20] In the eighteenth century, a profession was defined as 'any "calling, vocation, known employment" (Johnson), and it frequently turn[ed] up in the phrase "mechanical professions", meaning the trades of skilled workmen.'[21] Under these terms, authors who earned a living from their writing were, indeed, professionals. Since, as John Feather tells us, 'To make a living from literary writing was a good deal easier in the eighteenth century than it had been before,'[22] we can assume that more writers were able to pursue the profession than in previous centuries. But it was also true that writers' status had not increased at the same rate as their incomes. As Nigel Cross explains, at the beginning of the nineteenth century,

> Authorship was allowed to be the occupation of genius, or the hobby of educated men and women, but everyone else who wrote did so from base commercial motives and were scribblers, hacks and dunces. Robert Southey, who was about the only writer to make a comfortable living from authorship, attempted to protect his unique position by advising would-be competitors to give up their literary aspirations and accept their allotted rank in life ... The problem for the hack ... was how to avoid the undignified and humble rank of bookseller's employee and become a noble freelance like Southey.[23]

By 1830, things had improved somewhat in terms of status for writers, for, as Cross notes, 'the professional writer, as distinct from the genius or amateur, had sloughed off the reputation of hack and scribbler.'[24] Nonetheless, even at mid-century Cross admits that '[t]he common writer might have inched up the social scale but there were still many aspects of the literary profession that went against the grain of Victorian propriety.'[25] A marked change in authors' status, however, does occur after mid-century, and it occurs in part because of a shift in how professions were conceived.

In the nineteenth century, the word 'profession' takes on a different significance. Its wider meaning remains similar to the eighteenth-century usage, since it still refers to 'any calling or occupation by which a person habitually earns his living,' but its specific usage narrowed so that 'profession' was 'usually applied to an occupation considered to be socially superior to a trade or handicraft.'[26] The 'trades of skilled work-men' would be excluded from this new usage precisely because they had no claim to superior social standing. In 1861 the official government census listed 'author' for the first time alongside medicine and law as a profession, thus formally recognizing the migration of authorship from the realm of skilled workers to the realm of professionals.[27]

W.J. Reader observes that the middle class's 'characteristic activities: earning a living, raising the moral tone of society, and social climbing'[28] were directly linked to the emergence of new professions throughout the nineteenth century. Walter Besant's definition of authorship as belonging to the ranks of the 'nobler professions' captures nicely the way in which authors wanted to parlay their professional status into enhanced social status.[29] The characteristics of a noble profession are, he says:

> First of all, it must be independent: i.e., the members must not be servants of anyone: the barrister takes his work from the solicitor, but he is not the servant of the solicitor: next, it must be entitled to share in the national distinctions as much as a soldier, a sailor, or a statesman: and, thirdly, it must have in its gift great prizes, whether of distinction, or of money, or both.[30]

However, in true nineteenth-century fashion, even noble professions required some institution or structure that would not only govern the behaviour of its members, but also restrict membership and thus add prestige to the profession. Indeed, as Reader further suggests, 'An occupation's rise to professional standing can be pretty accurately charted by reference to the progress of its professional institute or organization.'[31] Authors had already tried to organize into a professional association prior to 1861. In fact, the first two attempts – the early eighteenth-century Society for the Encouragement of Learning and the 1843 Society for British Authors – coincided with authors' pressure for control of their work and better remuneration for it. In short, they wished a greater measure of independence. These associations were short lived.[32] By the late 1870s, a third attempt to organize writers was gathering steam. The motivation to establish an authors' union can be traced to a specific event – the work of the 1875 Royal Commission on Copyright. But an additional factor was the prevailing mood of the period with respect to the social status of professionals. Without this status, their independence was at risk.

Walter Besant stepped forward to remedy this situation. He had learned a great deal from the failure of the 1843 Society of British Authors, which he saw as chiefly due to the inadequacies of its founder. 'In every new society,' Besant wrote, 'it is one man, and one man alone, who at the outset determines the success and the future of the association. It is this one man who rules, infuses spirit, collects ideas, orders the line of march, lays down the policy, and thinks for the society.'[33] When he gathered together a group of twelve writers in 1883 with the intention of trying again, Besant followed his own precepts, installing himself as the one man around whom the society would be built. A working party of five, including Besant, was charged with the task of doing 'all things necessary for the foundation of the society.'[34] This group carried out its mandate, resulting in the February 1884 meeting at which it presented a 'Preliminary Prospectus' that was adopted by those in attendance. A new Council was elected, again containing Besant as a member, which was charged with drawing up a constitution and with regulating the activities of the society. Besant became the first chairman of the Society's Board of Management. In this capacity, he oversaw the rest of the necessary arrangements: enticing leading authors to join the board or the various subcommittees, finding a suitably prestigious president, and publishing the society's prospectus.[35] Throughout 1884, Besant carried on with his task, and in June, the Society was officially incorporated.[36] By the autumn of 1884, it was ready for business. Thus duly constituted, the Society of Authors publicly asserted its members' claim to professional status, which carried with it their implicit claims to proper remuneration and appropriate social standing. By 1899, Walter Besant could look back on how authorship was viewed in the eighteenth century – 'a beggarly profession: there was no money in it: there was no dignity in it: and it was not respectable'[37] – with the knowledge that his efforts had increased the dignity and respectability of the profession. Indeed, symbolic capital was flowing freely towards authors, with Besant himself being knighted in 1895.

If professional status depended on independence and 'great prizes' (financial reward), then control of literary property was crucial to achieving this status. Thus Besant's preoccupation with professionalization is allied with one of the central print culture concerns of his era – the ownership and control of copyrights. Copyright ownership and reform has been a recurrent theme throughout the eighteenth, nineteenth, and twentieth centuries. The history of copyright legislation is complex, and is dealt with well elsewhere.[38] What is important for this study is the way in which campaigns for copyright reform were used by authors to gain greater control over their own work.

The first copyright law, the 1710 Statute of Anne, was an essentially conservative piece of legislation, designed to deal with the problems arising from the lapse of the 1662 Licensing Act. As John Feather says,

> it was, in effect, a law designed by its promoters to defend a group of property rights vested in a small number of owners and shareholders. It lacked definition, especially of the key concepts of copies and rights, and, despite the amendments introduced as the Bill passed through the Commons, still left many loopholes for the ingenious ... Above all, it wholly ignored the authors of books, and certainly was not intended to confer any additional rights upon them.[39]

What is significant about this legislation in terms of authors' interests is that it 'merely assumed that a copy was in existence when it came into the hands of a bookseller. The law was for the benefit of the "proprietors", not the creators, of books.'[40] The eighteenth century witnessed a number of challenges to the Statute of Anne. The 1774 case of *Donaldson v Becket*, which eventually was settled in the House of Lords, was probably the most important of these.[41] One of the case's central issues revolved around a definition of authors' rights in their works. The Lords ruled that authors did have rights to their creations, and that those rights had been newly conferred by the 1710 Act. However, copyright in perpetuity was ruled not to exist and the terms created for it in the 1710 Act were upheld. The ruling effectively eliminated the legal basis for the monopoly control of copyrights that led to Donaldson's challenge. Yet it failed to alter existing trade practice in any significant way, for as the eighteenth century came to a close, most authors continued to part with their copyrights as the cost of getting their material in print.

'By the early nineteenth century,' as Mark Rose points out, 'the trade had adjusted to the limited copyright term, and many had a vested interest in it; it was authors such as Southey and Wordsworth who were now claiming that their rights should be perpetual.'[42] Southey's description of the author's situation in 1808 underscores Rose's comments:

My opinion is that literary property ought to be inheritable, like every other property; and that a law which should allow you the use of the trees upon your estate for eight-and-twenty years, and after that term make them over to the Carpenters' Company, would not be more unjust than that which takes from me and my heirs the property of my literary labours, and gives it to the Company of Booksellers.[43]

Modest changes were made to the Act in 1814, yet authors remained dissatisfied, and another round of revision began in 1836. The authors' contentions were similar to Southey's, with William Wordsworth, for example, arguing that authors ought to be able assign their copyrights to their heirs.[44] The pragmatic compromise eventually reached resulted in the extension of posthumous rights to copyright owners, though this did not satisfy many who continued to believe that their literary productions ought to be treated as real property – just like the trees on Southey's proverbial estate.[45]

By the 1880s, changing conditions in the literary marketplace heightened the urgency for further copyright reform. As Feather says, 'For authors, the newspapers and magazines were a major new source of income in the nineteenth and twentieth centuries, rivalling and perhaps often superseding the writing of books.'[46] Existing copyright legislation did little to protect authors' rights over their work in this area. Nor did it take account of the new copying methods or new publishing formats that arose in the last decades of the century – sound recordings, for instance, were possible from 1877 and were not included in existing legislation. It is this debate that Besant, and the Society of Authors, entered into in the 1880s. He joined with publishers and authors in lobbying Parliament and the public for amendments to the copyright legislation of the 1840s, seeking greater protection for copyright holders in Britain and abroad. Unlike the publishers, he was particularly outspoken about the need to have the law acknowledge authors' absolute right to control their work. Indeed, chief among the aims of Besant and the Society of Authors was 'to promote the recognition of the fact, hitherto most imperfectly understood, that literary property is as real a thing as property in every other kind of business: that it should be safeguarded in the same manner, and regarded with the same jealousy.'[47] There are two parts to Besant's case.

First, he took the same line of argument that extends back to the *Donaldson v Beckett* case of 1774. That is, he argued that a text should be treated as any other form of property, the owner's right to it being protected for as long as the property belongs to him or her. He was particularly concerned about the status of a copyright in terms of inheritance. Just like his predecessors, he did not succeed in changing the legal ruling that literary productions were not comparable to other forms of property. However, again like his predecessors, he did help to bring about an increase of the term of copyright to the standard of the author's life plus fifty years, which was central to the 1911 Copyright Act.

Because revisions to copyright law did not change the property status of literary productions, the second part of Besant's argument was the more important. Even though the *Donaldson v Beckett* case had confirmed authors' rights to their production, economic necessity and the custom of the trade meant that even in the latter part of the nineteenth century authors, ironically including Besant, continued to sell their copyrights outright. Besant knew that with the increase in demand for printed material and the various new ways of packaging and selling it, copyrights had become extremely valuable commodities. A single work could be sold many times over, and thus generate substantial income for the copyright holder. When publishers successfully exploited the copyrights they had purchased, writers had no legal way to force them to share in the extra income thus garnered or to compel them to obtain an author's approval of the format or place in which his or her work would appear. Besant, and the Society of Authors, advocated that authors not sell copyrights outright; they suggested that writers lease their copyrights for specific periods and formats. But Besant did not want to leave the authors' control over their work solely in the province of publishing contracts, knowing all too well the pressure that could be put on an author to part with the copyright in return for publication. He wanted to see the authors' rights to control their property protected by law, thereby ensuring such control for all authors, and not just those powerful, or astute, enough to negotiate good contracts. In this goal he was more successful, since the 1911 Copyright Act did, indeed, do just this. In it 'the author was explicitly in control of the work; the rights of translation, abridgement, dramatization, or any other from of adaptation, were clearly the author's and only the author's.'[48]

Authors' conduct had altered significantly from what it had been at the beginning of the century. They were a great deal more independent, in large measure because of the financial rewards available to them from an expanded marketplace and because of changes in copyright laws that made it possible for them to claim a greater share of these rewards for themselves.[49] Distinctions had also begun to flow more freely towards literary men and women, in the form of peerages and other markers of status; thus the cultural capital of authorship thrived alongside the economic capital. Besant's vision of the professional author – the 'respectable man of letters [who] may command an income and a position quite equal to those of the average lawyer or doctor'[50] – had, for many writers, become fact. Authors were thus better placed to press their case for a further advancement of their interests. Yet no matter how authors chose to situate themselves in the changing literary world, they all had to take into account the metamorphosis it was undergoing.

Transformation of Print Culture

It is a commonplace to state that the last quarter of the nineteenth century witnessed an extraordinary transformation in the book trade, yet the magnitude of this transformation is lost unless we have a sense of what those changes were and what impact they had. Simon Eliot has charted a number of the changes in various facets of the publishing world: his figures tell us that the marketplace boom hit almost all segments of the industry. For instance, 1299 Fiction and Juvenile literature titles were published in 1880, 2109 in 1900; 1835 Journals and 1033 Magazines were published in 1880 while 2471 Journals and 2328 Magazines were published in 1900. At the same time, employment in the book trade was up spectacularly: workers in Paper, Printing and Stationery increased from 187,000 in 1881 to 323,000 in 1901.[51] Periodical circulation figures also reveal the extent of the explosion in the marketplace. Altick notes that *Lloyd's Weekly Newspaper* – an illustrated weekly that competed for readership with the *Illustrated London News* – had a circulation of 350,000 in 1863 and by 1886 it had more than doubled to 750,000.[52] This growth occurred despite the advent of many new illustrated papers aimed at the same readership. Daily newspapers also showed strong increases in readership: *The Times* had a steady base of 50,000–60,000 in the period 1854–68. By 1882, this figure had risen to 100,000 copies sold per day. On the lower status end for daily papers, the *Daily News* had a circulation of 150,000 in 1870, and its counterpart, the *Daily Mail*, had a circulation of 543,000 in 1899.[53] The conclusion one draws from these figures is what the previous two sections have already demonstrated: more people were reading, and there was more for them to read.

Yet the raw figures only hint at the depth of the changes. The first distinction to make is that the increased readership did not all come from the same class or even from the same backgrounds within classes. Paul Delany notes a marked shift in market practices in the later nineteenth century, with the market moving from 'a vertical structure (a scale from highbrow literature to trash) towards a horizontal one by genres appealing to differentiated but formally equal groups of readers. Buyers would now be classified by their interests, gender, or life-styles, rather than their social rank.'[54] This is only possible if the material is priced so that class ceases to be a significant determinant in what one may purchase. The record bears this out, showing that as technology permitted cheap editions to be mass-produced, class barriers became less important. For example, J.M. Dent's Temple Shakespeare (issued 1894–96) 'reproduced the scholarly Cambridge text of the plays and sold for a shilling a volume' and 'for some time it sold 250,000 volumes a year.'[55] Dent introduced his Everyman's Library in 1906, selling classics of literature alongside contemporary works for a shilling a volume.[56]

A second important consideration is that the influx of new readers caused the literary marketplace itself to alter significantly so as to accommodate the different individual tastes and backgrounds readers possessed. Richard Altick states that price had less impact on middle-class magazine readers, who could afford a shilling for a monthly magazine, than did content. He points out that when *Cornhill Magazine* was launched in 1859–60 'the first number ... sold an astounding total, considering its price, of 120,000 copies.' However, as he says, its 'initial success ... was short-lived. Many of its first readers were attracted by its novelty but soon were repelled by its quality. They wanted shilling magazines, but they also wanted more fiction and a lighter literary tone than the *Cornhill* gave them.'[57] He argues that the same dynamics were at work in periodicals aimed at the working-class reader. Jonathan Rose's example of how the readership of popular literature crossed class and gender lines takes Altick's argument one step further by providing an example of how the marketplace and individual tastes can mutually influence each other. He points out that girls as well as boys read the *Boy's Own Paper*, which was a middle-class periodical filled with adventure stories, essays, and puzzles that attempted to inculcate middle-class norms and values. Later entries into the field, the *Gem* and the *Magnet*, which were similar in scope to the *Boy's Own Paper* though aimed primarily at a lower-class audience, had a large following of boys and girls in impoverished households as well as in wealthier ones.[58] Many other examples of how literature crossed the class divide can be cited from this time period; one notable example is that of Somerville and Ross's popular hunting stories, which were read by privates in the trenches of the First World War, by the King and Queen, and by everyone in between.[59] What Delany calls the 'stratification that established a stable division between high and low literary culture' and that permitted the 'domination of the literary scene by a compact group of canonical novelists'[60] had thus broken down in part because of the demand of the new readers and in part because of the effect that the tastes of new readers had on the marketplace.

In similar fashion, authors' newly acquired status and power altered the dynamics of publishing. After mid-century, when not only were there more publication opportunities and venues but also writers began to exercise more control over their own work, power relations noticeably changed. While only a few mid-century writers, such as Dickens, Eliot, or Hardy, had maintained ownership of their copyrights, and thus varying degrees of control over their literary productions, by century's end more and more writers were following their lead. As a result, authors' power increased, much to the discomfort of other members of the literary world, principally the publishers. Readers' increased prominence also shifted the power relations, as now a strong demand from readers for a particular type of novel influenced the book trade far more dramatically than it had at previous points in history. Thus, by 1900, the rules that governed the literary marketplace had changed utterly, leaving readers, writers, and publishers to find their own ways.

Emergence of the Professional Literary Agent

It was into this rapidly changing world that A.P. Watt stepped in the late 1870s. The conditions were ripe for someone like Watt who had the vision to see that a mediating figure was badly needed. Authors initially looked to agents for two specific functions. The first was tied to the extra economic capital an agent could acquire for writers. The horizontal expansion of the marketplace that accelerated after 1870 – new outlets such as illustrated newspapers or radio recordings and new markets such as colonial sales or translations – resulted in a proliferation of Henry Seidel Canby's publishing planes. Even prior to the market's horizontal expansion, as David Finkelstein notes, each plane was geared for 'different audiences with discrete and technically distinct codes, structures, and formats.'[61] Most authors simply did not have the expertise or inclination to learn enough about the various publishing planes to take advantage of the opportunities they offered. This situation did not alter after the market expanded horizontally. Because the agent's livelihood depended on successfully placing material for his clients, he had to be an expert on the various publishing planes, both at home and overseas. In fact, in many cases, agents were better versed in the inner workings of different planes than publishers; thus their expertise provided an important advantage for writers. A good agent, like Watt, could increase an author's income simply by placing material in the right market, in the right format, with the right publisher and at the right time. The 10 per cent commission he charged could be more than made up by the enhanced prices he could get for the writer. Second, employing an agent added to a writer's social status. It indicated to the world that the writer was a professional whose work was significant enough to be managed by another professional.

For publishers, agents also proved useful, despite the fact that their presence had considerable impact on author-publisher relations, a chief source of William Heinemann's animus towards agents. In the first place, publishers also employed agents to sell copyrights they possessed; thus they were able to take advantage of agents' knowledge in the same way as authors did. In the second place, publishers soon learned that agents could procure material for them that they might not have been able to acquire themselves. Much like newspaper syndicators such as Tillotson's or S.S. McClure, an agent developed a network of contacts, domestic and foreign, that spanned the spectrum of publishing planes; thus a publisher in search of a particular type of article or a story by a specific author could often acquire it through the agent's contacts. By the end of the century, publishers, somewhat grudgingly it is true, began to accept that literary agents were well situated to help them.

The introduction of agents into the literary marketplace had far-reaching consequences, as will be illustrated in the following chapters. Agents destabilized the author-publisher dyad, thereby causing changes in the interactions between authors and publishers. The author-agent-publisher triad that gradually became the norm also changed the existing power dynamics, thereby altering the ways in which authors and publishers competed for the limited capital available. Over time, the presence of agents prompted a shift in print culture as well. Thus though the social and material dynamics of 1870s Britain had created ideal conditions for the emergence of the agent, once the agent had assumed his place in the literary world, it began to change in consequence of his presence.

2 A.P. Watt: Professional Literary Agent

In 1975, A.P. Watt and Son celebrated its centenary as a literary agency. As Hilary Rubinstein, a partner in the firm since 1965, wrote at the time, 'Literary agencies, more than most businesses, depend for their success on the personality of their principals'; moreover 'many, probably most, do not outlive the lifetime of their progenitor.'[1] The firm's 'progenitor' – Alexander Pollock Watt – not only established the foundation for his family's business, but also established the profession of literary agency. Watt was, in many respects, an unlikely candidate for such a revolutionary position. He was a reserved man, who was described as having a 'very gentle manner,' an 'inborn dignity,' and 'profound religious feeling.'[2] These are hardly the qualities one would associate with someone who would redefine the working relationship between publisher and author and by so doing help shape the literary landscape of the twentieth century.

Watt was born in Glasgow in 1834; little can be established about his early years. We do know that he worked in an Edinburgh bookseller's establishment, that he married the sister of publisher Alexander Strahan, and that by 1871 he had moved to London to begin working as a reader for Strahan's publishing business.[3] By 1876, he was a partner in the second incarnation of Strahan and Company[4] and by 1878, he was operating as an advertising agent selling advertising space in Strahan's stable of periodicals. At about this time he began the friendship with George MacDonald that led him to establish his literary agency, although it was not until 1881 that Watt advertised himself as a literary, as well as advertising, agent.[4] By 1892, it was possible for an article in the *Bookman* to claim:

> There are few writers of Fiction in this country who are not familiar with the name of A.P. Watt, and perhaps the number is equally small of those

who are unfamiliar with the office on the first floor of 2, Paternoster Square. For it is there that the contracts are made under which, directly or indirectly, most important periodicals in this country, America, Australia, and elsewhere are supplied with the greater part of the novels and stories so necessary to their existence.[6]

In twenty short years, then, Watt had risen from the anonymity of a publisher's reader to the centre of the publishing world. The climb was anything but smooth and, in 1892, it was far from completed. Notwithstanding the favourable comments of the *Bookman*'s interviewer, Watt still had to convince many writers of his usefulness and often encountered outright hostility from publishers. At his death in 1914, however, the agent was a prime player in the publishing world.

Defining Literary Agency

Establishing Basic Business Practices

When A.P. Watt first began placing material for George MacDonald, he was acting as others had before him. He worked for his friend, initially at least, in an unpaid capacity. However, he soon saw commercial possibilities in his activities. His position at Strahan and Company made him well aware of the changes going on in the publishing world, and in particular the trend towards ever-greater commercialization of literature. He saw how publishers could extend their profits by exploiting new markets, but he also witnessed first hand the fact that many publishers were unable to take advantage of these opportunities. Watt was well placed to observe the challenges to the quality magazines published by his brother-in-law's firm from the illustrated weekly newspapers, such as George Newnes's *Tit-Bits*, which was first published in 1881. The new magazines employed different formats – including printing style, layout, and paper – which made them popular with readers and cheaper to produce. Magazines like *Tit-Bits* not only appealed to readers newly entering the literary marketplace, but they also drew readers away from existing segments of the market. Thus *Tit-Bits* and its confrères forced established periodicals to adapt existing business practices to compete with them. In addition, Watt's activities as an advertising agent, primarily for Strahan, but also for other firms, had enabled him to learn the rules and norms of different publishing planes, thereby providing him with a broad-based knowledge of the rapidly expanding marketplace.

This advantage was augmented by Watt's activities as an assessor of publisher's assets. He became intimately acquainted with the values of stock, materials, and, most important, copyrights. Thus, while Watt was still working for his brother-in-law, he was also educating himself about the literary marketplace. In the process, he acquired a valuable commodity that he was able to rely on when Strahan and Company failed, leaving him to find an alternative way to earn his living. His thorough knowledge of the inner workings of publishing became the capital of the business he was about to found, while his network of acquaintances, established and nurtured during his years working for his brother-in-law, formed the foundation of his enterprise. He was very well placed to establish himself as a powerful mediator between producers and publishers of literature.

The first consideration in setting up shop as an agent was financial. In the absence of any existing guidelines, Watt had to determine how, and how much, he should be paid for his professional services. Initially, he charged set fees for specific tasks – for writing letters, telegraph expenses, drawing up contracts, and so on.[7] This proved unsatisfactory, as the sums he charged were sometimes inadequate to cover the work involved. Very quickly, he settled on the commission system he had employed as an advertising agent. By charging a 10 per cent fee on the monies his clients earned from the transactions he handled for them, he set the practice that still exists today. Eventually, Watt's in-house agent-client contracts and the publishing contracts he negotiated for his clients included clauses stating that royalties were to be paid to the agent, who would, in turn, pass them on to the writer after deducting his commission.

The next task was to determine how an agent would relate to publishers and authors. Today we tend to think of agents as solely, or at least primarily, the representatives of authors, useful not only for their business knowledge but also for their skill in representing the author's interests in dealings with powerful publishers. In other words, we see the agent as the author's advocate. Yet when Watt began his career, he conceived of his position very differently. As he said in an interview in 1892, his business was to 'sell or lease copyrights,' and in conducting that business, he counted both authors and publishers as clients. In fact, Watt was widely employed by publishers, as he himself admits:

> my clients are not *all* authors, some of them are publishers! Yes; it's a fact, I could give you the names of some six or seven of the largest firms in Lon-

don, who, whenever they have any serial or book rights to dispose of, which for any reason they cannot handle themselves, invariably entrust the business to me. They, equally with my clients, recognise the fact that I, who do nothing but sell or lease copyrights, must know better than anyone else where to find the purchaser with whom the best bargain is likely to be made.[8]

The publishers for whom Watt handled business included Richard Bentley and Son, A. and C. Black, Chapman and Hall, Chatto and Windus, Macmillan and Company, Methuen and Company and Houghton, Mifflin and Company, Boston.[9] Essentially, Watt acted for publishers as he did for writers: he took their property, placed it in the appropriate market, and received a standard fee for his efforts. Thus at the outset, Watt situated himself between authors and publishers, working for both, but not allied directly with either.

Watt's comments tell us that the agent's principal task was to recognize a work that would sell. There was no sense in trying to place material for which there was no market, especially when the agent's earnings depended on a commission from the sale. Watt therefore defined the agent's primary role as that of an assessor and purveyor of literature, which meant that he assumed the position of house critic for his author clients, so to speak. For example, when Rider Haggard was working on a dramatization of his novel *Child of Storm* he wrote to Watt: 'Having no copy of *Child of Storm* with me, I have had to work from memory ... If you will get out a rough synopsis of your idea of what the various scenes and acts should be, I hope to be able to work it on the way home.'[10] Not all clients were as open to seeking or taking Watt's advice as was Haggard; nevertheless, Watt's advice to writers functioned as pre-publication commentary that often provoked them to alter their texts in slight or even profound ways. He gradually acquired considerable credibility and authority among authors because of his knowledge of what markets and publishers wanted. While many publishers were slow to accept agents, Watt's reputation for knowing good (and marketable) literature eventually led many publishers to trust his assessment of manuscripts. David Finkelstein, in his study of the Blackwood publishing firm, says that 'William Blackwood had initially been opposed to any such connections [with Watt or other agents]' but by 1894 'William was embracing those he had previously scorned.'[11]

Watt expanded the agent's role further by seeking out commissions for his author clients and also by ascertaining what publishers or editors needed and obtaining it for them. Previously an editor who wanted to commission a story had either to contact an author directly or send out word to the literary community through a cumbersome network of unofficial intermediaries. As Watt's reputation for providing quality work grew along with his client list, he became a logical first contact for editors in search of stories. However, although editors approached Watt because they were certain to obtain articles from his clients, the experience was not always pleasant. Ford Madox Ford wrote: 'I remember that when I edited the *English Review* I went to [Watt] to ask him for something by one of his clients and he was so patronising that I still feel like a worm when I think of it.'[12] Editors were not used to sharing power with agents, which may account for Ford's response to Watt, but they learned that contacting Watt first saved them much time and trouble. Watt would determine what the editor wanted and would then approach a writer with the editor's offer. A commissioned story meant a guaranteed sale, so many authors were happy to write to specific requirements. Often careers were started in this fashion; later, the established writer could command a high price for commissioned work or could refuse it altogether. Arnold Bennett, who started his writing career by scrambling to place pieces in the various literary magazines and periodicals of the day, provides a typical example of how a writer's attitude towards commissioned work modified as he became more successful. Although early in his career he was grateful for whatever commissions came his way, he later referred to this time as 'the humiliating part of my literary career.'[13]

Watt's position also brought him significant cultural authority. Indeed it brought him power of the sort previously confined to the other cultural mediators Janet Wolff identifies in her discussion of the sociology of art. 'In constructing the "great tradition" of literature or painting,' she writes, 'the role of publishers, critics, gallery owners, museum curators and journal editors cannot be overestimated. In the nineteenth century, there is a good deal of evidence that writers took into account the demands of the powerful mediators of the time in actually writing their novels.'[14] We can draw an analogy here between the role assumed by Wolff's cultural mediators and that of literary agents, such as Watt. As his agency grew, so did his influence; he was representing more writers, reading more manuscripts, advising more writers on the marketability of the work and the need for revisions. At the same time, as Watt's reputation for delivering high-quality 'product' to publishers grew, he began to exert a growing influence on the type of 'product' they wanted. His activities on behalf of both authors and publishers had a direct impact on the print culture because more of the 'product' – non-fiction books, novels, short stories, articles, drama, and poetry – passed through his office on its way to publication. By the end of the nineteenth century, Watt had, indeed, become a 'powerful mediator' in the sense that Wolff uses the term.

Author's or Publisher's Agent?

Not surprisingly, given that agents worked with both publishers and authors, one frequent charge levied against agents was that of divided loyalty. In 1899, an article in the *Author* commented on the morality and ethics of agents:

> It has been stated that certain agents take money from publishers in return for placing books with them. No proof of this allegation has yet been dis-covered, and one hopes that the thing is the invention of an enemy. It is needless to say that such a practice would be the most flagrant breach of trust. It would be exactly as if a solicitor was to take money from his client's adversary as well as his client.[15]

The adversarial relationship between publishers and authors is assumed here; it is clear that an agent who works for both sides is seen as no friend of the author. For the agent, however, a client was the person, or firm, with a copyright to lease or sell. As late as 1932, Raymond Savage was still arguing this role for the agent, stating,

> I am a *Literary* Agent whose business it is not only to act as an Author's agent but in any agency capacity which may be of benefit to authors, pub-lishers, editors or theatrical managers. Where I am acting on behalf of an author I am solely the author's agent, but in other cases I might act as a publisher's agent or again in a joint capacity.[16]

It is simple to say that the agent stands beside his client – whether the client is an author, editor, or publisher – as Savage does, but, in fact, the situation was more complex than that.

In any given transaction, the agent would be negotiating with a pub-lisher with whom he wished to work in the future. An individual author's needs would have to be placed alongside the agent's own long-term relationship with the publisher, but, at the same time, an agent who placed the publisher's demands before his author-client's needs could not hope to stay in business for long. To further complicate matters, publishers often became clients for whom the agent then negotiated with other publishers. The fluid nature of the business meant that the agent could not afford to alienate anyone. Watt notes this clearly when he comments in 1892: 'while I undoubtedly make it my business to get the best possible bargain for my client, I recognise the fact that that bargain is not a good one and not in the best interests of the author unless there is room for a fair profit to the publisher.'[17] Watt's approach was echoed almost fifteen years later by Curtis Brown, who wrote that the literary agent 'stands between the author and the publisher, and he ought to uphold better than either of them the importance of the greatest truism in trade, viz., that no bargain is ever really sound and honest without being profitable to both parties to it.'[18] Ideally, then, the agent walks a narrow line; he attempts to be fair to both publisher and author, and, by so doing, to serve the publishing industry as a whole.

The adversarial relationship between publishers and authors became more acrimonious as the nineteenth century drew to a close. Authors had long believed that publishers deliberately set out to cheat them. The *Author* frequently presented cases where unnamed writers had been badly treated by publishers who overcharged them for printing costs, corrections, and especially for advertising. Even established writers such as H.G. Wells complained to Watt that publishers were not treating them fairly in terms of payments owed to them.[19] In turn, publishers believed that authors were only interested in lining their own pockets. As Heinemann remarked in the *Athenaeum*, in his 'The Hardships of Publishing' article,

> [authors'] prices have gone up with leaps and bounds of late ... royalties are
> actually being paid which, with the increase in the cost of production, leave
> the publisher barely his working expenses; and ... [authors], as well as print-
> ers and binders, have a trades union which has formed a decided front,
> determined on concerted action, not perhaps *against* us, but *for* themselves.[20]

The agent needed to gain the trust of both sides in order to function properly. However, many authors would have agreed with warnings printed in the *Author* about unscrupulous agents and would have been sceptical about agents' claims to be on their side. Similarly, many publishers were highly critical of the agent's motivations and ethics. Indeed Spencer C. Blackett's remarks about agents affirm publishers' suspicions of agents. He begins by saying, 'The middleman in other businesses is, as a rule, to be relied on, and charges at the most 5 per cent.; but the literary parasites are not to be relied on, and charge the author 10 per cent.' He concludes with a warning to authors:

> avoid [agents] if you wish to succeed, as the best houses are closed to them; anything they introduce to a house worth cultivating is returned immediately the label is seen, for now the literary parasite is fully recognized as the grossest abuse of modern innovations.[21]

While Blackett's comments were hyperbolic – the leading publishers did deal with agents – his obvious contempt for, and fear of, agents illustrates the difficulty Watt faced in establishing trust with publishers.

Nevertheless, the basis of an agent's job is trust. The author must trust that the agent will do all he can to place the work, that the price negotiated will be the best that can be got for the work, and that in each transaction the agent places the author's welfare above all other considerations. The publisher must trust that the agent is negotiating fairly with him, that he represents the publisher's offers accurately to the author, and that the agent is not out to gain a price for the work which the publisher can never recoup. Blackett's comments notwithstanding, Watt won the trust of both sides. Mrs Belloc Lowndes's comments about Watt, though voiced from her perspective as an author client, would have been echoed by the majority of publishers with whom Watt did business; she said that he was 'a man of outstanding intellectual gifts and integrity.'[22] W. Robertson Nicoll makes a similar observation when he writes that Watt's 'work was largely that of a diplomatist ... Gradually ... he won his way to general confidence ... Of this there can be only one explanation. That explanation is that he was a very able and a very honest man doing a necessary work.'[23] His achievements were due as much to these qualities as they were to his business acumen. Competitors and successors who wished for similar results soon learned the value of conducting their business as Watt conducted his. In this way, he set the standard for future agencies.

Agents and the Field of Print Culture

Agents and the Transformation of the Literary Marketplace

Watt may not have invented the role of literary agent, but he certainly played a central part in defining and refining it. By the turn of the

century, other agents had begun to challenge his supremacy – notably
J.B. Pinker and Curtis Brown. But for almost twenty years, from the late
1870s through the late 1890s, Watt dominated, setting the standard
against which his competitors and successors were measured. His activities altered how publishing businesses operated and how literature was
produced. This, in turn, transformed the literary marketplace. His influence is both direct and subtle.

The direct influence can be seen by the ways that Watt, and the other
agents who came to occupy prominent positions, prompted a radical
shift in the balance of power in publishing. Agents undermined publishers' traditionally dominant position by forcing them to expose their
activities to public scrutiny – public in the sense of authors and agents.
They helped authors to empower themselves – by assisting them in their
fights for better financial terms and more control over their literary
property. Watt served as publisher for the first twelve issues of the
Society of Authors' journal – the *Author* – in which many debates about
authors' ownership of their work and reform of copyright legislation
appeared. He also sold advertising space for the journal. In both capaci-
ties, he was directly involved in the authors' fight for greater control of
their work.[24] But perhaps the best evidence of the extent of Watt's growing influence can be found in the virulence of the responses from the
party who apparently had most to lose – the publisher.

In the last twenty-five years of the nineteenth century, it was commonplace for publishers to point out the decline in literary quality that they
saw as a consequence of the expanded marketplace and the ongoing
commercialization of literature. Many held the agent largely responsible
for this. The most celebrated dispute between publishers and agents is
that which occurred in 1905 between the American publisher Henry
Holt and the London-based agent Albert Curtis Brown. Because Holt's
views are similar to those of many of Britain's powerful publishers, at
least initially, and because the exchange with Curtis Brown so fully elaborates the concerns of both sides, their exchange is worth looking at in
some detail.

Holt laments the transformations brought about by the increasing
sums of money paid to authors and the competition engendered by writers who hawked their wares in the marketplace. He places the blame for
the situation squarely at the door of the literary agent. He allows that
there might be 'a justification for a person so unbusinesslike as the
author generally is, supplementing himself with a business adviser to
look over contracts and royalty statements – a sort of lawyer and

auditor.' But he goes on to say that 'in carrying his functions farther, the agent has been the parent of most serious abuses,' and 'a very serious detriment to literature and a leech on the author, sucking blood entirely out of proportion to his later services; and has already begun to defeat himself.'[25] Such strong sentiments are surely incited by his real fear, not only for the condition of literature, but also, and more importantly, for the condition of publishers.

In his response to Holt, Curtis Brown presents a different assessment of the situation:

> Now it used to be considered good form for the author to know little or nothing about market rates, and to take whatever he could manage to get from his publisher without resorting to any systematic use of competition. When the agent came along and began to prove by expert knowledge of market prices that in many cases the author had not received as much as his work was worth in the open market, it was only human nature for that author's publisher to call the agent a villain.[26]

Brown's reasonable claim is that agents make the playing field level:

> The wise literary agent of to-day and of the future will act for the author on a policy of competition, it is true, but competition carefully tempered by regard for the value of friendly relations between author and publisher. The best arrangement between author and publisher is the one of closest touch on the literary side of the work, leaving the commercial side to be arranged between publisher and agent, on the basis of the value of the author's work in the open market.[27]

Implicit in Brown's remarks is the belief that the resulting redistribution of power among publisher, agent, and author will lead to a system that works better for all parties. While this is certainly open to argument, it is evident that just such a power-sharing relationship evolved. Despite their best efforts, publishers had no way to stop the rise of agents, for if they refused to deal with Watt or other agents, they risked cutting themselves off from a large number of writers and thus jeopardizing their firms' futures. Once Watt was firmly established, a new power nexus became inevitable.

Watt's activities also had a subtler, but equally significant, impact on the shape of literary culture that lasted well into the twentieth century. When one looks at Watt's client list – either the one supplied in his own advertisements or the list of contributors to the various volumes of *Letters to A.P. Watt* – a number of observations may be made.[28] First, Watt's clients were individuals who had proven themselves in the literary marketplace, as judged by the sales of their works. In many cases, they were also authors who had attained a measure of critical success, either in the form of favourable reviews from well-placed critics or in the accumulation of symbolic capital. Knighthoods were awarded to Watt's clients Walter Besant, Arthur Conan Doyle, and Rider Haggard, for instance, while Rudyard Kipling won a Nobel Prize for literature in 1907.

Second, it is clear that Watt did not typically expend energy or capital in the nurturing of unproven talent. He preferred to approach writers once they had established themselves. The way in which Rudyard Kipling became Watt's client provides a typical example. Harry Ricketts, one of Kipling's biographers, notes that within months of Kipling's return to London in 1889, 'he had become a phenomenon,' whose work had provoked 'a wide range of expectations ... even before his arrival in London.'[29] And Martin Seymour-Smith, another Kipling biographer, says that when Kipling arrived in London in October of 1899, he 'really was a rising young author.' Shortly after his arrival, despite what Seymour-Smith calls Kipling's 'general rule about the literary world coming to him,' Kipling 'called on Andrew Lang, who took him to the Savile club, where he would have soon met Hardy, Sir Walter Besant ... Haggard, Gosse, James, the literary historian George Saintsbury, and many others.'[30] Clearly, Kipling was moving in the sort of circles that would draw Watt's attention to him, and it was only a matter of time before the two met. In fact, within months of his arrival, Walter Besant introduced Kipling to 'the literary agent A.P. Watt, whom he employed until his death.'[31] While there is no doubt that Watt played a central role in Kipling's career from the time he took him on as a client (a fact Kipling acknowledged when he remarked to Olive Schreiner about Watt that 'he is very kind and nice and does everything for you except – writing your book')[32] – it is nonetheless the case that Kipling was already well launched in his career when he became Watt's client. Similar stories could be told about other Watt clients. Besant, who became a client of Watt's in 1884, had enjoyed a successful career as a novelist dating back to his collaboration with James Rice in the early 1870s;[33] Rider Haggard's *King Solomon's Mines* (1885) had attracted widespread critical attention, and within the year he signed on to Watt's agency;[34] and Arthur Conan Doyle, who joined Watt's stable of clients in 1890, had carved out a modest reputation for himself as a historical novelist and had already published the first of his Sherlock Holmes tales – 'A Study in Scarlet' and 'The Sign of Four.'[35]

Third, because Watt's clients were usually already successful, their works tended to reflect the prevailing literary tastes of the time. Granted, those tastes were becoming ever more diverse, as evidenced by the fact that George MacDonald, Rudyard Kipling, Marie Corelli, and Arthur Conan Doyle were all represented by Watt. However, Watt's clients were not often at the vanguard of literary experimentalism that later became associated with modernism (with the notable exceptions of W.B. Yeats and August Strindberg, for example), in large measure because such works had yet to capture sufficient attention from readers or critics to bring their authors the cultural or economic capital that would have drawn Watt's attention to them.[36]

The results of what might well be characterized as Watt's conservative approach were far-reaching. Because his was the leading agency of the era, a new writer's career could be given an enormous boost if he or she were added to Watt's client list. Joining Watt meant that all the contacts and experience of the firm were brought into play on the writer's behalf: doors were opened and opportunities provided that the writer struggling on his or her own might not have had. The obvious catch here was that the writer's work had to be the sort that Watt felt his agency could sell. Those whose works could not be slotted into an existing market niche were unlikely to be taken up by Watt. And as a result, they were more likely to have a difficult time finding a publisher willing to take a chance on their work, since as the twentieth century dawned publishers were relying more on Watt, and other agents, to provide them with marketable literature.[37] With as large a client base as he had, Watt might have been able to champion a new writer, knowing that he would benefit little from his actions in the short term, but also knowing that his other clients generated enough income to keep him solvent. If the new writer did catch on, not only would Watt's investment be returned, but also other clients might well be attracted to Watt, who might further exploit the market created by the demand for this new kind of writing. However, Watt's business model had little room for championing of new writers, a fact that would have consequences both for the profession of agenting and for print culture in general.

Ironically, Watt's conservative business practices proved beneficial to print culture for two reasons. First, the clients he represented continued to produce literature that met the demands of large segments of the reading public. Watt was adept at assessing what certain kinds of readers wanted and his firm continued to seek out writers who could supply them with the material they wanted even when many well-placed literary critics were beginning to champion the experiments of modernist writers. Second, as the literary marketplace evolved to accommodate new readers and writers from differing backgrounds, Watt's tendency to stick with established writers and markets meant that other literary agents emerged to assist new writers in taking advantage of the market's rapid expansion. As these new agents, such as Pinker, staked out turf in the broad print culture field, they challenged not only Watt's position as the preeminent literary agent, but also his ways of doing business. Thus because Watt was slow to change, his rivals provided an alternative that not only serviced an important emerging coterie of authors and publishers, but also enabled literary agency to adapt to meet the needs of the rapidly evolving print culture field.

3 Establishing the Agency Model: George MacDonald and Watt

George MacDonald – preacher, poet, and novelist – became A.P. Watt's first client in the late 1870s. MacDonald's background mirrored Watt's in that both were Scots, both had strong, Nonconformist religious beliefs, and both loved literature. More is known about MacDonald's early years than Watt's, though. He was born in 1824 in Huntly, in northeast Scotland, to a family that had once been prosperous, but had seen its fortunes slide over the years. Initially George's father (also named George) lived in a house next to that inhabited by his own mother, the contiguous houses having a connecting door between them. Young George's grandmother thus formed an early, and lasting, influence on his life. His father and uncle jointly ran the family bleach-works and farm, and from 1826 onwards both families shared a house on the farm. MacDonald's childhood is the stuff of Victorian novels. It is marked by the tragic death of his mother from tuberculosis when he was only eight; he and his brothers suffered bullying at the hands of his first schoolmaster, bullying which George and his brothers believed led to the death of his younger brother James; and he suffered frequently from severe bouts of bronchitis and asthma that forced him to spend long days quietly at home reading whatever books he could find, thereby sowing the seeds for his later literary career. At the core of his early years one finds him acquiring the profound religious beliefs which provided the foundations of his personality and his life, and which were instilled by his paternal grandmother, whose Nonconformist religious sensibility inspired the thirteen-year-old George to set up a youth temperance league.[1] And yet despite the tragedies and ill health that marked his early years, MacDonald always remembered his childhood with great fondness, recalling the long summer rambles with his brothers in the hills, the various activities on the farm, including horseback riding, which he loved, and the joys of family life in his boisterous farmhouse.

MacDonald left Huntly at the age of fifteen to study for the University of Aberdeen's entrance exams. He won a bursary and in 1840 enrolled at the university as a sixteen-year-old. As happens to so many young people, university proved a period of intellectual, social, and spiritual growth that was marked in MacDonald's case by his continuing interest in literature and his frequent spiritual searchings. He graduated with his MA in 1845, taking prizes in both chemistry and natural philosophy.[2] At this point, two professions appealed to him – medicine and science (chemistry in particular) – but his family's continuing financial difficulties rendered both choices impossible. The ministry was the option suggested to him by his friends and advisors, though MacDonald himself was unsure of this path. He therefore headed south to London, where he took on a tutor's post and continued his own studies informally with the hope that a change in circumstances and place would bring clarity to his situation. After two years as a private tutor, a job he found uncongenial, he decided that the ministry was his chosen profession, so in 1848 he enrolled in Highbury Theological College, from which he graduated in 1850.

In late summer of 1850 he took up his first real appointment as a pastor. The Congregational Church in Arundel initially hired him for a two-month temporary post, but then offered him the position permanently. He was reasonably happy during this period; both his personal circumstances – he married Louisa Powell in 1851 and they had the first of their eleven children while in Arundel – and his professional ones'– he enjoyed his work as pastor, particularly the weekly preaching, and he also found time to write – contributed to this happiness. Indeed, it is during his time in Arundel that MacDonald began to take the possibility of a literary life seriously. He wrote his first long work, the five-act dramatic poem *Within and Without*,[3] and he translated and paid for the printing of a volume of twelve of Novalis's *Spiritual Songs*. However, his unorthodox religious views were not in step with the beliefs of some of his flock, and, faced with the request from a significant number of his congregation to resign, MacDonald did so in late 1853, thereby ending his brief pastoral sojourn.

With the birth of his second child imminent, MacDonald was yet again faced with the dilemma of how to earn a living, though the situation was more difficult than before, since he would soon have four mouths to feed rather than just his own. He looked to Manchester, where A.J. Scott was principal of Owen's College (later Manchester University). MacDonald was not personally acquainted with Scott, but he admired him for his gifts as a preacher and his intellect, and they did have friends in common. MacDonald went to Manchester, introduced himself to Scott, and asked for his help. Though Scott could not secure a job at Owen's for MacDonald, the meeting between the two created a lifelong friendship that was to prove useful to MacDonald in a variety of ways. Scott may have helped MacDonald to secure some paying engagements as a preacher in Manchester, and in early 1854 he welcomed MacDonald, his wife, and his two daughters into his home. Shortly thereafter, a relative of Scott's offered MacDonald the use of a farmhouse in Alderley, where he recuperated from a bout of bronchitis and was able to write articles and poems that the *Christian Spectator* would publish on a regular basis from 1854 onwards. Soon the MacDonalds were living in their own home in Manchester with the bills paid by monies earned from MacDonald's preaching engagements and his literary output. In fact, shortly after settling into his new home, he rented a room where he could deliver his sermons without needing to worry about the approval of a congregation. In May of 1855, Longmans published *Within and Without* to generally favourable reviews, though it 'made very little profit'[4] and the family's financial circumstances were, as usual, dire. Louisa, who was visiting her sister Flora in Liverpool when the poem was published, was, as Kathy Triggs tells us, 'nearly desperate for money' at this juncture and Flora paid for her train fare back to Manchester. Once home, Louisa 'lived "on tick" for as long as she could.'[5] Nonetheless, the publication of this long poem launched MacDonald's literary career. Thus by 1855, the three central themes of MacDonald's adult life were set: he would continue to seek opportunities to preach independent of the sanction of a particular congregation or church; he would develop a literary career that would see him write in many genres; and he would be chronically short of money, depending on friends and family to make up the shortfall between his increasing expenses (due to his ever-growing family) and the income generated from his preaching and writing.

The 1850s and 1860s saw MacDonald's writing career begin to gather steam. In 1857 Longmans published his first volume of poetry, simply entitled *Poems;* it received solid reviews. In 1858, Smith, Elder, and Company published *Phantastes: A Faerie Romance for Men and Women,* which was also well received, though some reviewers were nonplussed by MacDonald's fusion of fairy-tale form with religious or spiritual truths.[6]

He was also building up his reputation and repertoire as a speaker, branching out to literary topics. In October of 1859 he accepted the position of chair of English Literature at Bedford College in London.[7] From 1859 until 1863, though he continued to write articles, poems, stories, and even plays, most of his income was derived from his lecturing and preaching. As a professor he made roughly £30 to £40 a year and he was able to lecture on his favourite authors, including Shakespeare, Milton, and the Romantics.[8] However, MacDonald continued to rely on the kindness of friends to support his large family. One generous friend and patron, Lady Byron, who had been so moved by *Within and Without* that she sought out its author and subsequently became a friend to both George and Louisa, left MacDonald £300 when she died. The money came at an opportune time, as George's son Greville relates, since Louisa had lost her purse and consequently they had no money to feed their children:

> They did not know where to turn next for help, and there was hardly enough food in the house for the children's dinner ... Then, my mother said, as the evening closed in, she and my father were standing hand in hand as if waiting for some answer to their prayers. It was in the little front drawing-room of Tudor Lodge, and the rain poured down upon the weeping ash that overspread the tiny garden. The postman walked up the steps, dropped a letter in the box, and with his double knock woke them from their quietude. The letter was from Lady Byron's executors enclosing a cheque for £300, a legacy of which they had not been advised.[9]

Circumstances turned around somewhat in 1863, when MacDonald's first Scottish novel, *David Elginblood,* was published.[10] He had written the novel at the urging of George Murray Smith, head of Smith, Elder, and Company, but Smith, Elder rejected it, fearing its spiritual and idealistic elements would make it unpopular.[11] Hurst and Blackett took the novel at the urging of Dinah Mulock (MacDonald's friend from Manchester days and a writer published by Hurst and Blackett), paying him £90 for the copyright. This novel sold steadily and proved to be MacDonald's breakthrough work, since it demonstrated to publishers that there was a market for the sorts of stories that he produced.

During the rest of the 1860s and into the 1870s, MacDonald's literary career flourished. Hurst and Blackett published a collection of his short stories under the title *Adela Cathcart* in 1864,[12] and the novel *Alec Forbes* in 1865. In 1866, George MacDonald joined the stable of authors published by Alexander Strahan, though he also continued to publish with others.[13] MacDonald remained with Strahan – placing serials in Strahan's various magazines, publishing many of his books with the company, and eventually editing *Good Words for the Young* from 1869 to 1873[14] – until 1884 when Strahan virtually ceased to publish under any imprimatur.[15] It was through MacDonald's relationship with Strahan that he met A.P. Watt. Watt 'served as Strahan's secretary, reader of manuscripts, and head of advertising.'[16] He undoubtedly met MacDonald in the course of his work, since it is likely that Watt would have had to meet with MacDonald about placing advertising in *Good Words*, as well as on social occasions at Strahan's home. When Strahan's financial troubles made it difficult for the firm to publish MacDonald's work or even to help him place it with other publishers, MacDonald turned, as so often in the past, to a friend to help him out of a difficult situation.

The Agent-Client Relationship

Friends First

In 1877, George MacDonald was, yet again, in dire financial straits and specifically in need of money to finance a move to Italy for the winter. His daughter Mary was ill with tuberculosis and he hoped that a gentler climate would improve her health. MacDonald himself was unwell again, and had decided to follow his family south in search of better health, which would allow him more time and energy for his writing.[17] From 1877 onwards, the MacDonalds spent winters in Italy, eventually settling near Bordighera, where they built Casa Corragio.[18] Yet despite the reduced costs of living in Italy, MacDonald's financial woes continued. Being so far from London, he had to rely on friends to assist him in all manner of literary business transactions – from arranging for copying of manuscripts and correcting of proofs to conveying contract terms back and forth between MacDonald and various publishers. Given Strahan's own precarious financial situation, he could not afford to buy MacDonald's works for the sums he previously had paid. Nor was he in a position to publish many of them, even at a reduced price, so in early 1878 MacDonald turned to Watt.[19]

Watt himself described the sequence of events that led to his becoming MacDonald's literary agent in his 1892 *Bookman* interview:

> When I started to sell copyrights, some fourteen years ago, the literary agent was an unknown factor in the world of letters. My friend, Dr. George

MacDonald, asked me to sell his stories, which I did – and I think I may say with great success. Dr. MacDonald found that my acting on his behalf in this way relieved him of an immense deal of trouble and worry, and he then, and has ever since, placed the management of his literary affairs entirely under my care. At the same time I was doing this for him it occurred to me that other authors might be glad to be relieved of what Mr. Besant has called 'the intolerable trouble of haggling and bargaining,' and one author recommending my services to another – for I never advertise, you know – I gradually came to take up the position I now hold.[20]

Watt's somewhat disingenuous account here does little to convey the importance of the relationship to both men. Nor does it reveal the gradual regularization of their business arrangements that eventually set the standard for agent-client relationships.

It is probable that Watt's first task was to place *Paul Faber, Surgeon* with Hurst and Blackett in 1878. Strahan had paid Macdonald £400 for the copyright, less than half the sum that Macdonald's novels had been garnering, but because of the firm's difficulties, it was unable to publish it.[21] Watt's position as an insider in the firm made it likely that he had access to it and was able to offer it for sale to other publishers, finally placing it with Hurst and Blackett. It appears that Watt was able to obtain at least an additional £50 from the publisher for MacDonald, thereby providing his friend with much-needed income.[22] Watt's placing of this book initiated a business relationship that was to last for almost thirty years and that was to be supplemented by a close friendship.

Agent-Client Business Relationship Established

From the outset, Watt was to find MacDonald a challenging client. In the first place, MacDonald was an established writer whose work spanned many genres. This meant that Watt could be called on to place a volume of sermons, a book of poetry, a 'regional' novel, or a children's story.[23] As a result, Watt had to be familiar with a variety of publishing planes in order to handle MacDonald's output properly. The second big challenge came from the fact that MacDonald viewed his literary work as an extension of his religious beliefs, using literature as another forum in which to preach his particular brand of Christianity. During the 1860s and 1870s the market had been good for this kind of work, but as the century wore on, fewer people were drawn to religiously or spiritually inspired material, particularly of the sort that MacDonald produced, and thus it became harder for Watt to sell MacDonald's works for anything approaching the prices they had commanded in the 1860s and 1870s.[24] Finally, Watt discovered that MacDonald was very unbusinesslike, an attitude that was also derived from his strong religious beliefs. Greville MacDonald's comments on his father's behaviour during the very bleak period in 1853 when MacDonald had left his post in Arundel with no promise of a future position or income provide us with an insight into how his father's profound faith governed his relations with the material aspects of life. Greville says that George MacDonald wrote to his father in Huntly:

> You must not be surprised if you hear that I am not what is called *getting on.* Time will show what use the Father will make of me. I desire to be His – entirely – so sure am I that therein lies all things. If less than this were my hope, I should die.[25]

Although MacDonald was constantly in need of money, because of his belief that God would provide for him and his family, he did not take the time or care to understand the market value of his work, trusting instead that publishers would pay him fairly. As Watt was to find out when he examined his new client's existing contracts, MacDonald's trust was not always well placed, a point that I will return to later in the chapter.

Thus, as he intimated to the *Bookman*, Watt was, indeed, helping to sell his friend's story at a moment when his friend desperately needed assistance. But we ought not to lose sight of the fact that he was also helping himself. George MacDonald's literary prominence provided enormous symbolic capital to Watt, who could point to his position as the manager of Dr MacDonald's literary affairs and use this as proof not only of his business skills but also of his trustworthiness.[26] His actions for MacDonald helped establish his own primacy in the emerging literary agency business and also provided him with a solid starting point in his new role in the print culture field.

Developing A Professional Relationship

Watt needed to establish his own business practices and credentials as an agent; therefore, he could not continue to act for MacDonald without some form of payment. It is virtually impossible to pinpoint the moment at which MacDonald began to pay Watt for his services;

however, we do know that from about 1882 onward he was handling virtually all of George MacDonald's literary affairs. The earliest documents in the Watt archive at the University of North Carolina, Chapel Hill pertaining to MacDonald deal with Watt's 1884 negotiations for the sale of *The Diary of an Old Soul.* Watt negotiated with C.J. Longman for the rights to it, for which he secured MacDonald 'a royalty of 20 per cent of the retail price' and 'An advance on account of royalties of £30.'[27] These terms were better than those offered by Longman, whose letter stated that the firm 'should prefer not to pay any sum in advance of Royalties as Dr. MacDonald has now for some time enjoyed two payments from us on account of work from which we are not yet receiving a benefit.'[28] It is likely that over the next three or four years Watt regularized his business dealings with MacDonald, bringing them in line with those he was forging with other early clients such as Wilkie Collins and Walter Besant.[29]

Professionalizing Agenting and Writing

In many ways, MacDonald belongs to a transitional generation of writers. As Simon Eliot, summarizing the various forces at work in the 1880s and 1890s, concludes, 'The whole concept of the "man of letters", not as an inspired genius nor as a picturesque bohemian, but as a workaday professional, on par in training, status, and (with a bit of luck) income with a lawyer or doctor, was the creation of this hopeful period.'[30] Writers in the final decades of the nineteenth century were caught up in the swirling forces of change in the literary world; Watt's interactions with MacDonald cast an interesting light on the shifting nature of this world.

MacDonald is a professional writer in both senses of the word as outlined in chapter 1. He depended on his writing for the bulk of his income. In fact, as Richard Reis points out, 'George MacDonald's works were best sellers … His novels sold, both in Great Britain and in the United States, by the hundreds of thousands of copies.'[31] Yet he also enjoyed the higher status that Walter Besant argued writers should be accorded because of their membership in a 'noble profession.' MacDonald had the air of a man of letters, a prophet or teacher who cared little for the financial aspects of writing, apart from his desire to sell his works so that he could support his family.[32] He cared much more for the moral and spiritual messages his works could convey to his audience. Indeed, in his biography of his father, Greville MacDonald perpetuated this image of a writer primarily interested in the spiritual wellbeing of others and largely disinterested in the material benefits of his literary output. The opening words of his biography convey this image clearly:

> This is the hundredth year since George MacDonald's birth, and the time is ripe for reminding the world of a spiritual genius whose art was so rare that, had he confined himself to poetry and purely imaginative story-telling, he could not have been almost forgotten. His fairy-tales and allegorical fantasies were epoch-making in the lives of multitudes, children and parents alike, and still are widely read. His novels, not only those which, conceived in his native country, inaugurated a new school in Scottish literature, but his stories of English life also, stirred the religious world to its depths and left their impress direct or mediate on the deeper thought of the whole English-speaking world.[33]

Yet the reality of his life reflected the degree to which MacDonald was already a professional writer prior to becoming Watt's first client. As Reis tells us, MacDonald's other activities were helpful, perhaps even vital, in creating a following for his popular fiction: 'his lectures were popular and widely attended; his poetry earned him at least passing consideration for the laureateship; and his reputation as a Christian teacher was vast.'[34] Greville, who accompanied his parents on their 1872 tour of America, noted the size and enthusiasm of the crowds who flocked to hear his father speak: 'The lecture was in the [Philadelphia] Opera House, packed full with 3,500 people ... He held the attention of that mass of quiet people as easily as the dozen of ten years before in his little study at Tudor lodge.'[35] Interestingly, his lectures were on literary subjects, rather than on the spiritual or moral topics that he had preferred in the 1850s in Manchester, thus suggesting that he was not so otherworldly as to be unaware of the need to tailor his material for the popular audience.[36] The tour, undertaken because it seemed a way out of another financial disaster, did not immediately alleviate the MacDonalds' pressing needs. Greville noted, 'I do not think my father brought home with him much over a thousand pounds; and he could perhaps have earned as much if the eight months had been spent in his study.'[37] However, Mr Redpath of the Boston Lyceum Bureau, which had arranged the Boston stop on the tour, reacted with indignation after the first lecture in Boston, apparently exclaiming, 'See here, Mr. MacDonald, why didn't you say you could do this sort of thing? We'd have got 300 dollars a lecture for you!'[38] Redpath's remarks underscored, yet again, MacDonald's apparent obliviousness to the direct financial potential of his considerable oratory and literary skills.

MacDonald was not a noticeable spendthrift, though his expenses were considerable because of his need to support his wife and their eleven children. The fifteen years from 1872 to 1887 saw him produce no fewer than twenty-four works of various sorts, including some of his most popular novels – *Wilfrid Cumbermede* (1872), *The Marquis of Losse* (1877), *Sir Gibbie* (1879), *Donal Grant* (1883) – and some of the imaginative fiction for children that was to become his lasting literary legacy – *The Princess and the Goblin* (1872) and *The Princess and Curdie* (1883).[39] Yet MacDonald's financial condition worsened after the tour. Why would this be?

The central problems MacDonald faced were similar to those of the majority of writers at this time. Because he sold his copyrights outright, he did not share in the extra profits generated when sales exceeded the sum he obtained from the publisher when he sold them his work, nor did he share in proceeds publishers could generate from the increasingly lucrative outside rights markets. Because he ascribed to the 'man of letters' approach to his writing career, he had no plan to manage the various facets of his professional life. Furthermore, because his literary output included sermons, fiction, and poetry, he had to contend with different publishing planes. This meant that he not only had to negotiate with a number of different publishers, but that these negotiations frequently required different strategies. Finally, because he was often out of the country or ill and because his belief that God would provide for him led him to neglect his business affairs, he had little time or inclination to assess the current state of the literary marketplace and thus was often at a disadvantage in negotiating prices for his works. All this was about to change, both for MacDonald and for the majority of writers, because of the emergence of the literary agent.

Literary Property

Selling and Buying Copyrights

As we have already seen from Watt's own descriptions, he initially conceived of the agent's role as the selling of copyrights. His narrow construction of his duties was in keeping with the prevailing practices in the print culture field in the 1870s, and his initial transactions did not deviate from these practices. In the 1884 sale of *The Diary of an Old Soul*, for instance, Watt sold MacDonald's copyright outright to Longmans in return for the 20 per cent royalty and the £30 advance. He was to act in the same way for other clients. For example, in 1889, the contract he negotiated with Richard Bentley and Son and Chatto and Windus on behalf of Wilkie Collins's literary executors resulted in the outright sale of Collins's copyright to Chatto and Windus:

> In consideration of the payment by Messrs. Chatto & Windus of Thirty Pounds (£30) to Mr. A.P. Watt and Thirty Pounds (£30) to Messrs. Richard Bentley & Son the first and second parties to this agreement [Watt and Bentley] transfer and assign to Messrs. Chatto & Windus the stereo plates and all remaining copyright in a story by *Wilkie Collins* entitled '*A Rogue's Life*'. [40]

He also performed this service for publishers who held copyrights that they wished to sell. In fact, he arranged a sale to Blackie and Son of what is described in the correspondence as 'Dr. George MacDonald's story for boys [likely "A Rough Shaking"].'[41] Blackie bought all rights and on 17 January 1889, Watt offered to place it serially. The firm replied on 18 January that

> we have had so little experience in selling copyrights to magazines that we must be guided by you in the matter of what we should ask – but we may say that we think we should get at least £250 for the magazine rights in this Country. As regards placing the story in America we fancy that a magazine that circulates in America *only* would require to be selected and from such a source we should get £100. We should like to know what magazines you would offer the story so that we might approve of same ... We were already aware that you charged 10% and hope that you will be able to place the story so satisfactorily as to insure you a substantial commission.[42]

Watt sold the American rights to the magazine *Atalanta*, which agreed 'to pay for serial use £250 (two hundred & fifty pounds),' the sum to be paid 'in twelve installments to Mr. A.P. Watt, Paternoster Square, at the end of each month of issue.'[43] The higher price certainly provided Blackie with evidence of the value of engaging Watt's services. MacDonald did not share in the profits from this sale because he had sold all rights to Blackie, but Watt managed to make three commissions: on the initial sale to Blackie, on the sale of British serial rights, and on the sale to *Atalanta*.

By the early 1890s, Watt was beginning to recognize the value of retaining the copyright for the author and leasing it for specific publication purposes rather than selling it outright. Watt was not the first to recognize the value of copyrights or that holding on to them meant that authors could exploit potentially lucrative outside rights themselves. In fact he was somewhat late in coming to this awareness. As we saw in the brief discussion of copyright in chapter 1, publishers had long been very aware of the value of the literary properties they purchased; indeed, Richard Bentley had been plying copyrights abroad and in various editions since as early as the 1820s. As for authors, Charles Dickens was taking advantage of his copyrights as early as 1855, and other writers whose work was in high demand soon followed suit. What Watt brought to the table, so to speak, was a broader perspective than could be found in individual contracts between publishers and authors. He knew the norms of the business: what kinds of arrangements were being made by particular publishers with their counterparts abroad, what kinds of contracts were negotiated by writers whose work was in demand abroad and in different domestic markets, and what sorts of options might be exploited by writers who had no knowledge of the possibilities inherent in exploiting outside rights if they retained them. Watt's insertion of himself into the publisher-author dyad is key here not because what he was advocating was new, but because his intervention carried with it the possibility that all authors could potentially exploit their literary property by hiring him to do it for them. To hark back to Jordan and Patten and Janet Wolff, for a minute, Watt became a powerful mediator in the publishing world when he began to advise clients to hold on to their copyrights and to allow him to exploit them on their behalf.

Some of the contracts Watt negotiated for clients from 1891 onwards began to reserve ownership of copyright completely to the author, permitting the publisher to produce the work in a particular format for a set period of time. Others sold the copyright for a specific publication format while reserving other publication rights to the author. For example, an 1891 agreement between Watt's client Edward Robert Bulwer-Lytton, 1st Earl Lytton, and Macmillan and Company for the publication of *The Ring of Amasis* contains this clause:

> It is agreed that the copyright of the said book is to remain with the said Earl of Lytton and that at the expiration of five years from the first day of July 1890 or at the expiration of any subsequent period of five years thereafter this agreement may be terminated by either party on giving three months notice of intention to do so.[44]

This text was originally published in 1863, so one would assume that Lytton had either retained his copyright or else he had reacquired it.[45] The contract makes clear, though, that Lytton did not retain full ownership of his copyright in other jurisdictions: clause 4 says that Macmillan purchased the colonial and American copyrights for £50. Nonetheless, the contract clearly shows Watt deliberately protecting his client's copyright, at least in England.

However, many writers continued to sell their copyrights for one reason or another, despite the exhortations of the *Author* not to do so.[46] A good example of this is Morley Roberts, who had routinely sold his copyrights up to 1895. His 1895 contract with Henry and Company for the publication of *A Question of Instinct* is typical of the contracts he signed. It contained the clause 'Fourthly, The copyright of the said book shall remain the property of the Publishers.'[47] A significant change is visible in the 1896 contract Watt negotiated for Roberts with J. Mentz and Company for a volume of short stories entitled *The Great Jester.* What is notable about this agreement is the following clause: 'the Publisher shall have the right during a period of seven years to print and publish a volume of short stories'[48] in return for an advance of £35 and royalties as outlined in subsequent clauses. Watt has leased Roberts's copyright for a specific purpose and for a limited time-period.

Because of the exponential growth in the literary marketplace and changes to International Copyright law, outside rights became valuable properties that agents could exploit on behalf of their clients. It is important to note here that Watt continued to work for publishers who had rights they wished to dispose of, but that from the mid-1890s he began to position himself more fully on the side of the author. Watt, undoubtedly under pressure from the Society of Authors' campaign for greater control of their own work, began to build into his writers' publication contracts clauses that reserved outside rights to the author. Perhaps his long association with Walter Besant had something to do with this change, or perhaps Watt recognized that if he did not move towards the role of primarily an authors' agent he would lose business to newcomers such as J.B. Pinker who expressly positioned themselves as writers' agents. Regardless of the motivation, Watt's recognition of the value of outside rights led to two different tactics.

The first was to write agreements that reserved all, or some, of these rights to the author. His contracts for George MacDonald from 1896 on reflect this approach. The contract between MacDonald and Longmans, Green for the publication of a book of poetry, 'at present arranged under the general title of "Rampollo; Growths from an Old Root; containing a Book of Translations old and new; also a year's Diary of an Old Soul,'" permits the publisher to 'issue an edition of the said volume for publication in Great Britain (and Ireland) its Colonies and Dependencies' under one set of terms and to 'the United States of America' under a different set of terms. Sales to the British market were on a basis of 10 per cent royalty on all copies up to one thousand copies to be sold at six shillings and a further twopence per copy on all sales over a thousand. The American terms were for a straight 10 per cent of the selling price for each copy, the price to be determined later.[49] Clause 5 of the agreement explicitly reserved 'the rights of translation' to George MacDonald. A later contract, for the 1897 sale of 'a new novel at present entitled "SALTED WITH FIRE"' to Hurst and Blackett, was even more protective of outside rights. Clause 7 stated 'That the United States rights, the rights of translation and dramatization together with the rights to publish said new novel in English on the Continent of Europe are reserved by the said George MacDonald.'[50] These kinds of clauses became common in contracts Watt negotiated for most of his clients from this time forward. Because of Watt's position as the major literary agent, similar clauses soon became the industry standard. Contracts were still written that did not contain them, but more often than not, it was inexperienced or impoverished authors without benefit of an ethical agent's advice who settled for such agreements.

Watt's second tactic was to repurchase as many of his client's copyrights as was financially feasible. This strategy was of major importance for a number of reasons. First, two important changes in international copyright laws – the 1886 Berne convention and the 1891 Chace Act in America – gave British literary productions a greater measure of copyright protection in other countries. The Chace Act was particularly important to British writers and publishers who wished to place their works in the lucrative American market, and though its protection was limited because of the requirement that books must be typeset and printed in America to be eligible for American copyright protection, it did provide a measure of protection that had not previously been available.[51] As a result of these copyright acts, it did become possible for the copyright holders, especially well-established writers, to insist on publication of authorized versions of the texts and then to exercise copyright privileges to protect their production, including legal action against publishers who pirated their work.

A second reason to repurchase copyrights arose because the growth in the literary marketplace meant that there were more ways of exploiting the sales of a particular copyright. The numbers of sale opportunities became dizzyingly complex: Domestic and Colonial book rights, American book rights, first and second serial rights, limited Domestic serial rights (restricting publication to Scotland alone, for instance, and then selling the rights to an English syndicate, or even to a London paper and a provincial syndicate), foreign serial rights, translation rights, dramatic rights, and so on. Each sale could generate new income for the copyright holder; thus an author who retained his or her outside rights could often earn far more from the exploitation of them than he or she earned from the sale of the work in book form.

A third reason to repurchase copyrights in individual texts was to enable the author to issue a set of collected works. For authors whose works were popular or who were held in high esteem, publication of collected works allowed them to exploit their reputation by reissuing previously published material and thereby derive new earnings from it.[52] This strategy was perhaps even more important to writers in the latter part of their careers when they might be producing little in the way of new material and thus the income obtained from sales of their collected work could provide a substantial windfall at a time when income from other sources might be scanty. However, since the prevailing practice had been to sell their copyrights to a variety of publishers, few authors (or publishers) were in a position to take advantage of this tactic. A collected edition of stories, essays, or sermons, for instance, often meant obtaining permissions from several publishers and also paying each firm for the use of each copyright it held. By first repurchasing the rights to each work, the agent avoided complex and protracted negotiations and also avoided having to divide the profits earned among a number of different rights holders.

Repurchasing copyrights proved to be particularly important to MacDonald, and later to the beneficiaries of his literary estate. These copyrights generated much-needed income for him in the late 1890s and early 1900s, which was a period when he wrote few new works. Watt appears to have begun the process of repurchasing MacDonald copyrights in 1894. On 31 May he wrote to Cassell, the current copyright holder of MacDonald's *The Wise Woman* (later titled *The Lost Princess*), inquiring about purchasing the rights. The reply came on 1 June: 'we shall be prepared to sell you the copyright for the nominal sum of Five Guineas.'[53] Watt then resold the work to Wells Gardner, Darton and Company. The contract, dated 8 April 1895, set the terms as follows:

(1) George MacDonald hereby assigns to the said Wells Gardner, Darton & Co. the exclusive right of printing and publishing in book form in Great Britain its Colonies and Dependencies and in English on the Continent of Europe the story at present entitled 'The Wise Woman' ... and in consideration thereof the said Wells Gardner, Darton & Co shall pay to the said George MacDonald the sum of £25.0.0 (twenty five pounds) and in addition thereto a royalty of three pence (3d) per copy on all copies which they may sell of the said story over and above the first four thousand copies.[54]

Clause 6 of the contract explicitly reserved 'all rights of translation' to MacDonald. In this transaction, Watt generated the possibility of significant income for MacDonald on a text that he had originally sold to Strahan in 1875. MacDonald immediately received approximately £17 – the £25 advance minus the 5 Guineas (£5.5.0) and Watt's 10 per cent commission – with the promise of more to come should the work sell well. By retaining the right to place the work in foreign-language markets, he might possibly make money there as well. Watt was to perform this sort of service frequently over the next few years for MacDonald. In fact, by 1903, spurred on by Greville, Watt was vigorously pursuing the repurchase of all MacDonald copyrights. An agreement dated 17 February 1903, between Greville MacDonald and Chatto and Windus, states that Chatto and Windus

being the proprietors of the copyright of a series of stories contained in ten volumes by Dr. George MacDonald, entitled 'Works of Fancy and Imagination' ... in which is comprised the undermentioned ... (1) 'Phantastes' ... (2) 'The Light Princess'; (3) 'The Giant's Heart'; (4) 'Shadows' ... (5) 'Cross Purposes'; (6) 'The Golden Key'; (7) 'The Carasoyn'; and (8) 'Little Daylight' ... agree to sell and Dr. Greville MacDonald agrees to purchase the remaining copyright in the above-named seven short stories and 'Phantastes' ... for the sum of Forty-Five Pounds (£45).[55]

This arrangement allowed Greville the opportunity to arrange for republication of some of his father's popular imaginative works with Blackie and Company and thus generated further income from property MacDonald had initially sold to Strahan in the 1860s.

Watt's decision to make the repurchasing of clients' copyrights an important facet of his agenting services was crucial because it provided authors with a revenue stream that on their own they frequently could not exploit. In some cases, Watt even provided the money for the repurchases, deducting the cost from commissions he earned from subsequent sales. It is evident that Watt advanced MacDonald money on at least one occasion. In an 1897 letter to Watt dealing with the sale of *Far above Rubies*, MacDonald says, 'I hereby authorize you to dispose of it [the story] at your discretion, and I shall be glad if after re-paying yourself the £100, which you have to-day paid into my account at Grindlay's, and deducting your usual commission, you will pay what balance remains to my bank account with Grindlay.'[56] It is possible that Watt also provided some seed money to help MacDonald repurchase some of his copyrights. Watt clearly gained substantial personal economic capital from this service, but he also gained substantial cultural capital as well. By establishing the principle of managing all of his clients' literary production, Watt consolidated his own position as an important figure in the print culture field.

Managing Literary Property

Watt's actions with regard to buying and selling of clients' copyrights can best be characterized as not only reflecting but also shaping the late nineteenth-century view of literature as property. The actions of all parties in the 1903 agreement – Greville (guided by Watt), Chatto, and Blackie – reflect the reality that as literature became widely regarded as property, its value was measured by the ways in which it could be exploited for sales to a growing number of markets. Watt, indeed, had become the manager of considerable properties that, in many cases, generated large and continuous incomes for his clients – and a steady stream of commissions for his firm. Watt was partially responsible for creating this reality through his canny manipulation of copyrights and, even more importantly, through the consolidation of so much of a writer's literary property in the hands of one manager. Publishers soon saw the value of courting Watt, for he could deliver the work of many prominent writers to them or he could withhold it, depending on what served his client's (and his own) interests best. His contracts, first with publishers and then his standard agency-client agreements, reflected Watt's evolution from purveyor of copyright to manager of substantial literary property.

In about 1890, Watt had begun to insert clauses such as the following in most contracts he negotiated for his clients:

That payment for the above mentioned story [by W. Clark Russell] shall be made by Messrs Trischler & Co as follows to Mr A P Watt of 2 Paternoster Square in the City of London on behalf of Mr W Clark Russell[57]

I call this the agency clause. It assumes a more uniform expression later in the decade, as is evident in the wording in MacDonald's 1895 contract with Wells Gardner, Darton and Company for the publication of *The Wise Woman*:

> The said George MacDonald hereby authorizes and empowers his Agents, Messrs. A.P. Watt & Son, of Hastings House, Norfolk Street, Strand, London, W.C., to collect and receive all sums of money payable to the said George MacDonald under the terms of this Agreement and declares that Messrs. A.P. Watt & Son's receipt shall be a good and valid discharge to all persons paying such monies to them. The said George MacDonald also hereby authorizes and empowers the said Wells Gardner, Darton & Co. to treat with Messrs. A.P. Watt & Son on his behalf in all matters concerning this Agreement in any way whatsoever.[58]

The significance of this clause cannot be underestimated. Not only does Watt clearly manage all interests in this particular agreement, but when we multiply this clause by the hundreds, if not thousands, of contracts that Watt's firm negotiated annually, his power becomes evident. Further evidence of the breadth of his influence is found in the fact that by the end of the first decade of the twentieth century, the majority of contracts went through an agent's hands before they were signed.

The agent-client contract was slower to develop, largely because Watt believed in accepting a client's word of honour on business matters. Yet as the agenting profession evolved, Watt reluctantly recognized that some form of contract was needed to spell out the relationship between agent and client. Although Watt did not have a formal contractual arrangement with MacDonald, by the late 1880s he was beginning to require such arrangements with other clients. For example, on 11 May 1887 Rider Haggard responded to Watt's request to formalize their business arrangements in writing:

> Thanks for your letter of 13 May – Our agreement then now is, You to receive 10% on Sales of English Editions of 'She' up to the end of present year –
>
> Also on sale of serial rights of Col. Mariten & Meeson & Addison. On monies received for literary work from all other sources (journalism excepted) your commission to be 5%.
>
> This agreement to be terminated at the will of either party –

Monies minus commission due to be paid over to my account on receipt, &
half yearly balance sheets to be rendered – together with your usual voucher.

If you will kindly signify your formal assent to this, I do not think any further document will be necessary. Please let me have a copy of my letter of
the 11th instant to put away with the papers –

I enclose formal authority to receive amounts due to me from literary
sources upon my account.[59]

Later contracts were more standardized, with the Watt agency requir-
ing writers to sign an agreement with them before they would act on the
client's behalf. Such contracts varied to some degree, but the important
clauses included the amount of the commission Watt was to receive;
exclusive representation by Watt; Watt's right to handle all literary materials; the term of the contract itself; the right for either party to end the
agreement if written notification to this effect was provided; and Watt's
collection of monies that the firm would then pay into the client's
account after deducting its commission. Although some writers refused
to sign such contracts or refused to honour all elements of them – H.G.
Wells was notorious for placing his own writings despite contracts that
precluded this[60] – the effect of agent-client contracts was to consolidate
even more power in the hands of leading agencies. Agents became
power brokers and their actions could, and did, affect not only the
careers of their authors, but those of editors and publishers as well.

Agents and Public Relations

In his introduction to *British Literary Culture and Publishing Practice 1880–
1914*, Peter McDonald recounts Edmund Gosse's well-known reaction to
Tennyson's Westminster Abbey funeral:

> Inside, the grey and vitreous atmosphere, the reverberations of music
> moaning somewhere out of sight, the bones and the monuments of the
> noble dead, reverence, antiquity, beauty, rest. Outside, in the raw air, a
> tribe of hawkers urging upon the edges of a dense and inquisitive crowd a
> large sheet of pictures of the pursuit of a flea by a 'lady,' and more insidi-
> ous salesmen doing a brisk trade in what they falsely pretended to be 'Ten-
> nyson's last poem.'[61]

McDonald's ensuing discussion suggests that the 'focus of [Gosse's] anxi-
eties was not ... the hawkers and their vulgar pictures – the counter-culture

– but the "more insidious salesmen" with their specious "last poem" and the seamstresses with their "little green volumes". He most feared the poachers within literate culture, not the philistines without.'[62] McDonald's argument may well be true, but Gosse was also afraid of the public itself, those people whose displays of grief at Tennyson's funeral disturbed and puzzled him. However, what Gosse failed to understand was the degree to which the literary world had already begun to accommodate this public. It did so not only through publishing lowbrow journals and cheap reprints of highbrow classics, but also through a deliberate positioning of literature, and its producers, as a cultural force. Writers had begun to assume the sort of public status that we associate today with rock musicians, movie stars, and superstar athletes. This may account for the public displays at Tennyson's funeral. For those who did not belong to the literate classes, Tennyson's death was important, though perhaps for different reasons. To them, he was an icon, and even if they had not read his work, his death was an event in their culture.[63] Gosse could not understand this positioning of writing and authors by the public and thus was afraid. He feared not only the incursions of the lower classes into high culture, but also, perhaps more interestingly, the power that this public could potentially gain in the print culture field.

In the 1890s, authors certainly were concerned about what literary culture thought of them, but they were also concerned with the opinion of the rest of society. Indeed, writers openly courted the attention of the very Philistines that Gosse dismissed. To this end, leading authors supplied illustrated newspapers with photographs of themselves for publication. They agreed to interviews, gave public lectures, and wrote memoirs and autobiographies, all of which fed the growing public appetite for information about and contact with writers. The 'New Journalism' so objectionable to Gosse and other supporters of 'high culture' routinely published gossip on writers' lives. Members of Gosse's self-proclaimed elite group even published material in the very journals to which they so strongly objected. As Nigel Cross says of Gissing, 'Gissing wrote to his friend Eduard Bertz in 1889: "Of course I should never dream of writing a story for a newspaper syndicate; the kind of stuff they publish, and the way they advertise it, is too ignoble." It was an untenable position for in the same letter he admitted "I cannot stand obscurity."'[64] The point here is that times were changing and the norms by which the print culture field was structured were also changing. Writers increasingly became public figures, whether they liked it or not, and the challenge became how to manage their public personae.

Here Watt, once again, led the way, recognizing that looking after his clients' literary affairs meant not only tending to the business transactions surrounding their works, but also managing their public images. It was important for an author's name to be recognizable to the reading public because name recognition resulted in sales. All the hard work of a publishers' sales and advertising staff paled in comparison to the boost to sales that could be generated from one well-placed picture or article. Publicity was a vital means of generating name recognition and to some extent it mattered little whether that publicity came from an excellent review in a leading newspaper or from a picture of the author on his yacht as it sailed off Cowes in a less desirable publication. Watt understood better than most of his peers that one of the most important tasks he could undertake for a client was to create and then sustain his client's reputation. Watt knew that reputation was business.

Watt took seriously his public relations duties for George MacDonald, though characteristically, MacDonald resisted Watt's efforts on his behalf. Apart from guessing his personality from his published work, some in George MacDonald's audience had other opportunities to become acquainted with the writer. MacDonald's public preaching and lecturing, beginning in Manchester in the 1850s and ending in 1891,[65] and his role as Mr Greatheart in the family's very popular, 'semi-professional'[66] presentations of *Pilgrim's Progress* from 1879 until 1887 contributed greatly to the public perception of the man. The image he projected was that of a Christian thinker, almost a mystic, whose religious views were decidedly Nonconformist. He was a passionate preacher who was, at the same time, somewhat remote from ordinary life and whose standards of moral conduct were perhaps out of tune with the changing times. Despite the busy public life that George MacDonald led up to 1891, Watt had very little success in his attempts to manage MacDonald's image. MacDonald had little time for the sorts of publicity-generating vehicles that Watt suggested. He refused to allow his publisher to use cuttings of comments Ruskin had made about his work in an Oxford speech, saying forcefully in a letter to Watt, 'I cannot and will not have those cuttings used for advertisement.'[67] He turned down Watt's requests to give interviews to the newspapers, writing in 1893, 'I can't do it, even to oblige you ... I never have and never will consent to be interviewed.' His telling comment to Watt in this letter is that 'I will do nothing to bring my personality before the public in any way farther than my work in itself necessitates.'[68]

Watt was much more successful in establishing and managing public personae for his other writers. Standard services included arranging interviews with prominent newspapers; collecting reviews of works and forwarding favourable ones to newspapers, prospective publishers, and current publishers for advertising purposes; and arranging for photographs to be taken and published in the illustrated papers. Other public relations activities were tailored specifically for individual clients' needs. One of the services the firm performed for Rudyard Kipling, for example, was to send out autographs to fans seeking them.[69] Watt also had to perform some damage control to protect his writers' reputations. Marie Corelli, for instance, had constant problems with the press and relied on him for advice and assistance. In 1906, she wrote to Watt, 'I would ask you (if you think it advisable) to get a private personal interview with the Editor [of the *Westminster Review*] on the subject'[70] of their continuing attacks on her. His advice not to react to the press brought this response: 'Thanks for your kindest letters and good advice. The annoyance I felt is past – I don't care about it at all now – and so far as the "Westminster Review" is concerned, it may go to – what do they say? blazes? – !!'[71] Whatever was needed to build a public persona for his writers, within the bounds of good taste and legality, Watt and his firm would undertake. Again, with Watt leading the way, this work became the norm for agents.

A final word on public personae needs to be said here, for it is likely that the most important public relations job Watt undertook was for himself. He applied the same 'reputation is business' dictum to his own positioning within the print culture field. There were two facets to establishing his reputation. First, Watt had to create a public presence in the publishing world, getting his name known among the editors and publishers who made the decisions about what would appear in print. And second, Watt had to reach beyond the circle of writers he knew from his own business and social life at Strahan and Company in order to attract a large enough pool of author-clients to place his agenting business on firm financial ground.

Watt's status as Strahan's brother-in-law and his own activities in the mid-1870s would have established a reputation in certain publishing planes, but this would not have been enough. His strategy here was actively to court business from publishers. He tirelessly wrote letters to editors and publishers of all sorts of publications. He offered to work on their behalf in the matter of outside rights and to obtain material from authors for them, and he insisted that he saw his work as not being allied solely with the author. For instance, he wrote to William Blackwood III in 1894, offering to 'assist [Blackwood] in any way to get the occasional works from the one or two writers you mentioned in your recent letter. If you will kindly let me have particulars as to exactly what it is you want and from whom, the matter will receive my immediate and careful attention.'[72] Acting as publisher for the initial volumes of the *Author* gave him credibility among those involved with, or aspiring to membership in, the Society of Authors. To further promote himself, Watt advertised in the trade publications, for instance, using the pretext of moving to new premises as a means of getting his name into the *Author* in 1895. The ad appeared on the back of the front page of the magazine. It first appeared in vol. 5, no. 4 in 1894 and ran in consecutive issues through vol. 7. It read:

A.P. Watt & Son
Literary Agents
Formerly of 2, Paternoster Row
Have now removed to
HASTINGS HOUSE, NORFOLK STREET, STRAND
LONDON W.C.

In addition, he drew attention to his services by advertising in the *Author,* and other publications read by authors, that his firm was uniquely equipped to deal with changes in copyright law. He also granted interviews and provided background information to journalists who wrote pieces on the literary agent for various publications.[73]

His most remarked upon publicity gambit was to solicit and then publish letters from satisfied clients. The publishers included many of the biggest names – Longmans, Green; Macmillan and Company; Richard Bentley and Son; and Chatto and Windus. Among the editors were George Newnes, W.C. Leng, and William Ingram. The contributions from authors were equally a who's who of the period; included were Wilkie Collins, Walter Besant, George MacDonald, Sir Arthur Conan Doyle, Rudyard Kipling, and Mrs Oliphant. The themes repeated over and over were, in Walter Besant's words, 'Not only have I profited from a pecuniary point of view, but my work can be carried on with far less stress and worry than it was when I had for a brief period to manage my own affairs.' Furthermore, 'You have been to me an agent with whom I know and feel that my interests are safe.'[74] The message was clear: if you joined Watt's clientele, you benefited from his associations with these publishers and writers.

Watt's public relations and business strategies paid off handsomely, since his name and activities were certainly widely known and accepted by 1905, the year of George MacDonald's death. It is evident that George MacDonald greatly benefited from his friend's management of his literary affairs. Arguably Watt benefited even more, for by 1905, he had risen from the ashes of a dying publishing firm to occupy a secure and powerful place in the print culture field. His profession was not universally welcomed, but there was little dispute that the road to literary success frequently passed through the offices of A.P. Watt and Son at Hastings House. His innovations in areas such as contract language, management of literary property, and public relations set the standard not only for literary agency, but also for publishing in general.

4 Testing the Agency Model: 'Lucas Malet' and Watt

Lucas Malet was the pseudonym adopted by Mary St Leger Kingsley Harrison, the younger daughter of the well-known Victorian theologian and writer Charles Kingsley.[1] Born in 1852, she was schooled at home by tutors and studied painting at the Slade School of Fine Art, with the intention of becoming a professional painter. Patricia Srebrnik describes her as 'in her youth ... a dutiful daughter' who gave up painting when her father 'insisted she become engaged to his close friend and assistant curate William Harrison.'[2] Yet she also displayed an independent streak that was in evidence when the Prince of Wales would come to visit Kingsley at Eversley in the early 1870s: 'Mary, who could not bear curtseying, would absent herself.'[3] This small act of defiance would lead to ever-greater acts of rebellion by Malet, who, as an adult, sought to create a space for herself in the literary world to which Kingsley's prominence was both an entrée and an obstacle.[4] Though she married Harrison in 1876, shortly after her father's death, the marriage was unhappy, and Malet 'apparently made no secret of her desire to escape from [it].'[5] She turned to writing, ostensibly to augment the family income, but more importantly because it provided her with the means to escape from a way of life that was uncongenial, even hostile, to her.[6] It also proved the means by which she engaged in her greatest acts of rebellion against the patriarchal Victorian values her father's life exemplified.

Patricia Srebrnik points out that 'Lucas Malet declared repeatedly that she was not indebted to Charles Kingsley for her literary ability' and her pen name 'was chosen to honor her paternal grandmother, whose maiden name was Lucas, and her grandmother's aunt, a Miss Malet.'[7] This tactic notwithstanding, reviewers frequently compared her with her father. She was nonetheless able to establish an identity for herself in the literary world at the end of the nineteenth century and into the first two decades of the twentieth. Indeed, her novel *The Wages of Sin* (1891) was critically acclaimed as 'the most striking of recent novels' and 'the book of the season.'[8] It was also highly successful financially, though Malet's business arrangements at this point meant that she did not share fully in the book's earnings.[9] By 1901, when she published *The History of Sir Richard Calmady*, she was one of the most popular writers of the day. As Janet Courtney, Malet's contemporary, wrote in 1932, 'who were the writers between 1885 and 1905 for whose newest novel the library public clamoured? ... after 1891, Lucas Malet.'[10] Yet Lucas Malet is not a name known to most early twenty-first-century readers and her writing has, until very recently, been out of print.[11]

A.P. Watt had many women writers on his client list, some of whom are far better known than Malet and who have retained a place, albeit a marginal one even now, in literary history. Why, then, examine the career of a writer as obscure today as Malet instead of one of these others? There are several specific reasons why Malet deserves attention, including her innovative writing, her enormous popularity during the 1890s, and the fact that despite critical acclaim during her lifetime she is now virtually unknown. In addition, Malet's relationship with Watt, and later his son Alec,[12] demonstrates some of the ways in which the standard agent-client relationship he developed with George MacDonald was not transferable to every client. Her refusal to be pegged solely as an 'authoress' and her desire not to be limited in her subject matter or style made her an interesting challenge for Watt. Yet, in many ways, Malet is a representative female client and as such she proves an interesting and instructive vantage point from which to assess Watt's interactions with his women authors. This comment is not meant to deny Malet's individuality as a writer, or to suggest a false homogeneity in women's writings of the 1880s and onwards. How Watt dealt with Malet demonstrates how he coped with emerging modes of writing and thus how he wielded his influence in the field of literary production in a time when avant-garde writers such as Oscar Wilde, Henry James, Joseph Conrad, and May Sinclair were challenging these norms.

The Agent-Client Relationship

Business First

Macmillan published Lucas Malet's first novel, *Mrs. Lorimer, a Sketch in Black and White*, in 1882. *Colonel Enderby's Wife* (1885), *A Counsel of Perfection*

(1888), and *Little Peter* (1888), all published by Kegan Paul, followed it. These novels attracted generally favourable attention, with the author being 'commended for her narrative power, for her gentle, ironic humor, and above all, for her subtle, detailed analysis of character.'[13] She published *The Wages of Sin* in 1891 with Swan Sonnenschein. It proved to be one of the most popular novels of the decade and at the same time it generated a storm of critical controversy. Patricia Srebrnik tells us that it was 'hailed as "the book of the season" according to C.E. Oldham … The *Scotsman* described the novel as "undoubtedly the greatest work of art this already successful author has yet produced … one of the boldest, most realistic … sketches of a … human soul, that the whole range of our fiction contains."' She also remarks, 'Some critics were disturbed, however, by the book's frank portrayal of an illicit sexual relationship. They were also dismayed by the possibility that Malet might share the religious and aesthetic views of her painter-hero.'[14] What most dismayed critics of this ilk was the fact that the author of *The Wages of Sin* was female; the subject matter was clearly not the sort that a woman ought to write about; in fact, it was unwomanly for her to even know about such explicit sexuality. The fact that the author was known to be the daughter of Charles Kingsley – whose high morals were widely admired – further condemned Malet in certain critical circles. The controversy surrounding *The Wages of Sin* notwithstanding, within ten years of first entering the literary marketplace Malet had established her reputation as a popular, innovative, and highly controversial writer.

Malet arranged her own publication contracts and was not satisfied with her treatment by publishers, in particular by Kegan Paul. She may have mentioned this to Thomas Hardy, with whom she had initiated a correspondence in 1892.[15] He suggested to her, in a letter on 18 March 1892, that 'Whenever you want to drive a bargain for a new novel I can recommend you to a man who will get you the best price possible.'[16] The man was his own agent A.P. Watt, whom he had recently employed successfully to arrange publication of a story in England and America.[17] Malet took Hardy's suggestion and contacted Watt later that year, beginning an almost forty-year relationship with A.P. Watt and Son.[18]

Upon assuming his role as her agent, Watt immediately set out to ascertain the status of Malet's existing works. He wrote to her publishers asking for information on copyright status, sales, stock on hand, and outside rights arrangements, and where possible he obtained copies of her contracts. He discovered that her literary affairs were in disarray. For instance, on 24 November 1896, he wrote to Swan Sonnenschein:

Mrs. Harrison (Lucas Malet) informs me that Messrs. Methuen & Co. have with her consent purchased from you your interest in 'The Wages of Sin'. A question has arisen as to whether Messrs. Methuen & Co. have purchased the Colonial rights of the book as well as the British rights. On this point Mrs. Harrison writes that the Continental rights were sold to Messrs Heinemann & Balestier for use in the English Library and that the American rights were sold to Messrs. Lovell, and that these arrangements were made by you at a time when she was unwell and unable to attend to business. I shall be glad to know whether in dealing with Messrs. Lovell you sold them United States rights only or whether the American rights included both the United States and Canada? I shall also be glad to know exactly what rights were sold to Messrs. Heinemann & Balestier.[19]

The response came the next day:

On 5th November 1890 we sold to the International News Co. a set of stereo plates of the Wages of Sin – nothing was said about American rights and the sale did certainly not include Canadian rights.

On 31 March 1891 we sold to Messrs. Heinemann & Balestier the right of publishing an English Edition for the Continental market only.

Both of the sums received were handed over in their entirety to Mrs. Harrison.[20]

Watt also discovered that, like many beginning writers, Malet had sold some of her copyrights outright to her publishers, though her practice seemed to vary widely. She sold the copyrights for *Mrs. Lorimer* and *Colonel Enderby's Wife*, but she kept them for *The Wages of Sin* and *Little Peter.* In the case of *Colonel Enderby's Wife*, she had sold the copyright outright to Kegan Paul, Trench and Company in return for their 'printing, publishing and advertising it firstly in three volume form giving her the sum of fifty pounds on receipt of the MS. fifty pounds on publication, one hundred pounds after the sale of one thousand copies and one hundred pounds after the sale of each additional five hundred copies.'[21] The contract goes on to spell out the various sums to be given Malet for publication in different forms, but what is clear is that Kegan Paul had bought all rights of publication by purchasing the copyright. As her reputation soared, she did not share in the increased sales of her previous works to the same degree that she might have done had she negotiated her contracts differently. Malet's literary affairs called out for professional attention of the sort that Watt had pioneered for George MacDonald.

Literary Property

Selling and Buying Copyrights

One of the early contracts that Watt negotiated for Malet was for the sale of American rights to *The Gateless Barrier* in 1899. The first clause of the contract stated:

> That the said Mrs Harrison shall assign to the said Dodd, Mead & Co. for the full term of copyright and renewals thereof the exclusive right of printing and publishing in book form in the United States of America a new novel ... [22]

Though the wording is somewhat obscure, the intent is not. Malet is assigning to Dodd, Mead the right to publish her new novel *only* in book form in America for the full term of copyright; Malet retains the option to exploit other rights herself. This arrangement is made clear in clause 5 of the contract:

> (5) That the rights of translation, the rights of dramatization, and all rights other than the above mentioned right of publication in book form in the United States of America are reserved by the said Mrs Harrison. [23]

At the same time, Watt was negotiating with Methuen for British publication of the novel. The contract with Methuen also protected Malet's copyright in Britain. Indeed, the agreement he arranged with Methuen permitted Malet to renew the contract at specified intervals or break it provided sufficient notice had been given to Methuen.

Later correspondence between Alec Watt and A.M.S. Methuen outlines clearly the nature of the various publishing agreements Malet had with Methuen. Alec wrote, on 16 March 1906: 'I now write formally to put on record the terms of the agreement at which we have arrived with regard to Mrs. Harrison's three novels "THE HISTORY OF SIR RICHARD CALMADY," "THE WAGES OF SIN" and "THE GATELESS BARRIER."' He continued, 'the agreement under which you are publishing "THE WAGES OF SIN" expires on the 9th of January 1911.'[24] The arrangements for the other two novels were more complex, but essentially, the contracts for each contained clauses permitting Malet or Methuen to end their arrangement upon appropriate notification of the intent to do so. In short, the Watts drew up contracts that attempted to guard Malet's long-term interests in her literary property – she leased the copyright rather than sold it – while nevertheless obtaining for her the best possible short-term benefits from the leasing of her property.

Watt's job was made more complex by the need to manage the literary property in different legal jurisdictions; here Malet definitely benefited from her agent's expert knowledge. Watt knew that the Chace Act required not only simultaneous publication in America and Britain in order to protect American copyright of a work, but also that the American edition had to be printed from type set in America. His concern about the timing of *The Gateless Barrier*'s publication is clear in his correspondence with its publisher. He wrote to Methuen on 20 February 1900, 'I shall write to Messrs Dodd, Mead & Co. informing them of the postponement of the publication of "THE GATELESS BARRIER" till August or September next, leaving you to arrange with them the exact date.'[25] In a subsequent letter, Watt again wrote to Methuen,

In a letter which I have just received from Mrs. Harrison she writes:

– 'I send you the slips as proposed by Mr. Methuen to be entered at Stationers' Hall. Please tell Mr. Methuen how much obliged to him I am for his kindness both in letting me have slip [*sic*] and in making this arrangement for securing my title.'

I think I am correct in supposing that you cannot register 'The Gateless Barrier' at Stationers' Hall without making some sort of publication and if you publish here and we do not publish in America simultaneously we shall lose our American copyright on the title and that portion of the story which is issued here only. Under these circumstances I must ask you kindly to let me have a duplicate set of the enclosed proofs in order that I may send them out to Messrs. Dodd, Mead & Co. with instructions to secure the American copy right on this portion of the book ... On hearing from Messrs. Dodd, Mead & Co. I would then advise you of the earliest date at which it would be convenient for them to take out their copyright in the States.[26]

Watt managed Malet's interests skilfully here, guaranteeing protection of her copyright in both America and Britain.

However, the Watts did occasionally sell Malet's copyrights in order to clinch a sale. As late as 1910, Watt sold the copyright of *The Wreck of the Golden Galleon* to Hodder and Stoughton for the sum of £250. The contract explicitly reserved the dramatic rights to Malet, but all others went to the publisher. Another clause stated that 'If the serial rights of the story are sold within a fortnight from date to the Editor of "The London Magazine" for publication in that periodical on a date not later than 31st of October next, the proceeds of any such sale to be divided equally between [Malet] and Messrs. Hodder & Stoughton.'[27] Such actions were likely driven by Malet's need for money; she was indebted to the Watts for £1000 and had other debts as well, which may have caused her to instruct her agents to agree to terms they might not otherwise have accepted. Equally, the sale of copyrights may have been seen by the Watts as the necessary price for selling Malet's work to the markets for which they believed it was best suited. For the most part, though, the Watts enforced the principle of retaining the writer's ownership of copyright, though the terms under which they leased the copyrights varied over time as Malet's reputation waxed and waned.[28]

Watt also attempted to consolidate Malet's literary property into her own hands, to be managed by him. As he had done for MacDonald, Watt sought to repurchase or reclaim copyrights where possible. Despite the enormous financial success she had from the sales of *The History of Richard Calmady*, which Patricia Lorimer Lundberg says earned her at least £10,000,[29] and despite the fact that sales for later books were often good – Lundberg notes that the 'first edition of 20,000 copies' of *The Far Horizon* 'sold within a day and Hutchinson [its publisher] immediately reprinted another 10,000'[30] copies – Malet's financial situation was seldom stable enough for her to enter into any arrangements with the Watts to repurchase copyrights that she had sold. In addition, her recurrent ill health prevented her from writing as much as she wished and she was behind in her obligations to meet contracts already undertaken. Indeed, she contracted with Hutchinson for a novel she then called 'The Book of the Wisdom of Damaris' to be published in 1902, but that novel was published as *Damaris* by Hutchinson in 1916, a full fourteen years after the agreement had been reached.[31] By that time, the advance she had received in 1902 had long been spent and any money *Damaris* earned first had to pay off the advance. Only then would Malet earn any money from this book. Her financial condition was precarious, at best, and was to remain that way for the rest of her life. Therefore, Watt was not able to pursue aggressively the strategy of repurchasing her copyrights.

The second avenue open to Watt was to renegotiate existing contracts, and in doing so seek to improve Malet's share of the profits for ongoing sales of her work. Here he was more successful. The continuing popularity of Malet's early works meant that they remained profitable for publishers, but changing economic and publishing conditions prompted publishers to market the books in different formats. In 1906, for instance, Leslie Willson, an editor at George Newnes Ltd, wished to publish a sixpenny edition of her works. Doing so would broaden the market penetration for Malet's work and generate a new stream of income for her. Malet was enthusiastic about this prospect, but worried about where the new profits would go – to her or to Methuen, whom she gradually grew to distrust – and she queried Alec Watt about how to proceed.[32] Alec responded by first informing her of the ownership of each of the texts she had mentioned – *Colonel Enderby's Wife*, *The Wages of Sin*, *The Gateless Barrier*, *Sir Richard Calmady*, and *Little Peter* – and the status of original agreements in place with various publishers. He remarked about *Colonel Enderby's Wife* that 'the agreement ... assigns the right of the book to the publishers, there is no five years or other similar clause and the agreement cannot therefore be broken without the consent of the publisher.'[33] Malet responded that 'I am disappointed to find that the copyright of "Colonel Enderby's Wife" belongs to the publisher. I remember your father told me that my agreements with Messrs Kegan Paul were anything but satisfactory! I believe this book would sell so well in a Sixpenny Edition, that I think we must eventually try to make some arrangement regarding it.'[34] Knowing that Methuen now owned the copyright, Alec approached them, seeking their permission for this undertaking. On 2 April 1906, Methuen replied, 'In regard to the proposed Sixpenny edition of Lucas Malet's COLONEL ENDERBY'S WIFE, we shall be happy to allow this to be done by Messrs Newnes if we receive 17 ½% of the sum paid to the author by them.'[35] Alec then arranged with Leslie Willson to include *Colonel Enderby's Wife* in the new sixpenny edition of Malet's work, though in the end, Newnes published only the sixpenny edition of *Richard Calmady*.[36] Watt continued to pursue publication of new editions of Malet's work – negotiating a contract in 1907 with Thomas Nelson and Sons for sevenpenny editions of *The Wages of Sin* and *The Gateless Barrier*; arranging in 1908 with Henry Frowde and Hodder and Stoughton for a new edition of *Little Peter*; and even arranging in 1911 for Methuen to bring out a two-shilling edition of *Colonel Enderby's Wife*[37] – and while the terms were frequently less favourable than Malet had become accustomed to, Watt was nonetheless able to continue to generate some income for her by this means.[38] In this way, Alec performed the same sort of service for Malet as his father had performed for MacDonald in consolidating as much literary property in the author's hands as possible.

Finally, Watt worked for Malet, as for all of his clients, in the area of outside rights. Only two of Malet's earlier novels had been serialized,[39] and despite Watt's attempts to place other material serially, his efforts on her behalf were not very successful.[40] He first attempted to have the follow-up novel to *The Carissima: A Modern Grotesque* appear in instalments in the *Queen* magazine in 1899, but despite a signed agreement, Malet never provided the novel to them.[41] Even something as routine as the sale of short stories created problems. The 1915 placement of the story 'Da Silva's Widow' in the American magazine the *Metropolitan,* for example, was fraught with difficulties. Mr Whigham, the editor of the magazine, informed Alec that he would pay the amount agreed to for this short story and 'that he [was] taking steps to sell the American serial rights.' Alec said that Whigham 'had no right to do' this, but he was willing to let him try 'provided he pays.' Alec concluded his letter to Malet, 'Indeed having received his cheque for "DA SILVA'S WIDOW", I take it that you will be glad to hear no more, either of Mr. Whigham, or "The Metropolitan."'[42] Malet replied to Alec:

> Many thanks for your letter, I am delighted Whigham sees the error of his ways and sends us a cheque. No, we will not protest against his sale of serial rights – This is an occassion [sic] surely to 'Take the cash, and let the credit go' – according to the advice of Omar Khayam. But what a ridiculous person to assert 'no magazine in the U.S. would publish such a story' – I quote from memory – and promptly sell serial rights. I do not wish, once the cheque is received, as you suppose, to hear more of him.[43]

Malet's willingness to take Alec's advice on dealing with this difficult situation shows just how fully she trusted her agents to make business decisions for her. Though Watt was able to place 'Da Silva's Widow' in England in *Nash's and Pall Magazine,* Whigham's refusal to publish the story in his own magazine and his failure to place it with another American magazine does suggest the difficulty that Malet (and the Watts) had in placing later material. They did have a small measure of success with the short stories Malet wrote during the period 1919–23, but Malet was not able to produce a large number of short stories, so this market was never fully exploited by her or her agents on her behalf.[44]

Some efforts were made to dramatize Malet's novels, but they were not very successful. An early effort in 1901 to dramatize *The Wages of Sin* came to nothing.[45] In 1926 Malet arranged for a dramatization of *Sir Richard*

Calmady with her companion Gabrielle Vallings and Louis Napoleon Parker as dramatists and George C. Tyler of the New Amsterdam Theatre of New York as the manager. The correspondence around this contract indicates that the performance was never carried out.[46] The Watts made every effort to exploit the growing film market, selling the rights of at least two of her books to film companies. Though she ran into problems with producers – Colonial Pictures, the American producer of *Sir Richard Calmady*, failed to produce the film as scheduled and also failed to pay the full sum of the contract agreed upon – the Watts' efforts were nonetheless vigorous and conscientious.[47] The Watts did exploit other subsidiary markets more fully. Translations of Malet's works were arranged in German, Swedish, French, and Italian, thus generating income for her.[48] Sales of her works to colonial markets were frequently arranged and the Watts also made every effort to reserve these rights for Malet in contracts they negotiated. If the publisher went on to exploit these rights, he did so with the Watts' approval, and the monies owed to Malet were spelled out contractually, either in the original contract or in one drawn up for the specific sale.

Thus, according to the template A.P. Watt had developed in his relationship with George MacDonald, Lucas Malet was professionally well served. A.P. Watt, or his sons, made every effort to find markets for Malet's work, to manage her literary property according to the highly successful model they had developed, and to look after all her literary affairs in a professional manner. The Watts also made efforts to keep her name before the public during her fallow periods, arranging for notices about her ongoing work to be placed in the *Bookman* and other periodicals, for instance. The indirect cultural capital Malet acquired because of the Watts' actions – Malet was a Watt client and publishers were more willing to consider her work than if it came to them direct from the author, for instance – helped later works find publishers. But the fact that their cultural capital was most useful in the mainstream markets they successfully plied and less well regarded in the emerging markets meant that the younger generation, those individuals who were to construct the canon of early twentieth-century literature, were less familiar with her work or possibly thought it outmoded, because of Malet's age and the venues in which her work appeared. Their views were to have a detrimental impact on her reputation and led directly to her obscurity by century's end. This is a point I will return to later in the chapter.

Friends

As we have seen, A.P. Watt began his agenting career by representing his friend George MacDonald. Many, though by no means all, of his subsequent clients also became friends, including Lucas Malet. In the forty years that the Watt firm represented Lucas Malet, A.P. and his son Alec undertook many non-literary services for her. They certainly carried on a friendly correspondence with her over the years and it is possible that A.P. Watt and his wife socialized with Malet. The kind of relationship that evolved predisposed the Watts to help Lucas Malet financially when sales and royalties diminished from about 1910 onwards.

Although it is not clear exactly when the relationship changed from a purely business one to a more personal one, it is evident by 1902 that a friendship existed between Watt and Malet. In the midst of a discussion about leaving Methuen to go to Hutchinson for the publication of her next book, Malet writes, 'I was so interested in hearing of the Fowler sisters [sic] engagements – Do let me know to whom, so that I may write to the delightful Ellen.' Evidently, Watt kept Malet apprised of gossip – both literary and personal – when she was out of the country. She adds a postscript to the letter: 'I hope you are well? Tell me when you write.'[49] A letter in March of 1902 to Alec about business matters contains these friendly words: 'My letters to you are also to your father – I know he will be distressed on ly [sic] account, to hear of Mr. Propert's death' and concludes 'Affectionate regards to your father.'[50] A few days later, again from Paris, Malet writes to A.P., 'I am afraid we shall not meet, unless you stay here on your way South. My house will not be ready till the end of the 1st week of April, so I shall remain here till after Easter. How charming it would be to have you and Mrs. Watt break your journey for a day or two here in Paris!'[51] The warmth Malet and Watt display in their letters to each other appears genuine, suggesting a real friendship existed.

It was not until 1909 that Malet signed an official agency contract with the Watts.[52] The absence of a formal contract between Malet and A.P. Watt most likely signifies his belief that she would treat him fairly and honourably. It also reflects Malet's trust in Watt to do the same. It is probable that the contract was arranged because Alec Watt was taking over more of the day-to-day business of the firm, and he wished to place all of their clients on the same legal standing with the agency. Furthermore, Malet's continuing financial difficulties, including outstanding debts to the Watts themselves, likely led Alec to seek a more formal arrangement with Malet.

Malet's financial position was increasingly precarious as the 1910s wore on, partly because she was unable to produce work as quickly as she needed to in order to generate new sales, partly because royalties from earlier works were beginning to diminish, and partly because she continued to live well beyond her means.[53] Malet turned to her agents for financial help. Patricia Lorimer Lundberg writes, 'On August 13, 1909, Malet ... had her attorney H.L. Roscoe conclude an indebtedness agreement with the Watts.' This came about because

> They had already lent her £500 and now added £500 at the interest rate of £5 per annum, in effect mortgaging the royalties promised in a contract with John Murray for a forthcoming novel, *Adrian Savage* (1911), signed February 1, 1909. Malet had begun the dangerous gamble of 'betting on the come,' spending her royalty receipts before she had begun writing the novels and earning the income. By November 1911, she would only be able to repay £500 to the Watts.[54]

After A.P.'s death in 1914, Alec continued to provide financial assistance to Malet. He arranged two life insurance policies for Malet as vehicles through which she could eventually discharge her debts to the Watts.[55] As Malet's solicitors at Field, Roscoe, and Company wrote, this was done 'in order to free the Eversley title [to her country home] and the amount which is owing will in future be secured by the Mortgage on the Policies which Mrs. Harrison is executing.'[56] Yet Malet eventually had difficulties paying the premiums for these policies, thereby engendering ever-greater financial debts to the Watts.

In 1922, Mr Emery of Field, Roscoe and Company informed W.P. Watt (A.P.'s son William)[57] that they 'h[ad] already advanced to Mrs. Harrison nearly all the money' that might have been gained from the insurance policies from which the Watts had hoped to recover their loans to Malet, and that 'it is no use crying over spilt milk.' The Watts now wished to transfer ownership of the policy from them personally to the firm. The lawyer advised William, 'I return the proposal to the Law Union which needs to be countersigned by your brother or by the firm if the Policy is to be made out in the name of the firm.'[58] Even when Malet sold The Orchard, her Eversley property, in 1922, her debt woes continued, since the three mortgages on the property amounted to £3100 and the price she obtained for it was at most £2170.[59] Deprived of the money they had advanced against The Orchard, Emery and the Watts stepped in to manage Malet's financial affairs, with Alec Watt paying off her £150 arrears to her bank, the National Provincial and Union Bank, and, as Lundberg notes, hoping 'for a large sale of *The Survivors* when it should appear early in 1923'[60] in order to recover at least some of their financial investment in Malet.

Even this assistance did not alleviate Malet's continuing financial distress; furthermore, the Watts' actions had the effect of reinforcing her belief that they would continue to provide for her, as her letter to Alec dated 10 January 1924 demonstrates:

> To take the letters as they come – First the correspondence with Mr. Emery – I had already written to him generally on the subject, and repeated a statement I had already made him – that I cannot give him a charge upon the book until I know what we get for it in America – This for the simple reason that your charges naturally stand first – that it [is] absolutely necessary I should set aside some part of the proceeds for arrears of income tax – and that I definitely refuse to be left with nothing in hand when these sums are paid. My nerve will go, if I work without cessation – I must pause now and then, and to do so I must keep some of the profits of this book unalloted before I have even earned them!! If you and Mr. Emery can carry out the plan you suggest as to the division of the Life Insurance, and this will enable you to go on advancing me a weekly wage on my work I shall be more than grateful to you.[61]

Emery wrote to Alec on the same day, 'The Policy is for £350 and the premium was £35, so that if you will send me a cheque for four sevenths of the premium – £20; this will be quite satisfactory, and I will attach to the premium a short Memorandum that the first £200 of it belongs to you as part of your security.'[62] At the same time, Alec began to pay Malet the weekly wage, both to provide her with the means to live so that she could write and as a hedge against future work that might generate sufficient income to make a dent in her debt to them.[63]

Though the Watts had limited any further financial drain on their personal purses, the family looked for other ways to assist Malet financially, for as Srebrnik notes, 'By the late 1920s Malet was so seriously ill with cancer and so deeply in debt that she could not always pay her hotel bills. In 1930 she was awarded a civil list pension.'[64] It is quite likely that the Watts lobbied for the pension. Alec was by now a Commander of the British Empire, and his firm's status as one of the country's leading literary agencies would have enabled him to make the right contacts on Malet's behalf. It is also likely that Alec had written in support of Malet's applications to the Royal Literary Fund for emergency funding.[65] His continuing friendship with her, and his determination to treat his father's friend with the same scrupulous care and attention as his father had, in all likelihood would have impelled him to act to better Malet's circumstances.

Malet, Watt, and the Changing Literary World

Lucas Malet's obituary in *The Times* stated that 'in the literary history of the last quarter of the nineteenth and the first quarter of the twentieth century Lucas Malet can hardly be denied a secure place.'[66] However, at the end of the twentieth century, not only did Malet not possess a secure place in literary history, but she had almost disappeared from it. There are a number of reasons for this disappearance that will not be addressed in this chapter.[67] Rather, I want to examine the degree to which her agents' handling of her work may have contributed to Malet's disappearance from the literary scene.

Initially, Malet appeared just the sort of writer that Watt usually sought out as a client. She was already a well-established author, having earned considerable critical attention with *The Wages of Sin*, and throughout the 1880s and early 1890s she established a good track record in terms of producing novels that sold well.[68] Even though she had deliberately distanced herself from her famous father, Charles Kingsley, she nevertheless came from a social background with which Watt was familiar and comfortable, thereby enabling him to create the bonds of friendship that marked his most successful agent-client partnerships. And, as we have seen, the Watts were conscientious in employing all facets of their agenting services to Malet's literary productions. It would therefore not be reasonable or accurate to claim that Watt, and later his sons, deliberately mishandled Malet's literary affairs or her career. On the contrary, the evidence proves that they worked as energetically for her as they did for any of their clients. So why did their efforts on her behalf not translate into the type of financial and critical success that Malet craved and that other Watt clients achieved?

The agenting practices developed by A.P. Watt, and used to considerable success by his firm, depended on two crucial factors. First, the writer needed to produce a steady stream of work that could be marketed in such a way as not only to exploit all publication opportunities for individual texts, but also to develop a following for the author. Second, knowing what markets were suited to each author's output was crucial, since it made little sense to offer a story to a periodical or publisher for which it was ill suited. The ideal client produced a new book every year, which could be serialized in a leading periodical prior to its publication in book form, and also wrote short stories or articles that the Watts could place in appropriate periodicals. Over a number of years, the accumulation of such material, preferably of the sort that would appeal to a well-defined segment of the reading audience, would result in increased recognition of the author and continuing demand for her work. Unfortunately Malet proved not to be the ideal client and Watt's agenting template failed to produce the results for her that it did for other clients.

Despite the fact that Malet positioned herself as a professional writer – revealing herself as such in the many letters she exchanged with Watt in which she discusses contract terms, advertising strategies that she would like to see employed by publishers on her behalf, and critics' opinions of her novels – she was unable to function effectively as a professional writer. Her inability to do so arose in part because of health problems and family duties, which meant that she did not produce material reliably or according to an arranged schedule, and in part because she refused to compromise her artistic sensibility in order to tailor her work to a particular market or readership. From the very beginning of her relationship with Watt, Malet's work habits caused problems. Her failure to write to an agreed-upon schedule was detrimental to Watt's attempts to keep new works coming forward to the public in a steady stream. There was a five-year lag between the publication of *The Wages of Sin* (1891) and her next novel, *The Carissima: A Modern Grotesque* (1896), and a further four years lapsed before *The Gateless Barrier*'s publication in 1900, for instance.[69] Publishers became leery of handling her work because of her growing reputation as a writer who could not honour her commitments. Typical of this are the circumstances surrounding the follow-up novel to the enormously successful *The History of Sir Richard Calmady* (1901).

Watt had arranged a contract with Hutchinson for a book that would capitalize on the brisk sales and popularity of *Calmady*.[70] Malet agreed to this arrangement in early 1902, but added, 'please if you come to terms with [Hutchinson], make it clear that I cannot be bound as to the date of completing the MS. – I do not know yet how big the book will be, and as I am most anxious it should be at least as good as the Calmady book, I must feel easy as to time.'[71] Her letter of 12 March 1902 contains this surprising news:

I should certainly like you to conclude the deal with Messrs. Hutchinson. Only there is this difficulty. I said something about a not unpleasant surprise – it takes this form of a quite new novel which has suddenly present [*sic*] itself! It promises, I believe, to be fine and original, but I am not sure yet as to its length ... I would rather write it before I attack 'The Book of the Wisdom of Damaris'[the follow-up to *Calmady*] ... What are we to do? ... But it is for you to decide whether we give this book to Mr. Hutchinson in place of Damaris.[72]

Although Hutchinson eventually published 'Damaris' in 1916 and they also published the novel that had so suddenly presented itself to Malet, finally titled *The Far Horizon*, in 1906, they could not have been happy with Malet's failure to produce the novel for which she had contracted with them. Malet's unpredictability increased as she aged, and it became more difficult for the Watts to place her work, as they could not guarantee to publishers the delivery times or even if the book contracted would be the book delivered. This clearly had an impact on her reputation. A steady stream of material meant that the writer's name was frequently in the public sphere. Notices of new books that were then followed by reviews and discussions of the books and the reviews in various periodicals helped to build and maintain the writer's reputation. Because Malet's works did not appear regularly, her name slipped from sight.

As we have already seen, Watt's tried and true methods did not work well for Malet. For example, her agreements to try serial publication were self-sabotaged, since she consistently failed to produce the works for which he had arranged contracts. Indeed, when she was unable to produce the agreed upon material for the *Queen* in 1902, she wrote to Watt, 'As you know, I do not care about serial publication.'[73] Malet also refused to work to order. She would not have her subject matter, or even the length of her works, predetermined for her.[74] Since these were basic components of commissioned works, she did not exploit this publication opportunity. Finally, even when the Watts provided Malet with an allowance, hoping that a regular weekly sum would enable her to produce material at a steady rate, she was not able to do so. In the end, it is clear that the Watts' standard methods did not work for Malet because she simply did not fit the professional author model upon which the Watts had based their agenting practices.

However, Malet's work habits are only part of the reason for the Watts' failure to manage her career successfully. At the heart of the problem was A.P. Watt's failure to understand at the outset of his relationship with her that the kind of literature she wanted to write would require him to cultivate more than one market for her work, since she not only wanted to earn a respectable living from her pen, but also wanted the freedom to follow whatever subject matter and write in whatever style she felt appropriate. In this failure he was not alone, since critics frequently debated about where to place Malet in the ever more fragmented literary marketplace of the era. As Patricia Srebrnik says,

> Critics agonized over how much latitude should be allowed a woman writer and struggled to assign Malet to a recognizably 'English' tradition of fiction. In the 1880s Malet's fiction was compared to that of George Eliot, while in the 1890s it was grouped with the works of the 'New Women' novelists, despite Malet's bitter denunciations of 'the *feministes*.' After her conversion to Catholicism in 1902, Malet's increasingly elaborate prose style prompted some critics to compare her to George Meredith and Henry James. Malet insisted that she was more influenced by Honoré de Balzac and Emile Zola than by any English author.[75]

That the 1890s and 1900s experienced a growing chasm in the literary marketplace between those writers who insisted on the primacy of literary art over popular sales and those who catered to the consumers of literature is a well-accepted characterization of the period. While this division is too crude to be supported by close examination of the careers of writers on either side of the divide, it is nonetheless the case that the rhetoric of art for art's sake versus popular literature was employed by many writers and critics in the period and subsequent to it. Malet's work straddles both categories and as a result she does not fit comfortably or fully into either one. Henry Seidel Canby's notions of publishing planes are well exemplified here; although Malet's output was fiction, thus belonging to one publishing plane, the fiction that she produced varied over her long career, which meant that her agents needed to understand the complexities and nuances of the publishing plane in order to market her work effectively. The Watts were normally very astute in discerning trends and shifts in the various planes, so it is interesting to note that in the case of Malet, they were less effective than usual and indeed had difficulty in knowing how to market her work.

It is evident from the publication venues that A.P. and then Alec Watt sought for Malet's work that their perception of her work was tied closely to the four novels she produced in the 1880s and to her 1891 breakthrough novel, *The Wages of Sin*. The first four novels portrayed 'women who [had to] learn humility and self-renunciation,'[76] earning Malet a place alongside other female writers, such as Mary Elizabeth Braddon and Mrs Oliphant, whose works also dealt with the moral and social complexities of late nineteenth-century women's lives. Even *The Wages of Sin*, which earned Malet critical condemnation because of its depiction of the illicit sexual relationship between the protagonist, painter James Colthurst, and his model Jennie, nonetheless continued her exploration of women's lives through its compelling portraits of the two women drawn into Colthurst's sexual and moral dilemma. Novels such as these prompted Watt to see his new client as a writer of moral and social fiction for women and he set out to situate her in the market accordingly. However, he failed to appreciate that by the mid-1890s, Malet's fiction was more closely aligned with emerging literary forms – such as aestheticism – and thus he miscalculated his marketing strategy from almost the beginning.

For instance, it is puzzling that Watt contracted with the *Queen* magazine for the serialization of the follow-up novel to the 1896 novel *The Carissima: A Modern Grotesque*. Lundberg calls *The Carissima* a '"masculine" or "horror" gothic in the Lewisite tradition' and says Malet's 'Readers could not fathom this dramatic change in Malet's style.'[77] Furthermore, she notes that 'Malet won few accolades and endured much negative criticism.'[78] This novel was clearly a departure from her early work, and readers must have wondered what Malet would produce next. In fact, she was working on both *The Gateless Barrier* and *The History of Sir Richard Calmady* and it is likely that the novel Watt had in mind to place with the *Queen* was the former. It too proved a departure from the early novels, and though it continued Malet's exploration of the supernatural, as Lundberg again tells us, 'it is dramatically different from *The Carissima*' since 'It follows the Radcliffean tradition, which employs the home as a site for an assaulted heroine to initiate her own rescue from the clutches of the villain, breaking through terror to establish control over her body and her home.' Furthermore, 'Malet complicates this tradition with a tale that explores an understanding beyond the natural but is grounded in complex realities of late Victorian, Modernist and wartime British concerns.'[79] That Watt thought the *Queen* a suitable home for Malet illustrates his misunderstanding of either Malet's new work or the *Queen*'s readership. The *Queen* was established in 1861 as a magazine '"for women", "about women" and "EDITED by a LADY"' and it proclaimed in its first number, 'When we write for women, we write for home.'[80] As Margaret Beetham notes, 'This "home" was neither the product of woman's moral management nor of her practical skills but a domestic theatre in which her femininity – defined in terms of beauty, dress and deportment – was displayed.'[81] It is highly unlikely that a magazine with this mandate would have been a suitable venue for a supernatural ghost story.

The contract was eventually cancelled in 1904, putatively because Malet's ill health prevented her from fulfilling the contract, as Watt states in his letter to Percy Cox cancelling the contract: 'Mrs. Harrison very much regrets that owing to ill health she will be unable to supply you with the story which you commissioned her some little time ago to write.'[82] However, between the signing of the contract in July of 1899 and its cancellation in 1904, Malet had published two novels – *The Gateless Barrier* and *The History of Sir Richard Calmady* – either of which might have been available for serializing in the *Queen*, so ill health seems a subterfuge designed to permit both Malet and Cox to save face. Indeed, *Richard Calmady* had created such a sensation when it was published that had Cox really wanted Malet to appear in the pages of the *Queen* he would certainly have held her to the contract rather than release her from its obligations. However, *Richard Calmady* was, according to Stephen Gwynn's review of it in the *New-Liberal Review*, not only 'the best novel since *Middlemarch* written by a woman' but also a 'story which it would be not only unwise but absolutely cruel to put into the hands of any inexperienced girl.'[83] The subject matter of the novel, he said, was 'the moral effect of deformity upon the deformed,'[84] and to deal fully with such a topic meant exploring the realms of passion, sexuality, and depravity in such detail that the 'story is one only for men and women.'[85] Gywnn's praise notwithstanding, the publication of the novel 'triggered extreme responses,'[86] and as Talia Schaffer suggests,

> Some critics found it difficult to evaluate the novel because its manifest virtues were precisely the ones most inappropriate for a female author ... At the turn of the century, the women's novels that achieved praise and popularity (though not necessarily critical respect) were light, humorous, charming texts that need not be taken seriously ... But Malet let her unspeakable subject peep through her aesthetic screen, writing books that were unmistakably daring, unarguably transgressive, probably unclassifiable, and almost certainly improper.[87]

The fact that Cox agreed to cancel the contract suggests that he believed that the work that Malet was now producing was unsuitable for the *Queen*.

This whole sequence raises the question about Watt's understanding of Malet's writing. His choice to serialize Malet's follow-up to *The Carissima* in a mainstream women's magazine like the *Queen*, whose readership would have found Malet's subjects and techniques at the very least unsettling, strongly suggests that Watt simply failed to understand the kind of fiction that Malet was writing and the market for which it would be suitable. The *Queen* was no more a suitable venue for Malet's work than it would have been for Thomas Hardy's later novels or Henry James's fiction.

Malet's gender may be one reason that the Watts failed to market her in a manner that would have gained her a foothold among the newly emerging critics whose views on literature were to shape the twentieth-century literary canon. In 'Malet the Obscure,' Schaffer suggests, 'During her fifty-year-long career, Malet participated in, and indeed helped to lead, the transition from the genteel Victorian romance novel to the iconoclastic modernist experimental novel.'[88] Her fiction often depicted sexually explicit issues such as incest, sadism, masochism, homosexuality, or physical and emotional deformity. She also employed techniques associated with aestheticism, including 'beautiful descriptions of hideous subjects,'[89] and a wide range of modernist techniques, including fragmented narratives, dislocated points of view, unreliable narrators, and oblique description.[90] Schaffer goes on to argue that Malet was 'comparable to Hardy, James, Wilde, Stevenson, and the other groundbreaking novelists of the turn of the century,' and that her obscurity can be blamed on the fact that 'the critics who admired their daring subjects and experimental styles condemned Malet for the same techniques.'[91]

Furthermore, as Elisabeth Jay notes with respect to Malet's contemporary Mrs Oliphant,

> Literary activity in the last decade of the nineteenth century was domi-
> nated by a male clubland taking its revenge for the long years of George
> Eliot's supremacy. Slowly a new literary myth evolved, the logic of which
> seems to have been something like this: George Eliot, now amongst the
> honoured dead, could be left upon her pedestal, with the sole provision
> that she continued her act of cross-dressing into perpetuity.[92]

It was this very clubland that staked out the 'purist' territory, to use Peter McDonald's term, in which the major literary experiments of the 1890s were carried out.[93] Malet's gender precluded her admission to the club, and thus not only denied her access to the publication venues these men controlled, but also prevented her work from receiving the critical approval that members of the clubland heaped on each other.[94]

As evidence of how pervasive this clubland mentality was, and in some senses still is, we need only look at the way in which just two highly respected current critics construct women writers' roles in the 1880s and 1890s. Peter Keating remarks in *The Haunted Study* that 'Discussion of the attempt to develop a woman's point of view in British fiction of this period [1880s and 1890s] is complicated by the simple fact there were no women novelists of a literary stature remotely comparable to that of James, Conrad, Hardy, Meredith, Bennett, Wells, Gissing, or a dozen other men. This situation was itself a specifically late Victorian phenomenon.'[95] This is a viewpoint that even a prominent feminist critic such as Dorothy Mermin accepts. In *Godiva's Ride*, she notes the enormous popularity of women's writing in the nineteenth century, saying, 'Nineteenth-century works by women, however, not only commanded large audiences but also entered the canon of high culture, in their century and our own.' She qualifies this comment by adding that 'almost all the works that did so were written between 1830 and 1880.'[96] According to these accounts, it would appear that the denizens of 1890s clubland had succeeded in excluding their female contemporaries from the realm of serious literature, since fiction written by women, which had flourished from the eighteenth century onwards, appears to have hit a low point by the 1890s.[97]

Despite the fact that several excellent recent studies have contested the account presented by Keating, including books by Patricia Stubbs, Carolyn Christensen Nelson, Ann Ardis, Lyn Pickett, and Jane Eldridge Miller,[98] the viewpoint he expressed does reflect the opinions put forward by critics writing during Malet's lifetime. As Gaye Tuchman and Nina E. Fortin point out in *Edging Women Out*, between 1880 and 1899, 'men of letters, including critics, actively redefined the nature of a good novel and a great author. They preferred a new form of realism that they associated with "manly" literature – that is, great literature.'[99] The consensus of these literary critics in the 1890s and into the 1900s was that women only wrote popular or middlebrow fiction. Women's work was relegated to literary magazines and newspapers aimed at a largely middle-class, and increasingly working-class, audience of women. Women writers often were actively discouraged from pursuing what publisher John Murray, in reference to Malet's 1909 work *The Score* termed 'painful subject[s].'[100] If women dared to write about 'painful subjects' such as violent murders, homosexuality, abortion, or moral depravity, they could escape critical condemnation only if their story made clear that such topics were presented as cautions to the reader about what happens when women stray from the socially and morally acceptable paths. Watt handled his women clients' works within this prevailing critical framework. Thus he and his sons continued to offer Malet's material to magazines that were aimed primarily at female readers, and by doing so they may well have denied her the very audience – the critics, readers, and writers who praised Hardy, James, Conrad, and other male writers – that would have assured her a secure place in literary history.[101]

Watt and Malet: Concluding Comments

A.P. Watt emerged as a literary agent at a propitious historical moment. In the last two decades of the nineteenth century, publishing was undergoing an unprecedented boom and conditions were ripe for professional writers to demand a larger stake in the business of writing. Watt's impact on the literary world was significant and long lasting. He developed the model for the profession of literary agency. He transformed the business practices of authors and publishers to such an extent that he came to occupy a central and powerful position in the book trade. By 1900, it seemed that Watt's power and influence would go unchallenged. Looking forward, however, we can see that just at the apex of Watt's personal dominance, the very nature of literature shifts again. The dominant forms of late Victorian literature give way to the emerging forms that were to become known as literary modernism.

Here Lucas Malet becomes a crucial and interesting case study. For Watt's ultimate failure to serve her as well as he served George MacDonald and others who helped him reach the centre of the literary field is symptomatic of how cultural fields work, according to Pierre Bourdieu's theories. Watt occupied a dominant position in the literary field and his client list reflected this position. Malet's post-1895 work existed in a liminal space, between the dominant late Victorian modes of writing and the emergent modernist modes. In order to serve her interests properly, Watt needed to position her at the juncture of dominant and emerging literatures. He needed to find publishers who knew how to market her work, and he had to be able to suggest editorial changes to her that would have allowed her work to appeal to the readership attracted by the emerging literature, while still retaining her share of the dominant market. In other words, he had to develop a strategy to situate her in both markets – the dominant and the emerging – in order to provide her with the best opportunity to succeed financially and critically. His failure to do so meant that her works did not find an audience that was learning how to read literature like hers. It remained unread by the very writers, critics, and readers who would come to dominate twentieth-century literature, redefining both the aesthetics and business practices of the literary field.[102] Schaffer is absolutely right when she says that 'To read Lucas Malet today is to participate in a history that demands a different explanation: a woman writer whose canonical imprimatur was later, apparently, revoked.'[103]

5 The Second Wave of Agenting: J.B. Pinker

By the mid-1890s, A.P. Watt's position as the only literary agent who mattered appeared unassailable. He was not without challengers, but most of them were unable to match his flair for business and his influence in the print culture field.[1] The pages of the *Author* throughout the 1890s and into the first decades of the twentieth century warned against unscrupulous agents, and its editor, Walter Besant, advised his readership to deal with established and trustworthy agencies.[2] He presumably steered many writers towards his own agent, A.P. Watt.[3] In publications aimed at book publishers and sellers, the agent's role was also hotly debated. Yet by 1895, a few individuals had emerged who were to challenge not only Watt's supreme position, but also the agenting template that he had established. These challengers form the core of the second wave of professional literary agency. Chief among this handful of men and women are Albert Curtis Brown and James Brand Pinker.[4]

Curtis Brown, as he was known, was an American who had come to Britain in 1898 as the representative of the *New York Press* and several other American newspapers.[5] His intention was to work as a newspaper syndicator – buying and selling material that would be syndicated in American or British newspapers. It was, according to his own words, 'a pure fluke'[6] that he became a literary agent. As Brown tells the story, 'It was stray chance that led me into a new corridor of publishing.'[7] He had gone to interview Pearl Theresa Craigie (who wrote under the pen name John Oliver Hobbes) for his syndicate; she asked him to let her know if he heard of an opening for serialization of a new novel she had finished. The 'very next day [Brown] happened to see the editor of the *Pall Mall Magazine*', who was in need of a story. Brown arranged for Hobbes's 'The Vineyard' to be delivered to the magazine, and thus was his career as an agent launched.[8] Brown's successful mining of the trans-atlantic market pushed Watt into this area, eventually prompting Watt to open a New York office.[9]

But a far greater threat to Watt's place as Britain's leading agent was J.B. Pinker, who not only mined the transatlantic trade, taking advantage of new international copyright laws, but also set his sights on carving out a niche for himself in the British marketplace.[10] By seeking out clientele that Watt chose not to pursue actively, he positioned himself as a distinct alternative to Watt. In doing so, Pinker became intimately involved in the transformation of literature that occurred in this period. Indeed, his client list contains many major modernist writers; at one time or another Pinker represented Joseph Conrad, Ford Madox Ford, T.S. Eliot, Henry James, James Joyce, D.H. Lawrence, Katherine Mansfield, John Middleton Murry, and Dorothy Richardson.[11] Pinker's influence grew throughout the 1900s and 1910s, eventually rivalling, and some would argue exceeding, that of Watt. Thus, the story of literary agency is as much about Pinker and the second wave of agents as it is about Watt and the origins of the profession.

Pinker and the Beginnings of the Second Wave

Pinker's Beginnings

There is little information about James Brand Pinker's origins, apart from the fact that he was born to James and Mary Brand Pinker in 1863.[12] No records relating to his education have been found, though his aunt Charlotte was a governess who later ran a school and his cousin Henry Richard Hope-Pinker was a well-known sculptor. It is likely, given such family connections, that Pinker's formal education was more than adequate for the occupations he was to undertake as an adult. According to James Hepburn, Pinker's first job was as a 'clerk at the Tilbury Docks.'[13] A couple of years later, he was a foreign correspondent in Constantinople, reporting mostly on diplomatic concerns for the *Levant Herald*. He had met his future wife, Elizabeth Seabrooke, prior to leaving for Turkey. Valerie Pinker, J.B.'s granddaughter, says that, according to family lore, Elizabeth and J.B. met 'when she was on her way to a ball in her horse drawn phaeton ... she saw a young man thrown from his bicycle into a ditch. She rescued him, but her family were not keen on the relationship – there was a gulf between her upper middle class background and J.B. came from working class.'[14] Elizabeth's father

died in 1888, and she sailed out to Constantinople, marrying J.B. on
21 June 1888. The marriage changed Pinker's material circumstances.
Elizabeth's family was very comfortably off, having earned their fortune
in the brewing business. Elizabeth likely brought a sizeable amount of
money to the marriage, probably enough to convince the Pinkers to
quit Constantinople shortly after their marriage and return to London.
Elizabeth's wealth likely also gave her husband the freedom to pursue a
literary career without having to depend solely on the income from it to
support his family. Upon returning home, Pinker sought out the position of assistant editor of the illustrated London weekly *Black and White*.
He was also reading manuscripts for a publishing house and, for a brief
time in 1896, was the editor of *Pearson's Magazine*, quitting this post
before the first issue appeared.[15]

His publishing experience can best be characterized as oriented
towards emerging literary markets. *Black and White* appealed to a
more self-consciously literary audience, showcasing the work of
younger, more experimental writers, while *Pearson's Magazine* catered
to a broader readership, its mandate being 'to entertain the great
public.'[16] His varied experience served him well. It brought him into
contact with the major publishers and editors of the day, allowing
him to develop the network of contacts that he would need as an
agent. He acquired an insider's knowledge of the material forces at
work in publishing, learned what would sell in what market and how
to place his clients' work accordingly, and thus became acquainted
with the rules and norms of different publishing planes. His work at
Black and White introduced him to many up-and-coming writers,
including contributors such as Henry James and Robert Louis
Stevenson, and staffers such as the editor C.N. Williamson, Eden
Phillpotts, Violet Hunt, and Mrs Belloc Lowndes, many of whom
later became clients. This provided him with a nucleus from which to
build his agency.

His training as a journalist, publisher's reader, and editor sharpened
his literary sensibility. He had a 'nose' for good literature and was astute
in assessing what material would sell well; indeed, Alec Waugh wrote of
Pinker that his 'shrewdness and knowledge of what the public wants
were invaluable to his authors.'[17] Although his formal education was
often inferior to his clients', Pinker's editorial suggestions frequently
improved the quality of their work. An example of his ability to size up a
story and provide candid but useful advice comes from his correspondence with Alice Williamson, the wife of his *Black and White* friend C.N.

Williamson. She wrote to Pinker in 1912: 'I thank you *very* much for *a* frank and friendly opinion, and *much* appreciate it, for I know it must have been hard for you to speak out, hating to hurt my feelings.'[18] A.A. Milne also sought Pinker's opinion of his work, writing to him in 1904 about whether a story he had written would be worthwhile reworking as a play: 'now I may be all wrong, but this story looks like an excellent curtain-raiser! I don't want to waste time in turning it into one, unless you think so too and can get a hearing or rather a reading for it from some manager ... so will you tell me whether you think it's worth while dramatising it?'[19] His preparation complete, Pinker opened his London agency in January of 1896, very rapidly establishing himself in the profession.

A New Literary Agency

Pinker's background was substantially different from Watt's both in terms of class – Pinker coming from the working class, Watt from the middle class – and in terms of their literary apprenticeships – Pinker's deriving from his time as a journalist overseas and his editorial work in periodicals aimed at an emerging readership, Watt's deriving from his work for an established publishing firm in which he carried out a number of duties including reading manuscripts and selling advertising space. Pinker's approach to literary agenting also differed sharply from Watt's, and in the course of establishing himself in the print culture field he challenged not only Watt's supremacy, but also the rules of literary agenting itself. An interview Pinker gave to the *Bookman* in April of 1898 describes the position he was in the process of staking out. The interviewer begins the piece with this leading remark: 'It was because he saw the great possibilities of a literary agency, and believed there was special need of a particular kind of agent, that Mr. J.B. Pinker forsook journalism proper for his present occupation.'[20] Pinker himself reinforces the interviewer's comments in his own description of why he established his agency:

> My idea was not simply to relieve the man of established reputation from the worry of business, but to take up the unknown man, the youngster struggling for reputation and bread and butter, and help him to build his reputation. To do this, of course, it is necessary first to decide that the man is worth working for, and then to give him ungrudging help – reading all his work, and giving any suggestions my experience prompts.[21]

He elaborates on this later in the interview, spelling out his position very clearly:

> Any business man can get good prices for a well-known author, but there's some fun in singling out a youngster from the crowd of unknowns and pushing him to the top. My ambition is to have a few clients, and add to the list each year some of the young writers who want help.[22]

For the readers of the *Bookman*, the comparison to Watt would have been unmistakable. And in case the reader missed Pinker's implicit criticism of Watt's practice of representing a large number of writers who had 'made it' at the expense of those who were struggling to establish themselves, Pinker commented:

> I do not think one agent can act for an indiscriminate number of men successfully; they are bound to jostle one another. Then it is physically impossible for a man to give close personal attention to each client when he has many. Naturally he gives the best of his time to the big writers. Of course one can have clerks who can pack up MSS. and dump them down wholesale in editors' offices, but that is worse than useless to young authors. You must take each one as if he were your only client, see that his work is as good as he can make it, and then run him as if he were the best man on your list.[23]

This last statement nicely outlines the position that Pinker took and that set him apart from other agents.

Pinker cultivated this image of himself as the agent different from others throughout his career. In other interviews and newspaper articles, he always presented himself as the champion of new authors and new literature, and even the ads he placed in various trade publications stressed this difference. A typical ad looked much like this one from 1901 – his listing in the section titled Agents in *The Literary Year-Book*:

> Pinker, Mr. J.B., Effingham House, Arundel Street, W.C. Literary agent. Mr. Pinker was formerly editor of Black & White, and reader of manuscripts for a well-known publishing house. He subsequently became editor of Pearson's Magazine, a post which he resigned in order to devote himself to the work of a literary agent. Mr. Pinker has always made a special point of helping young authors in the early stages of their career, when they need most the aid of an adviser with a thorough knowledge of the literary world and the publishing trade.[24]

In contrast, Watt's listing simply catalogues the names of over fifty prominent writers whom the agency represents. There is an asterisk that directs the reader's attention to the bottom of the page where we are told, 'To Mr. A.P. Watt is due the rise of the Literary Agent. He was the first to conceive and put into practice the idea of the Literary Agent, acting as an intermediary between authors and publishers and editors.'[25] This kind of public posturing by the two leading agents of the day – Watt the founder of the profession, Pinker the champion of new writers – speaks directly to their different views on agents' roles.

Challenging the Literary Agent Template

In many respects, Pinker managed his clients' literary property much as Watt did – protecting their copyright interests, consolidating ownership of literary property in their hands (managed, of course, by Pinker), exploiting the outside rights markets for their work, protecting and promoting their public reputations. He also provided his clients with editorial advice about their work, acting as both a sounding board for their ideas and a reader for their manuscripts. He even undertook the same sorts of personal services for clients that the Watts did for George MacDonald and Lucas Malet. However, the third quotation from the *Bookman* article succinctly articulates two ways in which Pinker's approach to agenting differed from Watt's. First, he positioned himself as the author's agent, in sharp contrast to Watt, who was still presenting himself as a literary agent for hire by authors and publishers alike. Second, he sought out young authors who were just establishing themselves and invested his energy, time, and money in shaping and nurturing their careers.

Authors First

As we have seen, from the beginning, professional literary agents were characterized as middlemen who brokered deals between sellers and buyers of literary property. One consequence of this conception of agenting was the ethical dilemma about where the agent's primary loyalty resided. The public debate surrounding this issue began to grow in the 1890s, with attacks by publishers on the 'parasitic' nature of the agent and countercharges from authors that good agents protected them from dishonest publishers. When Pinker entered the field, he, too, was forced to confront this question and to determine how he would respond to this central ethical dilemma. Although he did dispose of outside rights for publishers or editors, it is clear from his *Bookman* interview that his first allegiance was to the writer. Thus Pinker explicitly situated himself as the author's agent; in so doing, he directly challenged one of the most contentious elements of Watt's agenting template.

Important as this challenge was, it had a less significant impact on the transformation of the print culture field than did Pinker's positioning of himself as the agent of emerging literary talent. When Watt set up shop as a literary agent in the 1870s, he had spent many years learning what kinds of literary productions would likely interest publishers and readers and he knew what works sold where. With the need to earn a living from the commissions generated by selling his clients' work, he had to take on clients whose works he knew he could place with publishers and, as a result, his client list was populated by writers for whom there was already a market. Pinker, who was likely less driven to earn a living from commissions, could afford to spend time nurturing new talent, foregoing immediate economic gain for the promise of greater economic gain once the writer had established him- or herself. In addition, Pinker's orientation to the literary field differed from Watt's. Pinker's attitude was more closely aligned with that of the younger generation of the 1890s and 1900s that was challenging established individuals and institutions for the various forms of capital at stake in the field. These younger writers, critics, editors, and publishers viewed the world differently from Watt's generation: they were more likely to value innovation over tradition; they were as aware as the previous generation, if not more so, of the economic capital to be earned from their work and insistent upon receiving full value for their literary productions; and they were less concerned with upholding social or moral codes that they had inherited from their parents and grandparents and which they thought were outmoded. Pinker explicitly courted writers from this younger generation and in doing so he made three distinct alterations to Watt's customary practices. First, he sought out rising stars who had commercial potential but who had not yet found reliable markets for their work. Second, he set out to attract women writers as clients. Third, he deliberately sought to promote young authors whose works were more likely to provide him with symbolic/cultural capital than with economic capital.

Pinker and Rising Stars

Writers such as H.G. Wells and Arnold Bennett were pursued by Pinker. They had not yet achieved sufficient prominence to make them obvious targets of the Watt agency, but they were beginning to publish material regularly, their work was attracting critical and popular attention, and they could see the value of having an agent look after their interests.[26] Arnold Bennett, for instance, first contacted Pinker in January 1901 at a time when Bennett was struggling to establish himself after his decision in 1898 to take up writing for a living.[27] Peter McDonald's account of Bennett as 'a literary maverick [who] attempted to negotiate the treacherous dialectic that divided the purist from the profiteer, avant-garde from popular culture' and an 'adversarial journalist [who] eagerly exploited, and even insisted upon, the inconsistencies of his multiple careers as a serialist and a novelist'[28] provides a more nuanced and accurate portrait of this complex man than we usually get from scholars who settle for calling Bennett the consummate professional man of letters in the early twentieth century. Yet at the beginning of his career, in particular, though Bennett had already determined that he wished to 'lead a double life as a profiteering serialist and an avant-garde literary novelist',[29] to borrow McDonald's apt description, he leaned heavily on his new agent, trusting Pinker to advise him on the suitability of a text for a market and even to provide him with a monthly allowance of £50.[30] The two men's letters that still exist are a testament to their relationship. In them, we see that Bennett was forthright in his opinions and that he had a distinct sense of how to shape his career; nonetheless, they also reveal that he valued Pinker's advice. The correspondence over Bennett's series of Five Towns novels and stories provides a good illustration of how Pinker helped shape Bennett's career.[31]

Bennett brought his unsold novel *Anna of the Five Towns* with him to Pinker's agency in January of 1902.[32] Pinker placed it with the British publisher Chatto and Windus and sold its American rights to S.S. McClure, who published it in 1903.[33] Pinker next found markets for Bennett's series of short stories set in the Five Towns world he had created. This involved three distinct services. First, Pinker placed individual stories with appropriate periodicals. Second, he advised Bennett on when, and how, to issue collections of stories. Finally, he offered editorial advice on the material as it came in, thereby assisting Bennett in tailoring the work for the markets Pinker had identified.

An examination of Pinker's handling of the stories that made up the collection called *The Grim Smile of the Five Towns* illustrates the first point. In October of 1905, Bennett sent Pinker three stories – 'The Lion's Share,' 'The Baby's Bath,' and 'The Silent Brothers.' Pinker placed each one in a periodical, earning Bennett at least £3/3/ per thousand words for each story and also priming the audience for similar stories.[34] Each of these stories, along with 'The Death of Simon Fuge' – which is regarded by Bennett critics as one of his finest short stories – was republished in *The Grim Smile of the Five Towns*. The volume includes thirteen stories, of which at least half had appeared in print prior to the volume's publication.[35] Pinker negotiated with two presses – Chatto and Windus, and Chapman and Hall – over the British publication of the volume; Bennett had insisted on retaining copyright for the volume, and wanted to lease it for a period of seven years for a sum of at least £100.[36] Pinker placed it with Chapman and Hall, whose terms – including offering Bennett a royalty of 20 per cent – were more favourable than those offered by Chatto. Pinker then placed several of the stories from *Grim Smile* in American magazines, earning Bennett further income and expanding his readership yet again.[37] Finally, seven of the stories were republished in the New York edition of *The Matador of the Five Towns*, which was published by G.H. Doran in 1912.[38] The three original stories Bennett submitted to Pinker in 1905 thus appeared in three different markets – British periodical, British book, and American book – thereby gaining Bennett three payments for each of the stories. At the same time, because each publication went to a separate market, Pinker was broadening Bennett's audience and thereby creating new markets for Bennett to exploit.

On the second point, advising on the timing of publishing material, one of Pinker's greatest difficulties as Bennett's representative was to convince him that it was important to space out the publication of his works. Bennett was prolific, claiming, 'I could take long holidays & still produce as much as you would require from me.'[39] But Pinker insisted that flooding the market with too much work would lead to a diminution of Bennett's readership and thus to a decline in Bennett's asking price, possibly even to the demise of his career. Bennett eventually saw Pinker's wisdom, writing, 'It is absurd to pay an expert for advice & then only to take the advice when it agrees with your own views.'[40] Nonetheless, Bennett continued to produce a large volume of material, thereby creating a challenge for his agent's plan to keep a steady but not overwhelming amount of Bennett material before the public.

Finally, Pinker's editorial advice helped to shape the work Bennett produced. He relied on Pinker to tell him what would sell and where it would command the best prices. For example, Bennett wrote to Pinker in August of 1902, early in their relationship, soliciting input about a story he had written:

I enclose a short story, 'Nocturne at the Majestic' (6,300 words), which is meant to combine the virtues of the popular & the rather high-class short story. I shall be glad if you will read it, & let your acumen play upon it, & tell me whether it is the sort of stuff you can sell in good places.[41]

We do not have a record of Pinker's reply, but since the story appeared in the *Windsor Magazine* in May of 1904, we can conjecture that Pinker did find it the sort of stuff he could sell in good places.[42] Indeed, Bennett's later solicitations of further advice – writing Pinker in May of 1903, 'I should like to do a series of stories in the vein of "Nocturne at the Majestic". I contemplated such a series a year ago, & offered it to Tillotsons but they would not pay enough ... I shall be glad – apart from financial considerations – if you can fix it up,'[43] and again in 1904, 'Shortly I am going to do some purely humorous stories with a view to magazines ... What magazines had I better keep in my mind's eye while writing? And do you prefer "Five Towns" stuff or more general stuff?'[44] – lend support to this conjecture, for if Bennett had found Pinker's advice inappropriate or unhelpful, he would not have continued to ask for it. Even later in his career, when Bennett was fully confident in his own abilities as a writer and as a literary businessman, he still sought out and accepted Pinker's advice and assistance on a variety of matters ranging from income tax, to possibly providing an office for his secretary Miss Nerney to use while Bennett worked for the Ministry of Information during the First World War, to providing advice on how to deal with difficult publishers or editors.[45]

Pinker nurtured Bennett's career in the early years and then managed his literary property so successfully that Bennett prospered as a writer, leaving an estate worth £36,000 when he died.[46] Indeed, as James Hepburn notes, when the two started working together Bennett was earning 'about two guineas for a thousand words' and then twenty-five years into their relationship, '[Bennett] [was] worth two shillings and more a word ... and he earn[ed] £20,000 a year.'[47] Bennett's comments to his nephew about Pinker's sudden death in 1922 perhaps sum up the importance of their relationship: 'my agent, J.B. Pinker, died suddenly in New York last night. Apart from the fact that he was a very old friend of mine, he had the whole of my affairs in his hands. There is *no* other really good agent in England. The difference between a good and a bad agent might mean a difference of thousands a year to me.'[48] Gambling on these rising stars was central to the success of Pinker's agency because his clients' success led directly to his own financial success.

Pinker and Women Writers

While many of Pinker's female clients produced conventional work, with Baroness Orczy and Mrs Belloc Lowndes leading the way,[49] his female clients published all sorts of material. Pinker encouraged the women to try different markets and was proud of their achievements. Among his female authors, he counted Alice Williamson, Somerville and Ross, Rebecca West, Katherine Mansfield, Dorothy Richardson, and George Egerton. Alice Williamson, along with her husband C.N. Williamson, was a pioneer of a new form of literature: 'motoring' stories that were a cross between travelogue and short fiction. The author of a wonderful article on these stories in the *Bookman* for December 1906 positively gushes about the couple's success, saying at one point, 'His [Mr Williamson] were the hero's letters: the heroine's letters were Mrs Williamson's share of the work; and after the success of "The Lightning Conductor" in England and America, publishers would always have "more motor stories" from "the Williamsons," if they could.'[50] The author also makes the point that it was Mrs Williamson who was the moving force behind the husband-and-wife collaborations, saying that 'it was with little difficulty that she first persuaded her husband to throw in his lot with hers in the sail-boat of fiction.'[51] The writing team of Somerville and Ross – Irish cousins Edith Oenone Somerville and Violet Martin – are best known for their Irish hunting stories. Pinker actively encouraged them to exploit this masculine literary field, as chapter 6 will demonstrate. Rebecca West published all sorts of journalism and criticism as well as experimental fiction. She became Pinker's client around 1916, apparently referred to Pinker by H.G. Wells.[52] Her correspondence with Pinker is very informal, filled with accounts of her ill health and her daily life. It is evident that she relies on his business advice, though she has a strong sense of the kind of career she wants to create. In fact, she writes to him in 1918, 'The option on the next two books. That I don't think I can agree to. I have always meant if I could never to sign any contract – with anybody – with that clause as it seems to me quite unnecessary.'[53] Upon his death, she wrote a letter of condolence to his son, in which she said, 'I would like to tell you how much I admired your father both as a personality and a business man. I was not always able to take advantage of his good advice, owing to my health, but I was always deeply grateful for it and admired the touch of personal Instruction he brought to all his interviews.' She ended the letter: 'I hope I shall be able to look to you as I have to him for guidance in my business affairs.'[54] Based on the correspondence, she appears to have remained with the agency until the late 1920s, becoming a client of A.D. Peters (who founded his literary agency in 1923) sometime around 1928 or 1929.[55] Katherine Mansfield, George Egerton, and Dorothy Richardson also produced experimental fiction. Mansfield and John Middleton Murry, her husband and literary executor, were long-time Pinker clients, while Dorothy Richardson used Pinker early in her career.[56] Egerton, the pseudonym employed by Mary Chavelita Bright, provides a particularly interesting case.

The presence of George Egerton on Pinker's client list clearly illustrates his positioning of himself as the agent for new writers, and particularly for women writers who were carving out new territory for their fiction. Egerton's first collection of stories, *Keynotes*, published by the Bodley Head press in 1893, had created a sensation because of the stories' frank portrayals of female sexuality and desire.[57] It and her next collection, *Discords*, published a year later by the Bodley Head, clearly situated her at the forefront of the group of writers presenting new views of women in their fiction.[58] Though Egerton's work was treated harshly by many of the male critics of her day, who placed her in the New Woman category and wrote disdainfully of her fiction, she, like Lucas Malet, is regarded by a growing number of critics today as an important figure.[59] Ann Ardis, for instance, argues 'that the New Women novelists anticipate[d] the reappraisal of realism we usually credit to early-twentieth-century writers.'[60] She suggests that 'the precedent Egerton sets for other New Woman novelists [is] ... the acknowledgment that "nature" is something defined by culture as the place where culture's most cherished ideas and ideals can be kept safe from history.'[61] While we know now that her most important publications appeared before Pinker became her agent, at the time he undoubtedly expected that she would continue to produce stories that sold well and thus generate healthy commissions for his firm; however, there is another facet to his representation of her that is worth noting. Remembering that, as Pinker said in the *Bookman* interview, 'I pride myself less on the number [of clients] than on the worth of them,'[62] we may infer from Egerton's presence in the short list of names he gives the interviewer that he believed her work to be important. Pinker names Egerton as one of his clients in this early interview in order to cue both potential publishers and clients about the kind of writers he wanted to represent. By mentioning Egerton, Pinker tells the literary world that he is keen to make his name representing writers whose work is controversial, and, in particular, that he will represent women who cross the boundaries assigned to women writers in this period.

Pinker and Modernist Writers

In chapter 2, Janet Wolff's remarks about cultural mediating figures were invoked to situate the literary agent among the ranks of those individuals who influenced the production of art. I argued there that A.P. Watt assumed a mediating role between writers and publishers and in the process gained significant power in the print culture field. Pinker continues to carry on the same sort of mediating functions that Watt pioneered, thereby establishing himself as an important figure in the print culture field in the early twentieth century. However, Pinker's mediations go further than Watt's; indeed, in many respects Pinker becomes a literary patron, but a patron of the sort that Lawrence Rainey has identified as emerging in the modernist period: 'what had once been an aristocracy of patron-*salonniers* would now be replaced by an elite of patron-investors.'[63] Rainey's discussion of how patronage worked in modernism is complex and nicely nuanced, but despite his acknowledgment that 'the patronage of literary modernism was rarely the pure or disinterested support that we typically associate with patronage,'[64] he interestingly fails to include Pinker (or other literary agents) in his discussion. While a more extended discussion of Pinker's role as a patron of literary modernism occurs in chapter 7 – where his relationship with Joseph Conrad is examined – here I briefly want to establish Pinker's role in order to draw out more fully his distinctive position in the print culture field. There are two primary ways in which he functioned as a literary patron. First, he provided financial support for unknown or struggling writers, gambling on repayment of his financial investment at some future point, and in the meantime accepting the symbolic/cultural capital his actions earned him. Second, by employing his standard agenting services for modernist writers, he provided them with the same advantages as his more readily marketable clients; here again, he frequently gambled that his time and effort would earn repayment (in the form of economic or symbolic/cultural capital) at some future point. In each of these activities, Pinker consciously chose positions that set him apart from Watt, thereby pushing agenting in new directions.

The most frequently told stories about Pinker revolve around the money he advanced or loaned to struggling writers. In his 1898 *Bookman* interview, Pinker said that 'in some instances, I have worked for months for a young client without any return, [although] I find that the return always comes sooner or later.'[65] This is disingenuous, for it underplays the extent to which Pinker actually supported young writers in their lean years, as well as the fact that his efforts did not always bring a return. The most famous of these relationships is with Conrad. Less well known is the Pinker–D.H. Lawrence relationship; it nonetheless demonstrates Pinker's patronage of younger, experimental writers.

What is commonly known about the Lawrence-Pinker connection is that it dissolved because of Lawrence's anger over what he perceived as Pinker's failure to continue to support his writing career and particularly what Lawrence believed was Pinker's negligence in handling Lawrence's interests in America.[66] Indeed, those who were opposed to the growing power exercised by agents, and by Pinker in particular, gleefully seized upon the memorable phrase Lawrence used to describe Pinker: a 'little parvenu snob of a procureur of books.'[67] Yet Lawrence employed Pinker *because* he could procure prices for his works that Lawrence was unable to secure on his own. This disjunction between his aesthetic statements and his commercial desires was to characterize, and eventually undermine, their relationship.

Pinker was Lawrence's first agent. As Lawrence wrote in 1912 to Edward Garnett, his friend and informal literary agent: 'Pinker wrote me the other day, wanting to place me a novel with one of the leading publishers.'[68] It is likely that Pinker had an offer in hand from Methuen, as is evident from Lawrence's later comments to Garnett, in a letter from May 1914: 'Here is a letter which Pinker sent me, offering me £300 for English volume rights. There is another definite letter, later, which I have lost, saying "will you accept a three hundred pound advance on account of royalties in England."'[69] For the two years between Pinker's initial approach and this letter, Lawrence had used Garnett to funnel material to Pinker, thereby avoiding working with the agent directly. However, by the summer of 1914, Lawrence had lost confidence in Garnett. Lawrence, therefore, began to work directly with Pinker. In a 1 July letter to Garnett, he related the events that led him to take this action:

> I am awfully sorry I was precipitate at the last moment. I called to see you before I went to Pinker. Then you weren't in. And I hung a few moments on the pavement outside, saying 'Shall I go to Pinker?' And there was very little time, because we had to lunch with Lady St. Helier. And Frieda was so disappointed she couldn't have any money. And most of all, I remembered Mr Duckworth on Saturday.

'Well?' he said when I came in.
'Pinker offers me the £300 from Methuen', I said.
'He does?'
'Yes.'
'Then', he said, as if nettled, 'I'm afraid you'll have to accept it.'
Which rather made me shut my teeth, because the tone was peremptory. So I went to Pinker, and signed his agreement, and took his cheque, and opened an acc. with the London County and Westminster Bank – et me voila.[70]

The motivating factor here is obviously money. Lawrence needed it; Pinker offered it. This was to become the central feature of their relationship, which stretched from July 1914 until January 1920.

Pinker worked very hard for Lawrence, placing a number of his stories and articles, and arranging for Methuen to publish *The Rainbow* in England and for B.W. Huebsch to bring it out in America.[71] The arrangement was initially a good one. Employing his usual methods, Pinker found outlets for Lawrence's work, thereby providing the impoverished Lawrence with a small but steady income. Furthermore, Pinker also forwarded money to Lawrence pretty much on demand, advancing it to him in anticipation of future sales or royalties, which sometimes did not materialize. Typical of their interchanges during this period is this letter from Lawrence to Pinker in April 1915: 'Do get me some money, will you: I am at the end.'[72] In response, Pinker sent him some, which Lawrence gratefully noted in a letter in early May: 'Thank you very much for the £25, which will last me for some time.'[73]

By 1917, Lawrence had begun to complain about Pinker's failure to place his work – notably *Women in Love*. Lawrence came to believe that Pinker had failed to submit the manuscript to American publishers, and particularly that he had not sent it to B.W. Huebsch, who had published Lawrence's previous works in America. Lawrence's letters about this to Huebsch, who published the novel in 1916, reflect Lawrence's frustration about what he sees as Pinker's deceit. Indeed, in yet another memorable turn of phrase, he vented his anger about Pinker's handling of this novel: 'one could eat ones [*sic*] old shoes, while Pinkers and publishers were complaisant and vague.'[74] It is not clear, however, whether Lawrence's account of this affair is accurate. It would have been uncharacteristic of Pinker to fail to send the novel to Huebsch, particularly given that Pinker was also working with Huebsch on behalf of other clients and he could not afford to alienate the publisher. In fact, a July 1917 letter from Little, Brown and Company of Boston to Pinker declining to publish *Women in Love* because it 'is not especially adapted to our needs' and because the publisher felt 'that it is not as good as *Sons and Lovers* and that Mr. Lawrence has not made as good a presentation of his theme as we expected'[75] suggests that Pinker had indeed offered the novel to at least one American publisher. It is likely impossible this long after the fact to untangle the truth of this situation; nonetheless, what is evident is that Lawrence believed that Pinker was not handling his work in the manner that Lawrence wished it to be handled. This sentiment caused a breach in their relationship.

In addition, Lawrence reacted badly to Pinker's apparent reluctance to continue to supply him with money. He wrote to his friend S.S. Koteliansky in July 1917, 'I wrote and told Pinker I must soon have more money. He does not answer. Probably he does not want to advance any more.'[76] Despite Lawrence's comments here, it appears that Pinker did continue to advance him money, though not as freely as before. Lawrence eventually severed ties with Pinker in late December 1919, writing to him: 'I think there is not much point in our remaining bound to one another. You told me when we made our agreement, that we might break it when either of us wished. I wish it should be broken now.'[77] The estimates of the debt to Pinker that remained unpaid after Lawrence broke off contact range from £100 to £500 – not an inconsiderable sum.

Pinker's patronage came at a key period in Lawrence's career; it is arguable that without the financial support, Lawrence's career might well have taken a different trajectory. While it is unlikely that Lawrence would have altered his aesthetic stances, the contacts he later used were frequently ones that had initially been made by Pinker on his behalf. Had he not had Pinker's active support, he might not have had as ready access to the American market, for instance, in the late 1910s and 1920s. This would have had a significant impact on his income and might well have influenced the kind of writing he produced. Pinker's patronage of Lawrence's writing also went beyond supplying money. He fought against the ban of *The Rainbow*, offering to arrange a petition on behalf of Lawrence's right to publish it,[78] and Joyce Wexler notes that 'Pinker testified before the Westminster Tribunal'[79] on behalf of Lawrence. He continued to work for Lawrence even when he discovered Lawrence was making side deals with editors and publishers, deliberately cutting Pinker out of arrangements so as to avoid paying his commissions. To the very end, Pinker continued to treat Lawrence with respect, though Lawrence clearly did not reciprocate it. In fact, upon hearing of his death Lawrence wrote: 'As for Pinker, requiescat. – Ones [*sic*] enemies fall slowly but surely into oblivion.'[80]

Lawrence's continuing disparagement of Pinker highlights what Rainey calls the need for patronage 'to be disguised as something else if it were not to seem too at odds with the modern world.'[81] Lawrence was clearly unable to accept even Pinker's disguised patronage with any kind of appreciation, perhaps because, as John Worthen, one of Lawrence's biographers, says, 'Lawrence always felt an outsider not just in the working-class world he had left and in the bourgeois world he had in most ways not entered; but especially in the so-called literary world.'[82] Acknowledging Pinker's help would have left Lawrence indebted to Pinker, the epitome of the commercial literary world with which Lawrence had a love-hate relationship; indeed, it would have left him 'the literary man writing for the literary public,' to borrow Worthen's phrase – a position that Lawrence both desired and despised.[83] Better to attack Pinker, to denigrate his help, than to acknowledge that he accepted Pinker's support so that his works could reach the very market that he claimed to disdain.

Pinker's relationship with James Joyce provides a second example of his representation of a key modernist writer. One of the lingering myths about Joyce is that his writing found readers because of the work of a small, but loyal, group of friends and patrons who fought to ensure that it reached an eager audience. As part of their support of his talent they assisted Joyce financially, since the mainstream publishers and audiences, failing to recognize his genius, did not embrace his work and did not provide him with the material means to allow him to continue to write as he wished. Yet Joyce Wexler proposes an alternate assessment of the situation:

> the halo of genius blinds his admirers to traits all too evident to his contemporaries. In the morality play Joyce made of his life, he cast all who failed to hail his genius as villains. If the record is read retrospectively, however, Joyce appears as an unknown but highly recommended young writer whose career progressed steadily until he faced censorship ... Joyce embarked on his career as his predecessors had: he cultivated the influence of established authors and editors.[84]

Joyce also contracted the services of a literary agent, enlisting this literary professional in his battle to gain economic and cultural capital.

Interestingly, though Joyce employed Pinker – signing the standard agency contract that governed the relations between client and agent and which guaranteed the agent a commission on work he placed with a publisher – and though Pinker used his full array of services to handle Joyce's work – negotiating contracts, managing outside rights, assisting in public relations activities on behalf of Joyce – Joyce tended to treat Pinker much as he did other helpers or patrons in his circle, such as Harriet Weaver or John Quinn. Joyce expected Pinker to carry out the business that Joyce placed in his hands, but at the same time, he persisted in conducting his career as he wished – by negotiating contracts on his own, most notably – and he expected that Pinker would continue to work for him regardless of how frequently he breached their contract. Looking briefly at the Joyce-Pinker relationship will provide another glimpse of Pinker's role as a patron of literary modernism.

Pinker first approached Joyce in 1915, writing to him on 10 February: 'My friend, Mr. H.G. Wells, has drawn my attention to your serial story which is appearing in the *Egoist*, and I have been reading it with great interest. If you would intrust [*sic*] the book rights of your novels to me I should be very glad indeed to have the opportunity of handling them. I wonder if you are ever in town and could spare time to call and see me?'[85] Joyce replied to Pinker, 'I am obliged by Mr H.G. Wells' kindness and also by the friendly interest you express. Would it be too much trouble for you to write a line to Mr Ezra Pound? ... He writes to me to say that if you do he will interview you on my behalf and give you all the information you need ... You will understand also, from what he will tell you, that it will be impossible for me for some time to go to London.'[86] Evidently Joyce, and implicitly Pound, saw enough value in hiring a literary agent that Joyce took the trouble to have his friend interview Pinker, which suggests that both men were interested in the kinds of commercial success that other Pinker clients – Wells among them – enjoyed. What is more notable is the fact that even at the outset of their relationship, Joyce dealt with Pinker through an intermediary drawn from his inner circle. Throughout the next twenty years, Joyce frequently resorted to this tactic of having someone else deal with Pinker on his behalf, which allowed him to cultivate the image of the genius uninterested in the fruits to be gained from the literary marketplace, while nonetheless availing himself of the services of Pinker, who played a central role in harvesting those fruits for his clients.

Pinker's first task was to find a book publisher for *A Portrait of the Artist as a Young Man*; examining Pinker's role here will illustrate the challenges he encountered as Joyce's agent both because of the difficulty of placing the experimental material his client was producing and because of his client's inclination to make his own deals without always involving his agent. Pinker first went to Grant Richards because the contract the firm had negotiated for *Dubliners*,[87] which Joyce said that Pinker characterized as 'disastrous,' gave Richards the right of first refusal until June 1919 on any work Joyce wished to publish.[88] However, sales were poor for *Dubliners* and Richards was reluctant to publish *A Portrait* even at Pinker's urging. Pinker offered the book to several British publishers, including Duckworth and Heinemann, but was unable to secure a contract for its publication. On 6 December 1915, Joyce responded to an offer from Harriet Weaver, whose magazine the *Egoist* had been serializing *A Portrait*, about the possibility of her publishing the novel in book form. His postcard to her said, 'By all means telephone to Mr Pinker and also lay the matter before your staff and company,' and he even proposed terms to her: 'I undertake to buy for my account and pay for in advance 50 (fifty) copies at trade price.'[89] The same day, Joyce wrote to Pinker:

> The editor of *The Egoist* writes proposing to publish my novel, subject to the approval of the staff and publishing company. I have replied asking her to telephone to you. Perhaps you can see her. She has also sent me the address of their Paris correspondent but thinks that publication there would be difficult and unsatisfactory. I agree to this proposal if you do. I dislike the prospect of waiting another nine years before my next book appears – with the result which you know. All these schemes can be worked out simultaneously one against the other, can they not? In any case Miss Weaver's proposal is most friendly and I beg you to consider it.[90]

Pinker began to negotiate with Weaver, but as per Joyce's instructions, he continued his negotiations on other fronts as well. In January 1916, Weaver notified Joyce that her staff was prepared to support her in the publication of *A Portrait* and on 10 March 1916, Joyce wrote to her that 'I have written to Mr Pinker instructing him to draw up the agreement without further delay and to accept unconditionally, subject to his commission of 10%, whatever terms you propose.'[91] On 31 March he wrote to Pinker, 'I enclose agreement signed and initialized' for the publication of *A Portrait* by Weaver, but he also notes that 'Miss Weaver writes that seven printers have refused to set up the book and for this reason she prefers not to sign a contract.'[92] In fact, it took almost two years before the English edition of *A Portrait* was published. In the meantime, Pinker had been dealing with an American publisher, John Marshall, who had agreed to publish the novel, though eventually this fell through and B.W. Huebsch, who had contacted Harriet Weaver about the possibility of publishing the book, stepped into the breach. *A Portrait* was published in New York in December 1916. Pinker handled the contract between Joyce and Huebsch, and Weaver supplied the corrected text from which the novel was published. The first English edition, which appeared in February 1917, used the American pages, as Weaver had been unable to find an English printer willing to take on the task. Though Weaver's role is more frequently cited as the reason the novel finally appeared in book form, it is evident that Joyce relied on Pinker's assistance as well.

Pinker (and his sons, who took over the business upon Pinker's sudden death in 1922) continued to represent Joyce's interests in other publishing contracts, and over the years, the Pinkers had a hand in negotiations for the publication of Joyce's major works, though the process was often as complex as it had been for *A Portrait*.[93] What is interesting here is that while Joyce used publishers such as Harriet Weaver to place his material in little magazines and Sylvia Beach to bring out limited editions of his works, he looked to the Pinkers to arrange for publication of his work for a broader audience. In this he appears to have been engaged in what Rainey has identified as 'a tripartite structure within the productive apparatus of modernism,' by which he means that 'a modernist work was typically published in three forms: first, in a little review or journal; second, in a limited edition ... and third, in a more frankly commercial or public edition issued by a mainstream publisher and addressed to a wider audience.'[94] For example, the Pinkers arranged with Faber and Faber for the publication of *Pomes Penyeach* in 1932. Several private, limited editions of the poems had been published prior to then, but none had a print run of more than a hundred; thus the Faber edition marked the first broad market for the collection.[95] The publication of this volume of poetry is particularly noteworthy, since Faber was the publisher of record for most major poetry in Britain and their editions commanded a larger readership than Joyce's poetry would have reached in the little magazines or private editions in which he was usually published. The Pinkers also carried out their usual handling of outside rights, arranging for translation of various Joyce stories, and dealing with film rights, thereby providing further income for Joyce and also increasing his audience beyond the small circle of readers who would have had access to the private editions or little magazines in which his works originally appeared.[96]

The Pinkers were not without their difficulties in placing Joyce's work, however, particularly when they sought to place it in new, larger markets. A case in point is the problem they experienced handling Joyce's final masterpiece – *Finnegans Wake*. The Pinkers had negotiated a contract with Viking in America that would see Joyce's works marketed to a larger audience than they had reached before, given the resources at the disposal of Viking and the position it occupied in the American print culture field. As part of their work the Pinkers needed to coordinate the publication of American and English or European editions in order to secure American copyright. Faber's publication of *Pomes Penyeach*, for example, had to be coordinated with Viking's publication of it. The Pinkers initially tried to have the *Wake* published in extracts as Joyce requested. However, Joyce's publication of it in Europe in the small magazine *transition* jeopardized Viking's ability to copyright it in America and thus threatened their exclusive right to publish it. A letter from the Pinker office in New York (probably from Eric Pinker) to Ralph Pinker in the London office reads in part:

> This business is getting pretty tiresome, isn't it? I don't know what I can usefully say to you now about it except that as regards the publication of extracts in volume form the contract with Viking says in Clause 1 that publication shall be simultaneous in U.S.A. and England. Viking made the point before that TRANSITION is not copyrightable presumably because Holland is not in the Berne Convention. Also even if Viking took steps to make practical copyright such as Leon suggests[,] that does not prevent copies of TRANSITION or pamphlets coming into this country and being read by a lot of people.[97]

The frustration evident in this letter was not unusual, since the Pinkers frequently found that the agreements they had concluded or were negotiating conflicted with Joyce's own private deals. Furthermore, Joyce's explicit stance as an artist whose aesthetic need to see the text published in a suitably avant-garde journal like *transition* clearly worked against his implicit desire to earn the larger sums of money that the sale of his fiction by Viking might bring about. It is clear, then, that Joyce did entrust Pinker with his major works – from *A Portrait of the Artist as a Young Man* to *Finnegans Wake* – and though the agency had varying success placing them, the relationship between agent and client must have been of continuing value to both, since it lasted until the Pinker agency dissolved in 1937.[98]

What is particularly germane here is the fact that Pinker's patronage of Joyce was a gamble – Joyce's track record was not established when J.B. approached him in 1915 – much as Pinker's patronage of Lawrence had been a gamble. In this case, Pinker did not invest money in Joyce – there is no indication that he advanced him an allowance as he did Bennett and Lawrence, for example – but he invested both his time and his reputation. The measure employed by Pinker to assess the success of his investment in Joyce's career appears not to have been economic, but symbolic/cultural. By this I mean that the sums of money the Pinkers would have earned as commissions from Joyce were likely small, certainly during J.B. Pinker's lifetime, but the symbolic/cultural capital they earned by being Joyce's agent was large. Their association with Joyce would have established them as the literary agency that represented important, new writers, since Joyce was regarded as the leading novelist of the new generation. It is ironic to consider that this strategy is exactly the same as A.P. Watt employed when he set out on his career as an agent, for just as Watt had used his association with George MacDonald to situate himself in the print culture field in the late 1870s, so Pinker used his with James Joyce in 1915. The major difference, of course, is that when Watt took on MacDonald as a client he was taking on a writer who was already well established, while Joyce's position in the field was far from established when he became Pinker's client.

Pinker and the Print Culture Field

It is evident that Pinker's revisions to Watt's template had a significant impact on literary agenting. By the turn of the century, the ranks of literary agents had grown considerably. In part, this is because of the rapid expansion of the literary marketplace and, in part, because writers had routinely begun to seek out the services of literary agents. Newcomers to the profession looked to the big three agencies – A.P. Watt and Son, J.B. Pinker, and Curtis Brown – both as models of how to conduct their business and as rivals. Within this triumvirate, Pinker's innovations appealed strongly to smaller or newly established agencies. It was next to impossible for a new agent, or even an established agent whose firm was small, to induce well-established authors to leave the three big agencies. The connections and services provided for these authors by a Watt or a Pinker could not be as easily matched by smaller or newer agencies.

New agents had to seek out their clients in the ranks of authors who were not yet established or whose work rated less highly than that of the luminaries populating Watt's list of famous clients – much as Pinker had done when he started out. The fact that Pinker had prospered by doing just this provided new agents with a model of success that contrasted with Watt's.

Equally important, Pinker's actions had a significant impact on the print culture field itself. Early debates about the role of the agent had always conceded that an agent was 'Of every use to *the writer who has already created a demand*' for his or her work, but of little or no use to those who had not already done so.[99] By 1910, the usefulness of agents was still hotly debated, but there was a noticeable shift in the opinions about who could best benefit from an agent's assistance. Written in response to an article highly critical of literary and dramatic agents in the October 1911 issue of the *Author*, May Sinclair's thoughtful, and thought-provoking, letter indicates a real shift in the assumptions and terms of the debate. The first point she makes is that the issue was not about whether to employ an agent but about an agent's honesty. Sinclair argued forcefully that 'No doubt there *are* dishonest agents' and that

> It may be an author's misfortune if he encounters one of these, but it is also very much his fault. For there are plenty of people who can tell him where honest agents may be found. I, for one, can give the address not only of an honest agent … but an agent who, in my experience, has actually disregarded his own immediate interests in the interests of his clients. This honesty of his is no doubt his best policy; but I have also known him exert himself in ways where even policy could discern no profit.

She goes on to state as plainly as possible the central points of the debate surrounding the question of whether an agent ought to be employed by an author:

> the question is often raised whether an agent is really any good to anybody except the already prosperous or established author? Well, that depends on the agent; it depends also on the author; it depends very largely on the publisher. By knowing exactly where to place him, a good agent may be very useful to the promising unknown; by nursing a dying popularity into the semblance of a little life, he may still be useful to the too-well known. No doubt, with some firms, the unknown author will have a better chance, a perfectly fair chance, too, if he 'deals direct.' For, in the beginning, he is

a pure speculation to everybody concerned. Whether his chances will be equally fair when his commercial value is increasing, depends solely on the publishers' integrity. His exact commercial value is a thing no author at this stage of his career knows or can know. His publishers themselves may not know it. But the agent may know. At any rate he knows what other firms are prepared to pay.[100]

The argument was no longer 'ought agents to be employed'; the point was *how and when* to employ an agent. Clearly, the field had accepted the presence of agents as important players in the production of literature. Just as clearly, the central qualities of the agent, as outlined by Sinclair, are those which combined Watt's template with the innovations brought to it by Pinker. Pinker's influence was on par with Watt's.

6 The Agent and 'Popular' Literature: Somerville and Ross and Pinker

Irish cousins Edith Oenone Somerville and Violet Martin met for the first time in 1886. There was little indication over the summer of Violet Martin's visit to Castletownshend, the west Cork home of her Somerville cousins, of the unique writing partnership that was soon to be established. Nevertheless, in the course of the next two decades they would combine to write some of the most memorable fiction produced in the dying years of the Anglo-Irish Ascendancy. Although both women had begun writing separately prior to this meeting, it was the work that they wrote together as Somerville and Ross[1] that earned them a permanent place in the Irish canon.[2] Indeed, Ann Owen Weekes writes that 'Terence de Vere White, for example, finds [Somerville and Ross's] *The Real Charlotte* second only to "the great whale" (Joyce's *Ulysses*), and V.S. Pritchett calls it the best Irish novel of any period.'[3] Despite these laudatory remarks, there remains much controversy over the quality and importance of the work the two produced, and Somerville and Ross are not frequently mentioned alongside their contemporaries James Joyce and W.B. Yeats. Declan Kiberd perhaps best epitomizes the women's critical standing when he writes: 'Of all the major Irish writers, Edith Somerville and Martin Ross (whose real name was Violet Martin) are the most difficult to catch in the act of greatness.'[4] I do not intend in this chapter to debate the merits of their works; rather, I will focus on how the cousins' relationship with their agent J.B. Pinker shaped their literary output and how that output, in turn, helped to create their literary reputation. In the course of doing this, the chapter will also highlight the differences between Pinker's handling of his innovative female clients' work and Watt's handling of Lucas Malet's career.

Early Years: 1887–97

Somerville and Ross began their first collaborative novel in October of 1887. Edith's diary entry for 4 October notes, 'We began to invent a plot for a penny thriller, and Martin's diary entry for 21 October states, 'We stayed in and worried over the *Shockerawn*, an Irish tale of love and gore.'[5] Though Martin had to return to her home in Galway, they continued to work on their novel throughout the autumn and winter months. It was finished in spring 1888, and they sent the manuscript, now entitled *An Irish Cousin*, off to London publishers with high hopes. After an initial rejection by Sampson and Company, Richard Bentley and Sons offered to publish the book. Martin's diary entry for 2 December records her delight: 'Got a letter from Richard Bentley & Son announcing that the birthday of our lives has come and that he was prepared to publish the Shocker giving us £25 on publication and £25 on the sale of 500 copies. All comment is inadequate. Went dizzily to church twice. Wrote accepting terms with dignity.'[6] As Gifford Lewis notes, Martin then set out to arrange for their new novel to be reviewed in the right places by the right people (many of whom were relations or family friends). She even ensured that it was 'stocked by the Free Libraries that had been endowed by Andrew Carnegie.'[7] Lewis's subsequent claim that 'Had Martin not been related to such an influential circle it is likely that their career would have died at birth'[8] is an exaggeration. Nonetheless, it is arguable that Martin, who is here performing the business functions that a literary agent would have undertaken, greatly enhanced the chances that this first novel would be both a critical and a financial success. She was to continue in this role for the cousins' next two efforts: *Naboth's Vineyard* (1891)[9] and then the novel on which many critics have based their reputation, *The Real Charlotte* (1894). By 1895, they were busy, reasonably successful authors whose journalism brought in a modest but steady income.[10] The selling price for their novels also was steadily rising: they had received '£250 and ½ American rights'[11] for the sale of the copyright of *The Real Charlotte* to Ward and Downey. With the collaborative writing process working well, and given Martin's skill at promoting their work, it appeared that the cousins' writing career was successfully launched.[12] But by 1897, they were employing a professional agent – J.B. Pinker – to manage their literary affairs. What happened to bring this about?

Clients of Pinker

In 1872, Mrs Martin and her five daughters, including Martin, had left their family seat of Ross in Galway for Dublin. Martin's brother, Robert, now the master of Ross, had chosen to 'shut the ancestral house, place the collection of rents in the hands of an agent and himself continue his career in London. It was arranged that his mother should take her five daughters to Dublin where they had many relatives and the entry to the best society of the capital.'[13] Over the next decade or so, the agent embezzled money from the estate and, in essence, ran it into the ground. In 1888, Mrs Martin returned home; her two unmarried daughters, Martin and Selina, soon followed her. It was left largely to Martin to undertake the arduous task of rescuing the family home from the extreme state of disrepair that over ten years of neglect had caused. Hilary Robinson remarks, 'Until 1905 when her mother left Ross, almost all of Martin's literary earnings were spent on the upkeep of the house. And much as she loved her mother, who was herself well-read, intelligent with a fine sense of humour and a sharp wit, living with her meant little time to write in, even when the estate and the household cares gave her a few moments.'[14] Ross was to remain Martin's home for most of the next twenty years, although from the early 1890s she spent more and more time in Cork with her Somerville cousins. She finally moved to Drishane, Edith's home, in 1905, leaving Ross for good after the death of her brother Robert.

From 1895 onwards, Edith's own rather precarious domestic circumstances also became more difficult. In November 1895, her mother died after a brief illness. This left Edith to run the large household at Drishane for her father, including looking after the estate business and accounts. In 1898, her father died, causing further instability in the family, since his heir, Cameron, was only thirty-eight and wished to continue his career in the army rather than return to Ireland to manage the family estate. To make matters worse, their father's pension had accounted for a significant portion of the family income. As Maurice Collis notes, the financial situation at Drishane was difficult:

> As the pension died with [Colonel Somerville], could Drishane be kept up on the rents? Edith had no money except that which she made from her books, half of which went to Martin. Aylmer's income from his farm was small. Egerton had not yet succeeded his father, the baronet. As they all felt it would be dreadful to have to let or sell Drishane, they decided that each should contribute under Edith's general management.[15]

From this time until Cameron died in 1942, Edith managed the estate. As the political situation in Ireland worsened throughout the 1890s and into the first decades of the twentieth century, and the rent strikes bit more deeply into the estate income, more and more of Edith's money and energy were spent on maintaining Drishane. Her decision to take over the Carberry Hunt from her brother Aylmer in 1905 further worsened her financial circumstances. Every penny of her literary earnings was devoted either to maintaining the Hunt's hounds or to the estate. Her letters and diaries record her frequent money worries and her realization that she must write and be paid well for her writing in order to hold on to her family home and way of life. As Collis notes, this all exacted a heavy toll on Edith: 'Added to her griefs, Edith's struggle to keep writing while she supervised Drishane had been rather too much for her. She became run down and began to suffer from gout, a rheumatic disorder which in one form or another afflicted her for the rest of her life.'[16]

Not surprisingly, then, the women's letters are filled with references to their impoverished state; itemized accounting of their earnings from their literary efforts; and rants about the unreliability of editors in publishing material when they want it published and about editors' failure to pay them on time and at a level they felt was commensurate with the quality of their work. A fairly typical lament is this one in Martin's letter to Edith dated Thursday 18 September 1890:

> I *must* make money – so must you – and the Welsh Aunt [the working title for *The Real Charlotte*] is an awful business ... Hang the *Lady's Pictorial* – why wont [*sic*] they start these articles, or even answer my letter – Gibbons is a detestable creature and I have always hated him.[17]

Other letters discuss where to send material, how to get advances so that they could take the trips on which they based their travelogues, and how money earned was to be divided between the two. For example, Martin writes to Edith on 5 December 1894:

> I had this morning *another* cheque from B[lack] and W[hite] for £4.4 shillings. Two guineas were for the literary matter of the last two of the Beggars. Two for ditto of the first Quartier Latinity. The Beggars are now disposed of. I send the cheques as payable to you. There is £9.9 shillings altogether for us to divide – an almost impossible sum – It is I think £4 14 shillings and six pence each. Again, and in shame, I must ask to have my half. There are

Crowley, Jerry, Collins and others to face before I go home. I will lodge the
five guinea cheque in your bank straight away – and perhaps you will send
me a cheque for my beastly moiety.[18]

One thing that becomes clear is that their need for money drives their
decisions on what to write, where to place it, and how much to ask for
their work. Their judgment in each of these respects is not always good,
and in fact sometimes results in short-term economic gains that end up
costing them money in the long term. Edith's negotiations with Richard
Bentley and Company for the publication of *The Real Charlotte*, for example, are undermined because she asks for more than Bentley feels the
market can bear. The letter from the firm tells Edith, 'The price you
have fixed for the book when added to the cost of production and
advertizing [*sic*] is actually considerably in excess of the total receipts of
the work. I should therefore have some difficulty in persuading Mr.
Bentley for example – even if he did not look for a pennyworth of profit
out of the transaction – to buy for £200, the right of losing £50.'[19]
Though the cousins got £250 for the novel from Ward and Downey, the
fact that they sold the copyright to the publisher meant that they did not
share in any additional money the book's sales might have earned them
had they negotiated the contract differently.[20] Much as they might have
wished to manage their literary business as effectively as they both managed their respective family estates, the record suggests that they did not
do so. In fact, the women were stuck in the situation far too familiar to
many Victorian women writers – their domestic duties took time away
from their writing, yet they depended on their writing to permit the
smooth running of their homes.

The ever-increasing domestic duties left the women little time for their
writing. What time they had was too precious to spend in writing business
letters to editors and publishers or making the long trip to London to
deal with them in person. Nonetheless, these contacts were a central
part of literary life at the end of the nineteenth century. Edith and
Martin were more fortunate than most provincial writers because they
had a large circle of family and friends who were reasonably well placed
in the London literary world and who were willing to carry out business
tasks for them. Martin's obvious London contact was her brother Robert,
who, under the name Ballyhooly, had established himself as a successful
entertainer and writer.[21] She also sought help from others, including
Edmund Yates, founder of the *World*, whose assistance to the two women
early in their career was invaluable. Yates was particularly keen on

employing women; his staff included Mary Elizabeth Braddon and Mrs Lynn Linton, two of the leading popular women novelists of the day. The cousins' friendship with Yates and the degree to which they both depended on his literary help is evident in a letter Martin wrote to Edith on 4 August 1888 from Ross. She mentions a piece that she is working on, saying, 'I have been all day at intervals toiling over an article for the *World* anent Dublin and the horse show and I simply can't get the hang of it and *loathe* it. I doubt I shall send it if I finish it. I don't want to disgust Edmund all at once, and it is very foul.'[22] Martin began to publish regularly in the *World* in 1888. Even more telling is the fact that, according to Gifford Lewis, 'The naming of the R[esident] M[agistrate] [the main character in their hunting stories] as Major Sinclair Yeates is a tribute to Edmund Yates and not to the poet W.B. Yeats.'[23] Edith was also well placed in terms of family connections, though she was less skilled at using them than Martin. Nonetheless, Edith did her part, calling on family friend Oscar Wilde on 10 April 1888, for example, when he was editor of the *Woman's World*.[24] Edith's account of the interview paints an unflattering portrait of Wilde. She referred to him as 'a great fat oily beast' who 'pretended the most enormous interest' and 'assumed great interest in the Miss Martins and asked if they were married.'[25] Wilde proved of little help to the women, for, as Collis rightly suggests, 'The fact was that Edith could hardly have gone to anyone in London less likely to be of use to her and Martin … Under no circumstances could she have appreciated at its proper value his future oeuvre, any better than he could have appreciated hers and Martin's.'[26] Though the two women were to continue to call on friends and relations for help throughout the rest of their writing lives, it soon became evident that if they were to earn enough money and have their work properly looked after, they needed more help than their friends could provide.

It is interesting that Edith and Martin chose J.B. Pinker rather than A.P. Watt as their agent. That the cousins knew the London literary scene is clear from their letters to each other and to other family members and acquaintances. They certainly would have been aware of Watt's dominant position and it would seem likely that they would have sought advice from him. The modest reputation that they had begun to establish would probably have brought their name to the attention of Watt's firm. The kind of fiction that they had produced was also likely to appeal to Watt, given the moral tone and social commentary apparent in all three of the novels they had published by 1895. The generally positive reviews would also have been a point in their favour. Finally, some of their literary friends were clients of Watt.[27] In fact, in 1895, Martin wrote to Edith from St Andrews, where she was enjoying being feted by the journalist and critic Andrew Lang, that he suggested that they 'ought to employ Watts [*sic*] agent to work with publishers, adding that he was only a man for people whose position was assured.'[28] Why would they choose to employ instead an unknown agent, especially one who had just established his own firm?

It is possible that they were steered towards Pinker by one or more of their friends or relatives who were familiar with the various agents in London. It is more likely that they chose Pinker because they knew him from his capacity as assistant editor of *Black and White*, a magazine that had commissioned a travelogue from them and had published other pieces by them.[29] An early mention of Pinker occurs in a letter Martin wrote to Edith from the House of Commons in 1895. This trip to London followed on the heels of Martin's successful January 1895 sojourn in St Andrews. Martin is passing on gossip about literary acquaintances and tells Edith,

> [Armstrong, a family friend] told me that it was rumoured that Pinker had gone into partnership with [C.N.] Williamson in this *Hour* business – but he seemed to think it was a dubious spec. I said that Williamson had made B. and W. [*Black and White*] what it was – A statement that met with small enthusiasm. I also said the *Hour* wished us to travel for them. He said that we must not be enticed away from B. and W. and proceeded to ask if *I* could make any suggestions for the improvement of the paper.[30]

Though it was not until 1896 that Pinker established his literary agency, one may infer from Martin's gossip that Pinker was already looking for opportunities beyond his editorial duties. Many of Pinker's initial clients came from the rolls of *Black and White*'s editors and contributors, so it seems very likely that Williamson, whom Martin admired, may have steered her towards his friend. In any case, by 1897 the women had become clients of Pinker and remained with his agency until his death in 1922.

Business Relationship

In 1897, Edith wrote a letter to Martin in which she described a meeting Pinker arranged for her and which he attended as her advisor. It is probable that this was one of their first meetings, though, as is evident from this letter, they had been corresponding about other material that Pinker was trying to place for them. The letter, though long, deserves to be quoted at length because it captures the essence of the business relationship that was developing and it also illustrates Pinker's style as an agent. Edith writes:

> ... sure he [Pinker] can place it – I had suggested B. &. W. – (at *yr* suggestion) for 'Aran', but only in a letter, and I very stupidly forgot to speak of it; there was a good deal to say – He then asked me to come up to Lawrence and Bullen's, Henrietta St – Covent Garden, and took a hansom in the most dashing manner in spite of assurances that I preferred walking – En route he explained that the Art Editor and Sub-Editor of the Bad[minton] Mag[azine] were combined in the person of a Mr Hedley Peek, who was also a sort of partner of L. and B.'s: he explained also that Mr Peek's position was rather delicate between L. and B. and the Bad Mag people but that he might as a friend of both, buy serial rights for one and publication rights for the other – arrived at L. and B.'s we were marched right into the usual rather dingy office ... We began about the Silver Fox – they say it is to be published immediately ... I then asked of the Collected Works – they had not read them; they hinted at the idea that they ought to be all stories or all articles, but were not strong on that point. I said they were all Irish anyhow, and that we had often been asked to republish etc. – They then raved of the Bad Mag stories – Hedley Peek had got them – especially the grand filly – by heart, and both attacked me to know wch of us wrote which parts – by chapters or how – the usual old thing ... They all – including little Pinker – swore we had got hold of a very good thing in this serio-comic hunting business – 'To use the literary slang' said Pinker, 'this is *your own stuff*' and no one else does anything like it – H.P. said he liked immensely the start of Emily V. and Co., seemed to think if we could keep near that exalted level we shd do awfully well – ... He gave me to understand they will be glad of anything we write if we can keep to the G. Filly level and style. He said that as we propose to run the story serially we ought to arrange it to be not more than between 70 and 72,000 words, to be equally divided into 12 parts, not necessarily chapters, and to arrange a curtain for each part – He wld like, if possible to have all the M.S. by Xmas – with 6 drawings to show quality, and to enable them to decide if they would have more – If they liked the drawings they wld want about 70 (!!) and he wld – with great politeness – reserve the right to refuse or suggest corrections in any drawings sent in ... – Mr Bullen was very busy and fussed about in and out of the room and talked secretly to Pinker, and to red and glistening underlings, who came

perspiring in at frequent intervals with proofs etc – I think from the way he
spoke he wld be glad to bring out the short stories vol: he asked if we had
thought of a name – I said No – He said it was very important – H.P. said
something might occur to him and I said we would be thinking – the end of
all was that Pinker told me he thought they would publish the *S. Fox* in a
week or fortnight, and that then they might take hold of the short stories
and bring them out later in the autumn – H.P. said that as soon as ever he
saw the M.S. of Emily and co that he wld make Pinker an offer, and that we
could decide – He said he liked the Royalty System – I said that we always
liked it too, but that we should want a sum down, to wch he agreed I really
don't think there is any more to tell except that they begged me to come
and see them again as soon as possible, and to bring you with me as they
much desired the pleasure of yr acquaintance etc. ... [31]

There are several things going on beneath the surface of the conver-
sations that were taking place during this meeting. First, note the way in
which Pinker plays to his client's own sense of herself. He has sized
Edith up, deciding that the best way to manage her, and thus her literary affairs, is to flatter her own sense of importance as a writer while at
the same time finding a way to steer her towards the outcome he thinks
best suits her abilities. In this, he does what any good agent must do –
assess his client and learn how best to work with her. He begins by insisting that she ride in a hansom cab at his expense. Edith's tight budget
would not have permitted this luxury for short journeys, thus her objection to Martin, but Pinker's gesture evidently impressed her, since she
mentioned it in the letter. Next, he provides her with inside knowledge
about Hedley Peek's somewhat delicate position between the *Badminton
Magazine* and the publishing house of Lawrence and Bullen. By doing
this he not only prepares her for the meeting and the need to influence
Peek, but also creates a bond between Edith and himself as allies in the
game to get the best deal from the publishers. Then, at the outset of the
conversation, Pinker joins with Bullen and Peek in praising the R.M. stories, going so far as to state: '"this is *your own stuff*" and no one else does
anything like it.' Here he plays to Edith's writerly vanity, praising work
that he knows she is unsure of – it is not the serious 'stuff' that she has
been trained by her culture to think is the only writing worth undertaking. With three prominent literary men praising the work, Edith's sense
of its worth is bound to be influenced. Finally, Pinker withdraws from
the active conversation, choosing to sit in the background, talking quietly with Bullen while Edith and Peek discuss all manner of things

related to the stories themselves. Here, Edith is given the sense of being in control of her literary affairs; Pinker is placed in the position of her business advisor. As a result, when Edith complies with what Pinker advises her to do – write more R.M. stories – she does so in the belief that she has determined this course of action.

The success of Pinker's handling of Edith in this meeting is evident in the concluding comments in this same letter where she says to Martin:

> The end of it all is My Lady Anne, that you must come back to Drishane or else meet me in a desert place as soon as possible, get yr insides tidied up by Willy S., and buckle to. Some other Irish Devil who can hunt and write will rise up and knock the wind out of our sails, and we can't afford to be jockeyed like that ... I think on the whole it was satisfactory and worth the heaps of time, money and trouble of going up ...

Edith had been hesitant about pursuing the R.M. stories prior to the meeting with the publishers, as evidenced by her desire to get them to consider bringing out a *Collected Works* of Somerville and Ross that would include their previous novels. Yet by the end of the meeting, she is so anxious to start on the stories that she instructs Martin to go immediately to Drishane so they can begin work. It is reasonable to conclude from this change of attitude that she was skilfully managed by Peek and Pinker into doing what they likely agreed to beforehand: that Pinker would deliver to Peek more R.M. stories if he could convince Edith and Martin to write them.

The second thing to note about this meeting is the fact that Pinker took Edith with him to it in the first place. There really was little need for him to do so: he could have discussed the deal as easily with her in his office and then negotiated separately with Bullen and Peek. In fact, it was far more common for agents to serve as a buffer between publishers and writers; as we have seen, this separation of writer from publisher is one of the chief complaints both sides levied against agents. Yet Pinker chose to take Edith to the meeting and to permit her to believe that she virtually ran it. Certainly the tone and comments in her letter to Martin suggest that she is in charge and that Pinker is as subject to her charm and will as are Bullen and Peek. But Pinker's motivation was not solely to manipulate Edith into writing more R.M. stories. It is likely that he made the choice to include Edith in the meeting in part to gain favour with both his client and the publishers by indicating that he was not going to be an agent who kept the two apart.

Third, Pinker's use of this meeting for his own business interests is noteworthy. As an editor, he would have come into contact with most of the leading publishers, but it would have been in his own interests to firm up these relationships when he crossed the divide, so to speak, and set up shop as an agent. By bringing Edith to the meeting and then agreeing with Bullen and Peek about the desirability of the R.M. stories, Pinker does them a service. They want to publish more of them, but can only do so if they convince Edith of their aesthetic as well as financial value. When Pinker tells Edith 'no one else does anything like it,' he cues her that she is producing work that is not only in demand by the public, but unique. He is also reinforcing the not-so-subtle hard sell that Peek goes on to engage in with his subsequent flattering of Edith's ability as both writer and illustrator. In short, Pinker helps the publishers sell Edith on the idea of writing more of the stories that they want to publish. He is looking after her best interests – he will negotiate a contract that will be favourable to her and his assessment of the quality and marketability of the R.M. stories is astute – but he is also looking after his own interests by supporting the publishers' desires.

Fourth, it is interesting that Pinker orchestrates a meeting where Edith perceives the topic as not contracts but content. Contracts were the point on which many publisher-author relationships foundered; some also foundered over the issue of editorial control of content, but contract negotiations far more often poisoned the publisher-author relationship. Peek and Edith agree that the royalty system is preferable, provided there is an advance, but they also agree to leave the details of the contract up to Peek and Pinker. Edith is therefore free to think of Peek as a charming, cultivated man, a fellow artist and writer who sympathizes with her rather than as a hard-nosed businessman who insists that he have the right to refuse her illustrations if he does not like them. Yet Peek is both, as Edith's letter reveals. Pinker's presence as the business advisor permits his client to focus on what she does best – write and illustrate her writing. She goes away from the meeting enthusiastic about her next project and content that she will be well treated on both the business and the aesthetic levels by her new publishers.

This letter, written so early in the relationship between Pinker and the cousins, remarkably captures the working arrangements that were to persist throughout much of their twenty-plus years together. The pattern of praise followed by sound, practical business advice recurs throughout Pinker's letters to them, suggesting that he frequently found it necessary to 'manage' them as he managed Edith at this early meeting. For instance, he wrote to Martin in 1904 praising the latest instalment of the R.M. stories that he had read in manuscript form. He said, 'they are worthy of the RM's creators – and that is the highest compliment I can pay them.' But he went on to say, 'It is a great relief to my mind to have you started, and so well started too. I am hoping you will gradually get into the habit of work, and then we can perhaps have a novel to follow the "new experiences" and settle into a steady "book a year" rate of production.'[32] Apart from managing them so that they fulfilled their obligations, Pinker performed all the expected services of an agent – negotiating contracts, checking the publishers' accounts, collecting royalties, ensuring that his clients' works were properly advertised, and so on. He also arranged for press clippings of reviews and for copies of magazines in which their works appeared to be sent to them. In every respect, he was the model literary agent, managing them and their literary affairs with the utmost professionalism. Yet his services for the women went well beyond handling their literary productions.

Pinker, like Watt, was often asked to undertake personal services for his clients. For Edith and Martin, this often meant helping them with matters related to their estates. Edith, especially, relied on Pinker for non-literary help, asking him on more than one occasion to find owners for horses she (or her brother) had for sale. In 1899, for instance, she tried to convince him to buy a mare, asking him, 'Don't you want to win a hunt steeple chase somewhere next spring? I am sure she would do it for you – her price is £120 in Cork – (where she could be put on board the steamer by my groom.) A Curragh jockey *all but* gave me £100 for her at the Horse Show, so I think she is worth a good bit more.'[33] Edith's brother Aylmer wrote to Pinker on 1 January 1904, 'There is here an absolute past master or mistress rather of the art of jumping that might suit you. Only a cob 14.1 ½ 4 yrs sound, and as good a jumper as I have ever seen anywhere, if not the very best goes in harness. The owner a farmer asks £50 but £40 wd buy her I should say.'[34] Edith also asked Pinker to advise her on buying art and on selling her own. In 1902, for example, she wrote to Pinker about the advisability of purchasing a print of Rembrandt's *Descent from the Cross* for investment purposes, saying, 'I am sure, as you know everything and everyone you would not mind sending me a wire if you thought it worthwhile buying it.'[35] Such was their faith in his ability to arrange things that Martin even sought his help in obtaining the position of secretary of the Royal Automobile Club for her brother-in-law Colonel Dawson. Though Pinker was unable to procure it – because it had already been divided into three positions that had been filled by the time Martin made her request – Martin nonetheless responded, 'we value your kindness about it just the same.'[36] Theirs was clearly a business relationship that worked well, and much of the credit for this must go to Pinker, who managed the cousins' non-literary requests with the same skill and diplomacy as he managed their literary affairs.

Pinker and Somerville and Ross's Critics

At best, most Somerville and Ross critics have minimized Pinker's role in their literary career; at worst, they have suggested that his advice harmed them. One of their biographers, John Cronin, suggests that 'need for money forced [the women] to comply with [Pinker's] request [to write more R.M. stories] instead of devoting to their fictions the slow and careful preparation which had gone into the making of *The Real Charlotte*.'[37] This assessment of Pinker appears to be supported by Edith's published comments on their agent. An oft-quoted passage from her collection of essays *Happy Days* has been accepted as an accurate description of the working relationship between Pinker and the cousins. It appears in an essay entitled 'Étaples' in which Edith describes the genesis of their most popular work, the R.M. stories. Edith tells the reader that she and Martin had travelled to Étaples, she to paint and Martin to write, and while there they had ignored a commission to write more hunting stories for the *Badminton Magazine*. As Edith narrates the story, 'Other work intervened ... and we straightaway forgot all about Mr. Watson, and his Sporting Magazine.' Yet she was quickly reminded of her obligation, for as she says,

> ... we had a taskmaster, a little man of iron determination, a Literary Agent (which is the modern equivalent for an Egyptian taskmaster) and he did not forget. He did not indeed, like his Egyptian prototype, say, 'Ye are idle! Ye are idle!' But we knew he thought it, and when he wrote to us and alluded rather pointedly to our agreement with Mr. Watson, we decided that he was taking a liberty – *our* liberty – and for a further fortnight we continued to idle, defiantly and enjoyably. And then our taskmaster wrote again. In my diary, at the date July 16, 1898, appears the fateful entry. 'Heard again from X. He says Watson of the Bad Mag is shrieking for the hunting stories.'[38]

At this second urging, they began to work on the next R.M. story. Another passage from this same essay continues Edith's somewhat dismissive description of Pinker's (X's) role in their writing career. She notes that her sister and brother-in-law informed them that they were coming to visit and that she and Martin seized on this as an excuse to return to their 'idle' ways. Edith writes:

> Martin Ross and I found ourselves compulsorily established as guides and caretakers, and we accepted the change of masters without useless complaint, realising that our literary aims and responsibilities were for our young friends trifles as light as the idle wind. After all (we consoled one another) little X must learn that he can't always have it all his own way. We must sometimes sit (metaphorically) on little X. Therefore, sitting (metaphorically) on both Mr. Watson and our agent, we abandoned ourselves to the lawless holiday that our visitors expected of us.[39]

With remarks like this, it is little wonder that Pinker's role in their literary career has been understudied and under-appreciated.

Putting aside the deliberately playful tone that Edith adopts for this piece, it is still clear that the picture of Pinker that she paints is unflattering. This is surprising in light of the firm friendship that developed between both cousins and Pinker. Indeed, Pinker was a visitor to Drishane, where he enjoyed hunting with Edith and her brother Aylmer, and Edith and Martin both stayed with Pinker in London and enjoyed his hospitality at his Surrey estate. Strong evidence of the friendship that existed between the writers and Pinker comes from this letter that Edith wrote to Pinker after Martin's death: 'I have said nothing to you about our long friendship with you, and how my dear cousin relied on your help and counsel, but I think you know it. I, at all events, shall never forget it.'[40] In light of this remark, there must have been important reasons for Edith's minimizing of Pinker's role in the cousins' writing success.

Aesthetics and Literary Reputation

Edith and Martin shared the common belief of the print culture field they entered in 1890 that a writer's literary reputation rested on his or her 'serious' work. This belief was reinforced by the fact that the women's views of literary value – shaped by their class and education along with their life experiences – would have emphasized the primacy of cultural capital over economic capital, no matter how necessary economic capital was to the women's individual lives. Thus for the cousins, their literary reputation rested not on their hugely popular and financially lucrative R.M. stories, but on their critically acclaimed novel *The Real Charlotte*. Indeed, Edith says as much in *Irish Memories*: 'Very humbly, and quite uncontroversially, I may say that Martin and I have not wavered from the opinion that "The Real Charlotte" was, and remains, the best of our books.'[41] Edith's lighthearted recounting of how the R.M. stories came about permits her to maintain the position that they involved less work than the 'serious' novels, were less consciously crafted, and were therefore of lesser aesthetic value. The implicit message is that but for their 'Egyptian taskmaster' the public might have had fewer R.M. stories and more *Real Charlottes*.

The cousins' attitude to their work is reflected and reinforced in the comments of their contemporaries and by subsequent twentieth-century critical assessments. For example, Ernest Boyd's *Ireland's Literary Renaissance* includes an entry on Somerville and Ross that represents what has been until fairly recently the standard critical assessment of their work.[42] He writes:

> There has been a vast crop of entertaining fiction which has come to be regarded, especially outside Ireland itself, as 'very Irish,' as the characteristic contribution to the modern novel. The greatest of these disciples of Charles Lever were OE. Somerville and Martin Ross, whose partnership was terminated by the death of Miss Martin in 1915. Their fox-hunting, rollicking tales of serio-comic peasants and devil-may-care Anglo-Irish gentry gave to *Some Experiences of an Irish R.M.* (1899), *Further Experiences of an Irish R.M.* and *Dan Russell the Fox* the apparently irresistible charm of such literature for those who are satisfied with an effective convention. The popularity of the many volumes in this vein which these two collaborators published has somewhat overshadowed the real merit of the one novel of genuine power, originality and distinction which they wrote before they discovered the line of least resistance. *The Real Charlotte* (1894) is a Balzacian study of Irish provincial types, drawn with a seriousness and an impartial sense of reality, which serve to heighten regret for the subsequent squandering of the authors' great talent upon the trivialities of a superficial realism.[43]

Boyd's privileging of what he called Balzacian realism over serio-comic hunting tales is repeated in most critical appraisals of the women's work, where the R.M. stories themselves are often not even mentioned. For example, Declan Kiberd's important reappraisal of the Irish literary landscape contains a chapter on Somerville and Ross in which he focuses exclusively on *The Real Charlotte*. Kiberd says,

The bright, sparkling surfaces and fluent narrative method cannot conceal the dark undertow of *The Real Charlotte*, their greatest novel, published in 1894: while the form is jaunty with the ironies of good social comedy, the content is a tragic tale of the collapse of big house culture. This is what gives their writing its power to haunt the mind in ways that seem out of all proportion to its easy, middlebrow charm, for even as the style sings of hope the message is despair.[44]

He goes on to state, 'They [Somerville and Ross] have the moral courage in such a scene to raise problems for which they have no ready answer. *The Real Charlotte* thus becomes one of the very rare Irish narratives which is actually a novel in the comedy-of-manners mode, calibrating itself to the layers of a fairly complex (if restricted) society.'[45] Whether the novel offers the kind of full-blown realism that Boyd asserts it does or is a comedy of manners, as Kiberd suggests, does not seem to matter in terms of the general critical belief that the cousins' literary reputation rests on it. Certainly, the cousins agreed with this critical assessment.

Yet *The Real Charlotte* did not receive universally good reviews when it was published – indeed, many of the reviews, as Edith admits in *Irish Memories*, were highly critical of just those elements that Boyd and Kiberd praise. Edith wrote, for example, that 'One distinguished London literary paper pronounced it to be "one of the most disagreeable novels we have ever read"; and ended with the crushing assertion that it could "hardly imagine a book more calculated to depress and disgust even a hardened reader ... the amours are mean, the people mostly repulsive, and the surroundings depressing."' She concluded her comments about the reception of the novel by admitting that, 'on the whole, poor Charlotte fared badly.'[46] Added to this is the fact that the novel went out of print, likely when its publishers Ward and Downey went into receivership, so that by 1899 Edith was writing to Pinker to see if he could interest another publisher in taking over the copyright so as to arrange for another edition to be published.[47]

In contrast, the R.M. stories *are* what Somerville and Ross's literary reputation rests on. James M. Cahalan notes,

The *Irish R.M.* stories have enjoyed a persistent international popularity. They were first collected in three successive volumes of 1899, 1908, and 1915 – and subsequently they were published all together in 1928, have always stayed in print, and became known to many people through the British Channel 4/UTV/RTE television series that aired more than once beginning in the 1980s. An inexpensive, collected paperback edition sold briskly in Dublin following the 1991 rebroadcast of the television series there.[48]

Even the *Dictionary of Literary Biography* entry for the women allocates most of its space to a discussion of the R.M. stories, stating, 'The comic stories of Somerville and Ross have too often been dismissed as unimportant; the stories, however, reveal the authors' understanding of and attitude toward Ireland. And even when considered simply as entertainment, the short fiction is superb.'[49] More recently, other critics have begun to make a case for serious study of the R.M. stories, which suggests, perhaps, that they are as much a true measure of the cousins' work as *The Real Charlotte*. Cahalan, for example, follows a different critical path from that of his predecessors, focusing his study of the women's work on the R.M. stories, which he says were 'funny stories with a serious point behind them.'[50] He also suggests that along with James Joyce the women 'wrote some of the very best comic fiction'[51] to come out of Ireland. His assertion that 'Only recently have critics begun to understand Somerville and Ross'[52] seems apt.

Hilary Robinson makes the strong claim that 'Sadly, Pinker encouraged them writing [more R.M. stories] in 1899 when they were eager to write a novel.'[53] Elsewhere, Robinson even claims that Pinker 'worried and harried them into creating *The Irish R.M.*,'[54] presumably again at the expense of other more serious and important work. In these comments, Robinson echoes the standard critical view, including the implicit assumption that women should not write humorous fiction, as that, like, hunting stories, was a genre reserved for men. But Robinson also adds a piece of information that many critics omit: Pinker's role in the cousins' decision to produce more R.M. stories at the expense of more *Real Charlottes*. Yes, Pinker did encourage the women to write more R. M. stories; this much is clear in his enthusiastic support of Hedley Peek's request. But he did so not only because there was a ready market for them both serially and in volume form, but also because he thought that this was the literary form most suited to their talents. In a letter he wrote to Edith in 1899, Pinker makes clear what he thinks the cousins' literary strengths are:

I am rather sorry to see what you say regarding the Lawrence and Bullen novel, and I am not quite sure what to do in the matter. From the business point of view, you see, the contract is definitely arranged with Lawrence and Bullen, and if you lifted the sporting element from the novel, they would complain that we had not kept faith with them. Of course, they might or might not like the serious novel, but, at any rate, it is not what we undertook to let them have. This difficulty might be overcome by our giving them the option of cancelling the contract. From the literary point of view I think it would be a mistake. I think your happiest work is in this semi-sporting vein, and, moreover, there is, so far as I know, no one else who can touch you. If you and Miss Martin can give us more work like the *Badminton* stories, then I should say, from all points of view, that is the work to do. You did not ask for all this advice, but I feel sure you will not mind my offering it. I confess that I am very enthusiastic about the *Badminton* stories. We have had nothing like them since Lever died, and I am sure that I shall communicate some, at any rate, of my enthusiasm to editors. I am, for instance, sending a copy of the magazine to Mr. Harper, and I hope it will lead to a request for some stories for *Harper's Magazine*. Of course, when all is said and done, you and Miss Martin have to do your work in your own way, but I wish you would think over what I say, and, in the meantime, I will not open the matter with Lawrence and Bullen.[55]

Pinker's advice is not solely based on the commercial potential of the R.M. stories. He strongly counsels the cousins to write what he believes they write best. He bases his opinion on the quality and originality of their work. He recognizes that the R.M. stories will sell and that they will also generate favourable critical reviews because they are, simply put, good literature. An indication that the cousins took Pinker's advice is the fact that they continued to write R.M. stories for the *Badminton Magazine* and others, eventually accumulating enough material for two more short story volumes. Pinker's advice to the women was sound, both in terms of the steady stream of money that the stories generated for them and in terms of the widespread praise that the stories received. Certainly, the fact that they continue to be widely read over one hundred years after they first appeared suggests that Pinker knew what he was talking about.

In the mid-1890s, the cousins were in danger of being marginalized as Malet had been because the reception of *The Real Charlotte* tended to emphasize some of the same kinds of flaws that critics found in Malet's work: disagreeable characters and a story that was too depressing for the average reader. Violet Powell notes that '*The Real Charlotte* was received by the family circle with the usual volley of abuse, and its first reviews were equally disapproving. Mrs Somerville spoke for her familiars when she wrote to her daughter, "All here loathe Charlotte."'[56] Hilary Robinson notes that Mrs Somerville 'protested against the realism, the nastiness, the vulgarity of the characters,' and her comments on the book to one of

Edith's aunts have been 'echoed by modern critics: "Francie deserved to break her neck for her vulgarity; she certainly wasn't nice enough in any way to evoke sympathy, and the girls *had* to kill her to get the whole set of them out of the awful muddle they had got into!'"[57] As we have seen, the novel's initial critical reception was later modified, to the extent that leading critics such as Boyle and Kiberd regard it as one of the most important Irish novels produced during this period. The point here is that the initial reception of the text likely had some impact on the cousins' decision to focus on their R.M. stories; they were in desperate financial straits and, much as they wished to write another 'serious' novel, they were also aware that they were unlikely to receive as much money as they needed for another novel like *The Real Charlotte*. Equally important was that fact that they could continue the same kind of social criticism as found in *The Real Charlotte* but, by presenting it in a more palatable form in the R.M. stories, they could build a solid readership for the stories and thus earn the necessary money.

With Pinker's help, the women took a form that had existed on the margins of the literary world – the hunting story – and pushed it closer to the centre. The resulting accumulation of economic and cultural capital spawned a series of imitators who wrote similar serio-comic hunting stories in the hopes of cashing in on the cousins' success.[58] It also paved the way for future writers who would choose the short story over the novel and for those who wished to employ comedy as their preferred mode of discourse. That the early twentieth century is an age in which both the short story and comedy flourish has been frequently noted. It is not an overstatement to say that Somerville and Ross's success helped make space for both forms of writing. In this way, their work helped to alter the literary world; Pinker's assistance was crucial because he found ready markets for their work and kept them writing R.M. stories in the face of their own doubts about the stories' literary quality. Far from making them 'sell out,' he actually had the vision to see that their work would resonate with the changing nature of the print culture field and thus would garner the women much-needed economic capital in the short run and cultural capital over the long run.

Women Writers, Male Agent

Edith and Martin cultivated in private and in public the personae of professional female authors who had achieved a high standing in the literary world by dint of their own hard work. Both also were strong adherents of women's rights, becoming active in the women's suffrage movement. Edith frequently made speeches about women's suffrage and both she and Martin contributed pieces on the topic to various newspapers and periodicals. Their commitment to women's suffrage extended even to making a special trip to London. In 1908, Edith wrote to Pinker, 'Miss Martin and I hope to be in London on the 18th for a few days. We want to see the great Suffrage Procession on the 21st.'[59] The cousins joined the Munster Women's Suffrage League in 1910, Edith becoming its president in 1913 and Martin a vice-president.[60] This public self-presentation was reinforced by Edith's memoirs, which, as we recall, presented the cousins as professional authors firmly in charge of their writing careers. Indeed, her depiction of Pinker – 'little X' who 'must learn that he can't always have it all his own way' – contributed to the image of women fully in command of their own careers. Not only is Pinker's role minimized, but he is firmly put in his place. Implicit here is also the fact that he is a male servant to the female writers, a nice reversal of the Victorian paradigm that saw women as muses and servants to male writers.

Their public presentation of Pinker as their male servant belies their relationship with him. Their dependence on Pinker for business advice has already been established. They also relied on him for editorial advice. Their letters to each other and to him are filled with requests for him to comment on the content of the stories they submit to him. The women make clear to him that they want candid criticism: 'I asked what he thought of them, and said that we didn't want compliments but criticisms.'[61] More important, in terms of the writing of the R.M. and other stories of Irish country life, is Pinker's support for their incursions into largely male territory. Though critics and readers alike received the stories warmly, there was some consternation at the idea that they could have been written by women, since, as James Cahalan says, they were 'invading the male provinces of satire and hunting.'[62] In *Irish Memories*, Edith captures one of the standard responses to the fact that the R.M. stories were written by women when she relates the reaction of a male reader: '"First I read it at full speed, because I couldn't stop, and then I read it *very* slowly, chewing every word; and then I read it a third time, dwelling on the bits I like best; and then, and *not* till then, thank Heaven! I was told it was written by two women!"'[63] Pinker, as well as the cousins, would have found this remark both amusing and sadly reflective of a view of women's abilities that they opposed.

Pinker's views about women governed his treatment of the women's writing career. While he did not make public his views on women's issues, including suffrage, Edith indirectly relays them in a letter she wrote to him in 1913. She acknowledged Pinker's pro-suffrage position: 'Knowing yr views as to the Suffrage, I feel sure you will be pleased to hear that a little article we presented to an Irish "Suffragist organ", (named the "*Irish Citizen*") has been largely quoted from by the *Irish Times*! And, apparently as endorsing our views.'[64] Furthermore, the tone of the letter, Edith's triumphant announcement of their success to someone she assumes will share in her elation, suggests that Pinker not only supported women's suffrage, but also supported the cousins's activities. The fact that they could count on Pinker's active interest in, and support of, their suffrage activities attests not only to his ability as an agent to direct his writers to the genre and subject matter best suited to their ability, but also to his personal convictions that women ought to be treated equally with men.

Pinker's unstinting support of Edith and Martin's incursion into the realm of sporting literature is in direct contrast to the more conservative treatment of Lucas Malet's work by Watt. Unlike Watt, Pinker was an active partner, indeed, one might say an instigator, in developing a readership for Somerville and Ross's hunting stories. Because he was more closely attuned to the emerging forces in the field – writers, publishers, and readers alike – he was better able to assess what new genres or subject matters might catch on. He was also less likely than Watt was to be constrained by the prevailing positions allotted to women writers. As a result, one could argue that he not only created space for these two women clients, but also created space for other women writers who wished to invade previously male preserves in the literary field.

Authors and Commercialism

In her public erasure of Pinker's assistance, Edith seemed to be continuing the practice of divorcing the writer and the text from the commercial concerns of literary production. Unlike some of their contemporaries, such as Arnold Bennett, Edith and Martin preferred to keep private the practical difficulties they faced in getting their work finished and published, and also their need to make money from their work. The lighthearted account of the genesis of the R.M. stories in the 'Étaples' essay – with its implication that they could afford to be women of leisure – is only one example of the disingenuous public portrait they cultivated.

Edith begins *Irish Memories* by stating, 'These vagrant memories do not pretend to regard themselves as biography, autobiography, as anything serious or valuable. Martin and I were not accustomed to take ourselves seriously,'[65] thereby further shaping the public perception of the two of them as ladies of a certain class who happened also to write stories. But the situation is more complex than the cousins simply choosing to keep to themselves the harsh realities of their lives as professional writers. Edith's pejorative description of Pinker as 'the modern equivalent for an Egyptian taskmaster' who 'must learn that he can't always have it all his own way' sets out the hierarchy between authors and agents that Edith and many of her contemporaries were keen to perpetuate. Writers determine what to write and when to write, not 'little men' who are agents (or editors, publishers, or critics, for that matter). The split between the creator of art and the seller of a commodity is a convenient fiction which Edith supported strongly, both in the way that she and Martin presented themselves to the world and in their public statements about their agent and his handling of their business affairs. While this prevailing attitude and its specific manifestation in modernism will be dealt with more fully in chapter 7, it is important to explore it briefly here because it does have a direct impact on how the relationship between Pinker and the cousins was presented to the world.

Edith and Martin enjoyed the literary life, meeting other authors, listening to their work being read, reading reviews of their work, reading and replying to letters from fans, receiving honours, and so on. For instance, they were thrilled when they were informed that the King and Queen had read and enjoyed the R.M. stories.[66] In fact, a delighted Edith wrote to Pinker: 'I heard yesterday, through one of the Royal Equerries, that the King convalesced on the book [*Some Experiences of an R.M.*] after his last illness and that it was of more use to him than Sir Frederick Jeeves![his doctor].'[67] On another occasion, she wrote excitedly to Pinker about two American fans of her work: 'I heard from Mr. Roosevelt's daughter, with a postscript from "Teddy" himself!'[68] They also relished being considered important writers whose work was not only commercially but, more importantly, critically accepted. Martin's reception by Andrew Lang in 1894 had given them a taste of what it was like to be highly regarded by their peers and they both saw the benefit of being seen to be in the company of prominent literary men and women. Martin's account of 1905 reading of two R.M. stories by Frank Fay at the New Century Club in London provides us with a glimpse of the public personae they cultivated. She says:

I was there before 4 and met a luncheon to the Imperial Colonial Press vis-
itors just emerging. I was introduced by Mrs Rentoul Esler to one or two
Australians – all doosed civil. Then upstairs I met Miss Woolf – a kindly nice
little thing – and two or three more of the authors, among them Beatrice
Harriden; Dr. Margaret Todd was to have been the boss of the show, but
her sister was ill so Miss Mytton took it on – ... I had to sit in the front
corner of the front row with the Board people. I was asked if I would say
anything and firmly replied that I should rather not – having discovered
that there were appointed people to say all that was needed. Miss Mytton
introduced Fay, in a very excellent little speech, full of praise for our work,
and of Fay – with sympathetic reference to your accident and your absence.
Fay then did the Patrick's Day Hunt, leaving out a short bit in the middle.
He was *excellent* – ... After Fay finished another of the authors got up and
proposed a vote of thanks to him – an extraordinary little Irishman who
writes the critiques for the *Lady's Pictorial* also murmured a few words – and
there was an end – and most people went off at once – ... [69]

Martin clearly enjoyed the attention of fellow authors, the press, and the
public, while at the same time she offered the world the picture of the
shy, retiring authoress who chooses to have others present her work and
accomplishments to the public. In many respects, this is the portrait that
both women wished to have the world accept as genuine and which they
themselves believed to be an accurate depiction of their authorial selves.

But their private papers reveal just how thoroughly involved with the
commercial side of their literary endeavours they were. Both saw themselves as professional authors, a belief underscored by Martin's response
to a request that she provide a piece *gratis* for a memorial book for her
brother Robert. Martin wrote to Edith about this request:

> The gist of it all is the book is to be crown octavo – and as well as I could
> make out, my part is to be about 15000 words! He said 'about twelve col-
> umns of *The Times* – but you write all you like, and we can select what is
> wanted' – I at once said that I was too busy to write stuff that might not be
> wanted, and he seemed quite surprised – I dont [*sic*] think he at all realises
> the position, or that I am a professional writer.[70]

Her sense of their standing is reinforced by Pinker, who treats them
as thorough professionals who should always charge the going rate
for their work. For example, he agrees with Longmans' stance that if
Miss Jones of the *Times* book club republishes some of the R.M.

stories, she ought to pay for them. Pinker says, 'I think Longmans are right in exacting payment for these extracts. It is a very common way of trying to make a book without expense, and as these applications from their very nature are complimentary, authors' hearts are softened; but I do not really see why these permissions should be given without charge.'[71] Clearly, the women were intimately aware of the commercial aspects of writing and they were determined to be treated as professional writers who were to be paid fair market value for their work.

How do we reconcile the contradictory stances adopted by the women publicly and privately? On the one hand, we could simply agree that the conception of the author as a leisured amateur still held sway, and that Edith and Martin were in good company in their public presentation of themselves. On the other hand, their view of themselves as professional writers is consistent with the views about authorship that Walter Besant was constantly advocating in the *Author*, and it could be said that they are very much of their time in their private defence of their commercial worth. Closer to the truth is a recognition that by the turn of the twentieth century writers embraced a fundamental paradox of authorship: the joining together of the amateur and the professional views of what constituted an author into a thoroughly modern, two-faced stance: the public amateur and the private professional.[72]

Because Pinker occupied a mediating position, he was able to cater to both aspects of his author clients' needs, thereby allowing them not to have to embrace one aspect at the expense of the other. He treated his clients as professional writers by involving them in all commercial aspects of their literary production. At the same time, he accepted that they were artists who needed nurturing and support during the process of creating their works. Further, he did not threaten their public profile by seeking to become a celebrity himself. Pinker was content to stay in the background, to watch his writers gain acclaim, and to earn a good living from his activities. He accepted the paradox of authorship and made it work for his clients and for himself. Indeed, he exploited it and in doing so, he changed the print culture field in ways that are still being felt.

The End of a Successful Partnership

Martin died in 1915, but Edith continued to write under both of their names. She employed Pinker until his death in 1922. However, by the late 1910s she was writing to Pinker to ask him to discontinue his services for her because she felt she could no longer afford to pay him the 10 per cent commission and still make enough for all her expenses. Despite the ending of their business association, it is clear that their partnership with Pinker was an integral part of Somerville and Ross's success as authors. Without Pinker's close attention to the business side of their affairs and his constant encouragement of their writing, it is likely that Somerville and Ross would not have produced the R.M. stories that consolidated their reputation among the twentieth-century's finest Irish writers. Equally possible, without Pinker's astute management of their career, both might have been forced to give up their estates and their way of life. As it was, even with Pinker negotiating the best prices for their work and protecting their copyrights, they still endured lifelong financial difficulties. Without Pinker, one can only imagine what might have happened to them.

7 Building a Career:
Joseph Conrad and Pinker

The previous two chapters have argued that J.B. Pinker's adaptation of A.P. Watt's agenting template affected not only how literary agents conducted business but also the literature that was produced during the early twentieth century. In both chapters, a central argument was that Pinker's willingness to vary his standard business practices contributed to the eventual success (economic and/or critical) of these writers. This chapter will develop the argument further by examining Pinker's relationship with Joseph Conrad. The chapter initially travels some familiar territory as it sketches out the associations between the two men. It examines their business relationship, assessing it as an example of the agenting template that Pinker had established as an alternative to Watt's; then it looks at their friendship, discussing it in terms of its importance for Conrad's writing career. Once this ground is covered, the discussion pursues a line of recent critical work on the materiality of modernism that, in the words of Joyce Wexler, suggests that modernist writers were aware of the fact that 'to become published authors in the first place, they had to reconcile competing models of authorship.'[1] In particular, it will look at the ways in which Pinker's patronage of Conrad enabled the writer to enact what I referred to in the previous chapter as the fundamental paradox of authorship in the early twentieth century, although in Conrad's case the paradox takes on a slightly different form: the public face that of the artist who disdains popular success and the private face that of the professional author who demands remuneration on par with what popular writers were receiving. Pinker's activities on behalf of Conrad not only illustrate how he helped Conrad to confront the 'competing models of authorship' present in the early decades of the twentieth century, but also constitute a paradigm employed by other modernist writers. The chapter subsequently examines how Pinker's innovations, particularly his patronage of Conrad, altered the dynamics of both the profession of agenting and the business of publishing.[2]

But before launching into the chapter proper, it is important to say that the significant role played by J.B. Pinker in Joseph Conrad's career has been openly acknowledged.[3] Conrad's many biographers have discussed both the business arrangements and the close personal ties forged by the two men in their twenty-year friendship. For instance, Frederick Karl comments that 'Pinker nurtured [Conrad] in his apprentice years, [and] they had become inseparable friends, true survivors of the publishing wars.'[4] Jeffrey Meyers puts the case for Pinker's importance in Conrad's life as strongly, remarking that Conrad

> was as grateful for Pinker's faith as for his cash, recognized that their relationship was based on friendship, not business, and said 'He has stepped gallantly into the breach left open by the collapse of my bank; and not only gallantly, but successfully as well. He has treated not only my moods but even my fancies with the greatest consideration.' Conrad later told his young Polish friend Joseph Retinger that if it had not been for Pinker he would have starved.[5]

Conrad also acknowledged his agent's importance to his life and career when he wrote to Eric Pinker following his father's sudden death in 1922:

> Twenty years' friendship and for most of that time in the constant interchange of the most intimate thoughts and feelings created a bond as strong as the nearest relationship. But you know enough of our grief here and our sense of inseparable loss. There are no words of comfort for such a blow. I can only assure you of my affectionate friendship.[6]

This strong bond between agent and client not only permitted Joseph Conrad to write the modernist masterworks he did, but also placed Pinker near the centre of the modernist movement in literature. Yet while Meyers, Karl, and other biographers and critics have made sure that Pinker's role as Conrad's man of business has not been overlooked, it will become clear as the chapter unfolds that they have failed to understand the full impact of Pinker's activities for Conrad.

Business Partners and Friends

Conrad: A Writer, Not a Man of Business

Joseph Conrad was notorious for his inability to manage his own money; for most of his life he relied on financial help from family and friends to meet even the most basic of daily needs. One of Conrad's most important early literary friends was Edward Garnett, who was a reader for the firm of T. Fisher Unwin when Conrad first encountered him in 1894. Garnett was to assume for Conrad the position of literary mentor and financial advisor, and, in part, it is through Garnett's influence that Conrad began to establish his literary career.[7] While Garnett appears to have borne Conrad's constant neediness with grace and tact, he was also aware of the impossibility of providing him with the necessary support on an ongoing basis. Frederick Karl suggests that as early as 1896, Garnett was recommending that Conrad seek out the services of a literary agent to manage his business affairs.[8] Garnett attempted to steer Conrad towards A.P. Watt, which is something Conrad acknowledged in an 1896 letter to Garnet: 'As to Watt I think I ought to know him.'[9] Nothing came of this initial suggestion, and for another four years, Conrad continued to rely on Garnett and other friends for their literary, as well as business and financial, advice and support.

In August of 1899, Conrad received his first overture from J.B. Pinker and rebuffed it with typical self-deprecation. He replied to Pinker on 23 August that

> My method of writing is so unbusiness-like that I don't think you could have any use for such an unsatisfactory person. I generally sell a work before it is begun, get paid when it is half done and don't do the other half till the spirit moves me. I must add that I have no control whatever over the spirit – neither has the man who has paid the money.
>
> The above may appear fanciful to you but it is the sober truth. I live in hopes of reformation and whenever that takes place you and you alone shall have the working of the New Conrad. Meantime I must be content to pander to my absurd weaknesses, and hobble along the line of the least resistance.[10]

A year later, on 19 September 1900, Conrad agreed to Pinker's proposition that he represent him. His letter to Pinker sets the initial terms of their business dealings:

Your letter found here my collaborator Mr Ford M. Heuffer [Ford Madox Ford] and this circumstance allows me to answer your proposal with the suggestion that you should take in hand a joint work of ours which is nearing completion. Whether this is what Constables want I don't know but our meaning is that you should handle that stuff with a free hand: that is *serialise it* and arrange for book form ...

As to my own singlehanded work I can't say anything nor hold out any hopes. I wish that in Am[erica]: you would give McClure the first chance. The title of the book is *Seraphina*; action in West Indies, Havana and England. It concerns itself with the last of the pirates in those parts. The hero is English.

Would you let me know how it strikes you. Yours faithfully

Jph Conrad

PS The serialising is *the important* part.[11]

On this tentative note, their partnership began.

When Conrad signed on with Pinker, he had already published three novels (*Almayer's Folly, An Outcast of the Islands*, and *The Nigger of the Narcissus*) and *Lord Jim* was in the process of becoming a novel.[12] He had also published four short stories that were collected together in *Tales of Unrest*.[13] Several articles, including one on Alphonse Daudet, had appeared in various magazines.[14] He was at work with Ford Madox Ford on *The Inheritors*, which he gave Pinker to place.[15] Despite this activity, and the generally positive reviews his work generated, Conrad's finances were in a terrible state. He was constantly short of money and had even arranged in December of 1900 to have his publisher, William Blackwood III, stand as a surety for a £200 loan taken out against his life insurance policy.[16] It would thus be an understatement to say that Conrad failed to manage his literary property effectively.

In fact, as Meyers notes, 'Conrad's first eleven books were brought out by six different publishers ... His first eight American editions were published by seven different firms.' Meyers continues, 'Conrad was not good at dealing with publishers, felt wounded when they rejected his terms and was crushed when told that his books had lost money.'[17] A case in point is Conrad's reaction to T. Fisher Unwin's handling of *Tales of Unrest*. Conrad wrote to John Galsworthy in January of 1898 that Unwin 'is trying to play me a dirty trick. He got possession of the whole manuscript [*Tales of Unrest*] under pretence of placing the *Return* (serially) and now suddenly writes that he is tired of trying for it – so concludes to publish the book at once!' Conrad claims, 'Neither in previous letters nor in conversation did he ever give the slightest hint of such an intention. In fact the scoundrel pretended a desire to delay pub^{on} till autumn.' Despite his evident anger over Unwin's 'dirty trick,' Conrad says he 'wrote temperately that I object absolutely' to the publication of the volume of short stories.[18] However, he appears to have conveniently forgotten that in October of 1896 he had agreed to supply the complete manuscript for the collection by March 1897. In fact, he discussed the terms of Unwin's offer with Edward Garnett in letter dated 16 October 1896 in which he says that Unwin 'wants the work [*Tales of Unrest*] delivered on *March 97* at the latest. He engages himself to publish within *six* months of delivery.' Conrad's comment on that part of the arrangement – 'That also is all right'[19] – leaves little room for him to later argue that Unwin had no right to publish the book once he got hold of the manuscript in early 1898. Clearly, Conrad was not dissembling when he informed Pinker about his attitude towards the business aspects of his chosen profession. He really did 'sell a work before it [was] begun, [got] paid when it [was] half done and [didn't] do the other half till the spirit move[d] [him].' Without a doubt, in the managing of Conrad's literary property, Pinker had a substantial challenge on his hands.

His first task was to place a new story called 'Typhoon' that Conrad was composing in the autumn of 1900. The two men's interactions around this story set the tone for their business partnership for the next twenty years, so they are worth studying in some detail.

Conrad wrote to Pinker on 8 October 1900:

> This word is to inform You [*sic*] that you shall have *two* stories from me to place serially, of which one shall probably be ready by the 14 inst. It is not the story I spoke you [*sic*] about; it is nothing so horrible and deals with a lot of Chinamen coolies and a few seaman on board a steamer in a gale of wind in the China Seas. Its title is *Typhoon* and length as far as I can see 12000 words. Why however I mention it now is because it struck me casually that it is quite the thing that finds room in Xmas numbers. I may be too late with the stuff by this time, for that purpose, but here's the suggestion.
>
> The other story shorter and much more horrible shall be finished early in Nov^{er}. I fancy I can do it in about 5000 words. I'll forward it to you in due course.
>
> And now I go back to my MS.[20]

There are several things to comment on here. First, Conrad had already mentioned this story to David Meldrum, Blackwood's editor and another in the line of Conrad's literary advisors, in a letter written on 14 February 1899. The letter is in response to Blackwood's advance of £100 for their agreement to publish in volume form three tales by Conrad: 'Youth,' 'Heart of Darkness,' and 'Lord Jim.'[21] In his letter to Meldrum Conrad says, 'I have two more stories in my head which would run the copy to 120000 words, but I can't possibly be ready with them before say – July.' In the postscript to the letter, Conrad elaborates on three, not two, stories:

> In that case the stories: 'First Command'; the one about a Captains [sic] wife; 'A Seaman' sketch; and 'Equitable Division' (a story of a typhoon) would perhaps find hospitality in the Maga [Blackwood's Magazine] and go to make another Vol, later on.
>
> Of this idea I've said nothing in my letter to Mr B'wood, but put it before you, should M. B'wood stick to the may [sic] publication and Jim is ready, which last upon my conscience I dare not promise.[22]

In effect, Conrad is offering 'Typhoon' to Meldrum for publication in *Blackwood's Magazine* a full twenty-one months before he tells Pinker that 'it struck [him] casually that it is quite the thing that finds room in Xmas numbers.' This disingenuousness was typical of Conrad in his relations with Pinker. Conrad frequently did not know in advance that his stories would grow beyond the size he projected for them, but he was usually aware of what material he had promised to whom. His profound dislike, and even embarrassment, over his financial dependence on Pinker, coupled with his need to assure his agent that he was working on what he said he was (even when that was not the case), meant that he resorted to manipulations in order to keep the money coming in. This distortion of the truth becomes more marked in the middle years of their relationship – about 1908–15 – though it is found throughout the twenty years they worked together.

The next step in this chronology indicates that Conrad had *already signed* an agreement with Blackwood for the publication of this story in July of 1899 – a full fifteen months prior to his letter to Pinker. We know this from the letter he wrote to Meldrum on 31 July 1899, saying, 'I make note of the new agreement entered into with Mr B'wood. £5 *per 1000 words serial rights (in England) and 20% book. No advance.*'[23] The agreement was for another volume of short stories to be published after the one intended to include 'Lord Jim' and 'Heart of Darkness.'[24] Given the previous letter, it is reasonable to assume that Blackwood would expect that a story about a typhoon would be one of the three stories. On 3 January 1900, Conrad again wrote to Meldrum:

> When the end is delivered [the volume of short stories to include 'Lord Jim' and 'Heart of Darkness'] I hope Mr Blackwood will be kind enough to send me at least £80 (100 if possible). I have innumerable bills flapping about my ears! Thereupon I shall proceed to write 20000 words (either *A seaman* or *First Command* or a *Skittish Cargo* ['Typhoon'] or any two of them to make up the number) for publication serially when he thinks fit and convenient ... [25]

Evidently, Conrad still intended Blackwood to have this story, both for serialization and to fill out the volume of three stories to which he had already agreed.

The next stage of negotiations occurred on 19 May 1900. Conrad wrote Meldrum about several issues, among them Blackwood's proposal that 'Lord Jim' stand alone as a novel and not form part of the volume of three short stories. Because of its importance in our chronology about 'Typhoon' and because it vividly reveals Conrad's attitude towards the business of writing, it is worth quoting from this letter at some length:

> I think that the conditions of production should be altered a little. I wouldn't think about it, much less say anything, if it was not a matter of self-preservation almost. I must be enabled to draw breath or I will choke. I've been gasping for months now and doing my best all the time too. The question is what Mr Blackwood will do for me? What I suggest would be this: –
>
> *Lord Jim* should be considered separately of course. It will be (it seems incredible) of, apparently, 100000 words or very little short of that. In fact it shall take the place really of that *second book* to follow 3 tales which we have talked over and which was to be paid at the rate of £5 p. 1000 (serial) with a shilling royalty but *no* advance on book form. However the circumstances are not the same if only for the reason it is going to appear first – and besides *Lord Jim* was not meant when we settled the terms. On the other hand it is a long story – a novel – and this, I am told, is an advantage from the publisher's point of view. What I would propose then would be that Mr Blackwood should pay me at the rate of £5 p. 1000 but that the

whole sum £200 should be put as on account of a shilling royalty. This would make the serial payment (assuming 100,000 words) to be at the rate of £3 p. 1000 – 10/- higher than the serial rate of the short stories volume that was to be. I engage myself to furnish between 30 and 40 thousand words to complete the vol: of stories at the old rate of £2.10 per thousand if Mr. Blackwood should wish to use these serially. But as Maga has been pretty full of Conrad of late I would try to serialise them elsewhere reserving them for Mr Blackwood's vol without further payment – naturally – since *that* volume has already been paid for.

Just to make the urgency clear, Conrad included a postscript: 'PS I would be rather anxious to know the result of this.' Leaving aside the fact that he is renegotiating the terms of his agreement long after receiving large advance payments, Conrad is also renegotiating the terms for the second volume of short stories that was to include 'Typhoon.' Now *Lord Jim*, in novel form, is to take the place of that volume and Conrad wishes to be free to sell the stories, *already contracted*, to other magazines for serialization, though he reserves at least one of them to take the place of *Lord Jim* in the first volume of stories.

As if that is not brazen enough, Conrad then attempts to close the deal by telling Meldrum that another publisher wants his work and is willing to pay him well for it, though he prefers to remain with Blackwood. His letter continues, making this point clearly:

I ask for these terms with the less hesitation because I know that Mr X ... (pardon this discretion) would give me £200 on acc^t of royalties for a long book. Hang Mr X. The fact is I don't hesitate because if I hesitate I am lost – like many a better man; and if I AM worth anything I had rather be helped over the stile by Mr Blackwood than by any publisher in the three kingdoms. The long and short of it is I want £300 to pay my debts (which are not great but very awful) and to go abroad for a couple of months. I fear I must go, and that soon, or I shall become a complete idiot. My nerves are like fiddle strings. I think of going to Bruges directly I deliver the last of Jim. Hueffer is going too and we shall bring two-thirds of a novel from there or the devil's in it! Should the length of *Lord Jim* not cover my demands Mr Blackwood would always have that collaboration novel to fall back upon. (He said he would like to see it). But the crux is that I must have (from somewhere) the 300 in question. For *L.J.* I had already £165 I think – maybe more; (my wife is out for the day and has locked her drawer so I am not certain). I had £65 this year and fancy a 100 (or 130?) last year.

> Of course I am aware that Mr Blackwood may with perfect fairness
> return to the original plan. In that case I say – very well. Let the whole
> thing appear in Septb[er] or never appear. I am so utterly weary of myself
> (not of my work) that I verily believe that I don't care. I ought to have been
> writing MS instead of this. There's a tidy pile ready and it seems good stuff
> too. [26]

In due course, Conrad did arrange new terms with Blackwood for both
the novel and the first volume of short stories. *Lord Jim* was published by
Blackwood in 1900; it took the place of the second volume of short stories for which Conrad had already contracted. 'The End of the Tether'
took the place of *Lord Jim* in the collection that included 'Heart of Darkness' and 'Youth.' It was published in 1902 and cleared Conrad's debt
for the first volume of stories for which he had contracted with Blackwood in 1898.[27] With that, Conrad met his obligation to Blackwood for
the two books he had contracted with them. But what of 'Typhoon'?

Conrad continued to work on the story over the summer of 1900,
writing to Pinker in November 1900: 'I send you 33 pp of my
Typhoon, all but two thirds of the whole. (7000 words or 7500).'[28] He
delivered the manuscript to Pinker on 11 January, 1901. He wrote
Pinker on 14 January:

> On reckoning up with the situation I see that I must take advantage of your
> proposal.
>   Would you, therefore, advance me as much as the prospect of placing
> the story would justify – leaving you on the safe side.[29]

Pinker advanced him £100 the day following his letter despite the fact
that the story had not yet been sold. Pinker attempted unsuccessfully to
place it in *Blackwood's Magazine*, eventually he arranged for it to appear
in *Pall Mall Magazine*. Conrad would not have been happy to see this
story published not in his beloved *Maga* but in the lower-status *Pall Mall*;
nonetheless, he would have been please to have it placed with a publisher, since he had likely already spent the advance from Pinker.[30] However, it was not published until the January–March 1902 issue, a full year
after Pinker had advanced Conrad payment for the story. It finally
appeared in volume form, along with three other stories, in *Typhoon and
Other Stories*, published by Heinemann, not Blackwood, in 1903, thereby
clearing yet another outstanding arrangement Conrad had made prior
to enlisting Pinker's services.

In the end, then, the story that he had envisioned, and sold, to Blackwood in February of 1899 was not even finished until January of 1901. And when it did appear in print, it was in a magazine owned by someone other than Blackwood. Finally, it never did form part of the second volume of short stories for which Conrad had signed a contract with Blackwood in July of 1899. No such volume was ever published. Instead, 'Typhoon' appeared in volume form under the Heinemann banner in 1903. This convoluted and highly irregular publishing history of one short story is no aberration in Conrad's career. In fact, it is in many ways representative of the kind of business arrangements that he had made prior to employing Pinker. Pinker's challenge was to find ways of honouring existing agreements while at the same time putting Conrad's work on a much more businesslike footing. His attempts to do so met with much resistance from Conrad, but, as we will see, Pinker's actions over the next two decades did, eventually, place Conrad in a sound financial position.

Reforming Conrad's Business Practices

Pinker's approach to handling Conrad's literary business followed the by now familiar path: consolidating management of all of Conrad's literary property in Pinker's hands; finding markets for new works; and working with Conrad to raise his public profile. In each of these areas, Pinker faced distinct challenges, and in meeting them, he was forced to alter his own agenting practices to accommodate his frequently difficult client. As is evident from the brief history of the convoluted journey that 'Typhoon' took to press, Pinker faced a major challenge in his primary task of consolidating the management of Conrad's literary property. Conrad had several outstanding arrangements with publishers at the time he engaged Pinker. He was well aware of this stumbling block to Pinker's usual methods, as he acknowledged in this letter to him in January of 1901:

> I feel I am not fair to you with all my reservations of book-rights to certain publishers and so on. However, later on, when I've cleared up my position vis-à-vis Heinemann – principally – we may be able to put our connection on a sounder basis, as far as *you* are concerned.[31]

Conrad had mortgaged his future work in order to pay his current bills, and though he had every intention of honouring his commitments, his mode of composition meant that he was ill suited to do so. Conrad wrote to his friend Ted Sanderson on 15 June 1899, for example, about the mess he had got himself into over the premature sale of *Rescue*. His comments vividly illustrate his awareness of his difficult situation:

> I am in a state of deadly, indecent funk. I've obtained a ton of cash from a Yank under, what strikes me, are false pretences. The Child of the Screaming Eagle [S.S. McClure] is as innocent as a dove. He *thinks* the book he bought will be finished in July while I *know* that it is a physical and intellectual impossibility to even approach the end by that date. He sends on regular cheques which is – according to his lights – right, but I pocket the money serenely which – according to my lights – looks uncommonly like a swindle on my part ...
>
> But as I don't wish to see Your door closed against me I hasten to inform You, that, partly from fear and partly from remorse, I have invited the Yank to lunch here to-morrow. In that way I return some part of my ill-gotten gains and may have an opportunity to break the fatal news gently to him.[32]

Compounding his challenges, Pinker had to deal with the fact that Conrad had published his works with a variety of firms, had sold some copyrights outright and leased others, and in almost all cases had taken payments for works in advance of finishing them and was thus in debt to many of the firms who had published his works.[33] And to make matters even more difficult, early in their relationship, Conrad still acted on his own with publishers, making arrangements without informing Pinker of them until after the fact. One such occasion concerned the novel *Rescue* that Conrad had sold to both Heinemann and McClure. On 28 January 1902, Conrad wrote to Pinker:

> On consideration of a thought which occurred to me after I left you I shall approach B'wood myself ... I have seen the books at H.[einemann] and McClure coming in I have arranged the affair of serial rights of Rescue.
>
> I have got them back in America as well as in England. He has given me these back on the only condition that from the proceeds I should repay the sum he advanced on *acct*. That is *£180*. The book-rights in America he keeps of course – and the book right[s] in this country remain with Heinemann who has also advanced me £180 on 17½% royalty. After that we shall be free! And You shall run the show.[34]

Pinker set about sorting out this mess with characteristic energy. He first had to deal with the fact that his client was accustomed to making his own arrangements with publishers. For instance, Conrad's attempt to clear up his contractual situation with Blackwood apparently provoked an objection from Pinker, which in turn prompted this mollifying response from Conrad: 'I feel I owe You an apology for the way I changed my mind; I trust You never supposed that it had anything to do with *you* personally. It would have been too absurd.'[35] Not surprisingly, given Conrad's history of making deals that permitted him to continue to write as he wished, it was Conrad, not Pinker, who initiated the plan that attempted to resolve this situation. On 25 February 1902 he wrote to Pinker setting out his scheme in some detail:

> Rather more than a year ago I've insured my life with the Standard life in two policies one *A* for £600 and the other *B* for £500. Together £1100 ... I have managed to pay the premiums which amount for the policy *B* to £9.13 *half yearly*. On that *B* policy however I borrowed from the Ins^{ce} Comp^y itself the sum of £250 at 5% p.a. with the proviso that the capital is to be repaid in installments of £25 every half year. My banker *Watson* of 7 Waterloo Place was *one* of the sureties on that agreement. And as the Comp^y required *two* sureties M^r Wm. Blackwood is now the other ... My difficulty, the incubus, is the obligation of paying off the borrowed capital – that half yearly £25. This is always the difficulty; and I have a positive dread of the Insur: Comp: coming down on my sureties ... I owe them now altogether £225 the half year's interest and the premium in all £*240.5.6* of which the *40.5.6* must be paid off this time ...
>
> I could not and would not ask you to help me with this payment. It would be of no use, because next June the same difficulty would occur. But if you could see your way to do something in appearance much more considerable and in reality much more business-like, I would propose this:
>
> That you should *pay off* the Insurance C^o completely (£240.5.6 as near as I can reckon to a shilling or two) and I would *assign to you* my policy *B* (for £500) which your action would totally liberate. My work passing through your hands ... would always cover the yearly premium to the Comp^y of roughly £19 per year and the interest to you at say 6% on £240.5.6 – again roughly about £15 per year – or a few shillings less. Together £36 or so per year. Of course I hope to write more than that – but when making me advances on short stories or on a long novel you would keep in mind that charge. Your capital would be secured by the policy and as my position improved we would reduce my indebtedness to you, the policy remaining assigned to you *absolutely* till the last pound has been paid off.[36]

In a letter written three days later, apparently in reply to Pinker's response to this proposal, Conrad goes even further by entrusting past as well as future works to his new agent. He writes:

> I wrote you *all* that I had thought on the matter and this accounts for the length of the letter. Here I only repeat that if there is a way of giving you a legal lien on the proceeds of my *future* work (including 'Romance' but *excepting 'Typhoon' and B'wood volumes*) and also in three of my past publications, namely: *Outcast of the Islands, Tales of Unrest, Nigger of the Narcissus* – I am perfectly ready and willing to do what's necessary.[37]

This astonishing offer was accepted by Pinker, who paid off the capital and signed Conrad to his standard agency contract.

While Conrad still felt the need to encourage overtures from publishers or editors interested in his material, for the most part he honoured his exclusive arrangement with Pinker, steering requests for material to him. For example, this is his November 1902 reply to an inquiry from the Northern Newspaper Syndicate about supplying them with an article:

> Mr. James B. Pinker Effingham House Arundel S[t] W.C. is my literary agent, to whom I've forwarded your communication of the 25th inst. I beg him at the same time to keep your request in view. No doubt something of the sort you desire will be finished in good time next year, since this is the form I like best (30–40000 words) and have a subject or two in reserve in that shape. Then with the work before you, you could judge of the suitableness for your public. But I could not bind myself for delivery at any specified time or discuss in any way the nature of my story.[38]

Though the past business arrangements were still terribly tangled and caused considerable trouble for Pinker when arranging for republication of early work (especially for the later *Collected Edition*), from late 1902 onwards Pinker was able to take control of Conrad's literary property. He ensured that all of Conrad's contracts were dealt with by his office and that copyrights were retained and exploited fully on Conrad's behalf. However, ensuring that copyrights were retained was occasionally a challenge, as Conrad's constant need for money sometimes led him to come up with desperate schemes. In one case, Conrad tried to sell the copyrights of *Lord Jim* and two as yet unwritten stories first to McClure and then to Blackwood in return for an immediate infusion of cash. That his agreement with Pinker precluded this kind of sale did not seem to register with Conrad, who pursued this idea for several months. Pinker apparently opposed the plan, but Conrad persevered on this course until Blackwood eventually declined the deal.[39]

Yet there was a complication to business as usual that Pinker did not foresee. As Frederick Karl says, 'the two began to head into another kind of "collaboration," in which Pinker advanced money for which copy was not yet ready, assumed the role of Conrad's banker and financier, and took on the elder counsel's role in the relationship to the older man.'[40] As we saw above, he had already taken an active role in Conrad's financial affairs, though any risks he took were at least in part offset because of the arrangement to which they had agreed. And as we have seen, Pinker was prepared to risk his own money in the backing of writers who he believed would eventually find an audience and thus enable him to recoup his initial investment, such as Arnold Bennett, to whom he provided an allowance early in their relationship. However, Conrad did not have the track record that Bennett had, nor was he as prolific a writer or as reliable in meeting his publishers' deadlines, so Pinker's cash advances to Conrad carried a higher risk. But this was the practice that Conrad had developed with his previous literary mentors – Garnett and Meldrum – and publishers – Unwin, Heinemann, and Blackwood. In 1895, in fact, he had even nicknamed Unwin EPL, Enlightened Patron of Letters,[41] thus unintentionally declaring the role that he required all his literary mentors to assume – that of his patron. He would expect no less from his agent.

Pinker responded to Conrad's implicit designation of him as his literary patron by adjusting his customary business practices in order to supply Conrad with financial support. In the absence of Pinker's letters to Conrad, one has to read between the lines of Conrad's letters to Pinker to find the agent's reaction to this new kind of business arrangement. For example, on 8 January 1902 Conrad wrote angrily to Pinker:

> I fail to apprehend what inspired the extraordinary contents of your letter which I received this morning. All you had to do was to say yes or no. Mine was written fully not to get the easier at your pocket but from another motive – not worth explaining now. But it was never intended to give you an opening for a lecture. It will take more than the delay in delivering S[eraphina] to you to make *me* a failure; neither do I believe it will put you into the B[ankrupt]cy Court.[42]

Reading between the lines, one infers that Conrad wrote to Pinker asking for money and in his response Pinker proffered unwelcome advice to Conrad. Given Conrad's comment in the last sentence, the advice was likely to do with timely delivery of material and the folly of spending advances for work that had not yet been sent to the publisher. Unfortunately, we do not have Pinker's response to this tirade, but we know from Conrad's letter of 12 January that Pinker sent Conrad money as a result of this blast. I will return later in the chapter to a further discussion of Pinker's patronage of Conrad, but for now it is enough to say that the initial stage of their relationship settled into a familiar pattern for Conrad. He would demand money from his new 'enlightened literary patron' and Pinker would acquiesce, though not always as promptly or as compliantly as Conrad expected.

Even Pinker's patience and forbearance were stretched to the breaking point by Conrad's constant requests for money and his failure to submit material on any sort of schedule. Willing as he was to provide Conrad with advances so that he could write the kind of stories Pinker knew he was capable of writing, in order to manage his client's career properly he needed to have a reliable stream of material. Conrad had to finish projects in a timely manner and in the format agreed to, or else Pinker's arrangements on his behalf were jeopardized. But as is evident, Conrad was rarely accurate in predicting the format, length, or completion date of his many works. One theme that runs through his letters – to friends, publishers, and Pinker – is that of Conrad announcing the start of a new 'story' which he assures his correspondent will be of somewhere around five to ten thousand words. Frequently, the story grows and its promised completion date extends months, and sometimes years, beyond the time frame Conrad initially projects. Pinker's requests to Conrad to supply copy in a timely manner prompted angry outbursts from Conrad. He frequently chastised Pinker for failing to support his art and for caring solely for its commercial aspects. As he says later in the same letter quoted from above, 'Pray do not write to me as if I were a fool blundering in the dark. There are other virtues than punctuality. Have you the slightest idea of what I am trying for? Of what is my guiding principle which I follow in anxiety, and poverty, and daily and unremitting toil of my very heart.'[43] Needless to say, this was an issue that went beyond Pinker's representation of one writer. If Pinker could not supply material to publishers when he had promised it, his own standing in the print culture field was at risk.

Finally, in the autumn of 1907, Conrad and Pinker reached an informal arrangement; Pinker would supply Conrad with an annual allowance in return for submission of a set amount of written material from Conrad. Conrad's letter of 13 August 1907 to Pinker clarifies their new agreement: 'In the terms of your letter of 6th Aug '07 (in which the strict limit of £600 a year is established) I reckon that this year begins on the *10th* of this month the day of our arrival here. In other words that I may reckon on £600 between this and the 10th Augst 1908 – I on my side writing in that time 80 000 words at least; this 80 000 words being the words of a *novel* not short stories.'[44] In practice, Pinker would supply Conrad with a weekly allowance of £6 and additional money as requested up to the maximum of £600 a year, thereby ensuring a regular stream of money that would enable Conrad to deal with his living expenses. Despite his good intentions to abide by this agreement, Conrad was already seeking to reopen its terms as early as January 1908. By July of 1908, the situation had deteriorated even further. At this stage, Conrad was some £1500 in debt to Pinker, who seemed to be at the end of his patience. In mid-July, Conrad wrote a letter to Pinker that illustrates just how dire things had become:

> You must not treat me as a journeyman joiner. Am I to understand that if the book is not finished by say 10–15 then You will drop me on the 15th of Augt. I don't inquire whether it is You *can't* or *won't*. From the practical point of view it amounts to the same thing. Hall Caine takes two years to write his books. J.C. may be allowed some time. If your idea is that my stuff is unsaleable then all I can say is that I haven't made it so. If I must starve or beg I won't do it *here*. That's all I have to say really. Consider whether it would be good policy (from a practical point of view) to drive me away. This is nothing but a *statement of the case*. Don't take it in any other spirit. I have not vice to prevent me working and I am willing as soon as practicable to get away into a most economical hole imaginable and write there night and day. I can't believe that my reputation has gone to pieces suddenly.[45]

Pinker did not cut off relations, but he did alter their arrangement to one that 'was strictly an exchange of cash for work delivered, four pounds per thousand words.'[46] This arrangement lasted until 1915, though it caused a serious strain between the two men that culminated in an estrangement in 1910 that lasted for two years.

In terms of finding markets for Conrad's work, and especially new markets for it, Pinker was reasonably successful. The difficulty was always the lack of a steady stream of work, but Pinker nonetheless managed to sell what Conrad did produce and he placed it in an ever-widening circle of publications. Prior to engaging Pinker, Conrad had mostly restricted his publication to a select few magazines and publishers: Unwin, Heinemann, and Blackwood for books, and magazines such as *Savoy, Outlook, Cornhill, New Review,* and of course '*Maga.*' One common feature of these publications is that they were what Peter McDonald calls 'high-class literary and political magazines.'[47] As McDonald suggests, Conrad was positioning himself as a 'purist.' He saw himself as an author who consciously chose to '[shun] worldly claims and rewards' in return for the 'compensatory attainments: in particular, the achievement of what [Conrad] called a "literary reputation."'[48] Yet as McDonald's argument points out, Conrad needed to earn his living from his writing, so he was not as free to embrace this position as were others who had independent sources of income. However, Conrad's aspirations to achieve a 'literary reputation' meant that he could not admit to his friends in these literary circles that he wished to reach a wider audience in order to earn sufficient income. In fact, this was something he had trouble admitting to himself. Here Pinker provided a means to solve this problem. Conrad could conveniently shift the responsibility for his work appearing in less prestigious journals to Pinker's shoulders, while still accepting the income Pinker's efforts generated for him.

Pinker began creating larger audiences for Conrad's work with the very first piece Conrad placed in his hands. 'Typhoon' was published in the *Pall Mall Magazine,* a journal that Conrad would not have approached on his own because it was not in the same 'purist' category as *Maga* and the others. But the *Pall Mall Magazine* had a larger circulation and a broader readership base, so Conrad's story found an audience it might not otherwise have reached. Conrad may have felt it was a less worthy outlet for his work, but he was aware of the benefit of increasing his readership. His comments to David Meldrum about Pinker's placement of 'Typhoon,' though typical in his damning with faint praise the less prestigious journals, reveal just this: 'To appear in P[all] M[all] M[agazine] and the Ill: Lond: News is advantageous no doubt – but I only care for *Maga*, my first and only Love!'[49]

Over the next several years, Pinker continued this deliberate widening of Conrad's audience. By 1905, for example, he was arranging for material to appear in the very mainstream *Daily Mail* – it published three pieces that later became part of *The Mirror of the Sea.* One might consider that Conrad, the purist, would have seen the appearance of his work in the *Daily Mail* as a distinct lowering of his status, and he did believe that. However, he rationalized his publication in the *Daily Mail* by claiming financial need and by also disparaging the quality of the product he provided them with, as this letter to H.G. Wells dated 7 February 1904 illustrates:

> I've started a series of sea sketches and have sent out P[inker] on the hunt to place them. This must *save* me. I've discovered that I can dictate that sort of bosh without effort at the rate of 3000 words in four hours. Fact! The only thing now is to sell it to a paper and then make a book of the rubbish. Hang![50]

In the same year Pinker also arranged for publication of material from *The Mirror* in, among others, *Harper's Magazine*, the *Fortnightly Review*, and the *Standard*.[51] These venues would have appealed to very different audiences; two of the periodicals Conrad would have thought suitable – *Harper's* was one of America's leading political and literary magazine; the *Fortnightly Review*, under the editorship of W.L Courtney at this time, retained the prestige it had earned under the editorship of George Henry Lewes – but the *Standard*, although favourably rated by Conrad (he claimed it was the only newspaper he read),[52] would have been viewed as less prestigious than either *Harper's* or the *Fortnightly Review* and distinctly less prestigious than *Maga*. The fact that he was publishing 'this sort of bosh' in important periodicals such as *Harper's* or the *Fortnightly Review* seems to have passed without comment from Conrad, though the irony is obvious enough. Thus, while Pinker would have seen this expansion of Conrad's readership as a positive, it is doubtful that Conrad shared his views, though he did need the money that it could bring him.

The final standard way that Pinker looked after his clients' business affairs was to raise the author's public profile. His challenge in this task was as great as it was in the other two areas. Conrad's nature did not dispose him to the kinds of public relations activities that Pinker undertook for his other clients. Indeed, Conrad's dislike of the publicity aspect of literary culture is evident in this letter to David Meldrum, who had requested a photograph of Conrad:

> I had rather not; moreover I haven't got a photograph, not a single copy; and I won't sit on purpose as two years ago I've refused to do so for Dr Robertson Nicoll who wanted to put me into the Bookman.

A criticism of a book is all right, but my face has nothing to do with my writing.

If I were a pretty actress or a first rate athlete I wouldn't deprive an aching democracy of a legitimate satisfaction.

In '96 a photograph of me appeared in the *Sketch* I think. I let myself be persuaded. Two columns of colossally stupid letter press accompanied it. No more.[53]

He also turned down invitations to take part in formal literary gatherings. Karl says that Conrad declined an invitation from André Gide to spend ten days engaged in organized group discussions about literature at the Abbey of Pontigny in 1912. He notes that this 'was the kind of affair Conrad would not even consider, first because of his obsessive need to turn out copy, and second because of a constitutional dislike of literary meetings or forums of any kind.'[54]

However, even with respect to publicity, Conrad's somewhat contradictory attitude to the business of writing is evident. Aware of the need for good reviews, he frequently pushed his literary advisors, including Pinker, to ensure that 'quality' journals published reviews of his work. Like any writer, he commented on reviews to his friends and agent, rejecting the unfavourable ones as by those who were not capable of assessing his work and rejoicing in the favourable ones. A fairly typical Conrad response to a negative review comes from this letter, which he wrote to John Galsworthy in August of 1908. Conrad goes on at length about the reviewer's inability to judge his work, but a small excerpt should suffice to indicate his views:

There is an ass who tells me in Dly News on god knows what provocation that I am a man 'without country and language.' It is like abusing some poor tongue-tied wretch. For, what can one say? The statement is gross and palpable and the answer that could be made would be incomprehensible to nine tenths of the hearers who would not have imagination enough to believe that a complex sentiment can be true.[55]

By the end of his career, Conrad was particularly keen to have his stature as a writer suitably acknowledged. He turned to Pinker for help in a campaign to have his work considered for the Nobel Prize in Literature in 1919. On 15 February 1919, he wrote to Pinker about the possibility of a nomination: 'That was in the air last year; and as it is an international thing and less in the nature of an honour than of mere reward, we needn't have any scruples about acceptance if it ever comes our way.'[56] They strategized about how to arrange matters so that *The Rescue*'s publication dates would fit the time constraints of the award, since Conrad had long nurtured the belief that this novel was worthy of such a prestigious honour. These plans came to nothing, but it is nonetheless interesting to see that Conrad was willing to employ his agent to boost his public profile when it suited him.

Despite all of the difficulties Pinker encountered in managing Conrad's affairs, their long business partnership must be deemed a success. During their twenty years together, Conrad produced work that earned him critical acclaim and he eventually earned a sizeable income for his efforts. Pinker's managing of Conrad's affairs is, at the very least, part of the reason for Conrad's eventual accumulation of economic and cultural capital.

Friends

One of the most interesting aspects of the Conrad-Pinker relationship is the lasting friendship that developed between two men whose life experiences and temperaments were fundamentally different. Pinker's new-found wealth and the elevation in social class provided by his marriage to Elizabeth Seabrooke had enabled him to adopt the trappings of the life of a gentleman. He was an extremely sociable man, who enjoyed dining with his many clients and friends, hosting weekend parties at his estate in Surrey, and participating fully in country life. Indeed, he loved to hunt, sharing that passion with many of his clients, including Somerville and Ross. Yet the values instilled in him during his early years remained central to the way he lived his life and carried out his business. He respected hard work and expected those around him to work as hard as he did; he knew the worth of money and could not understand Conrad's cavalier attitude towards it; and he retained a sometimes unwarranted admiration for men whose family connections were socially superior to his. Conrad retained his own class sensibilities, his attitudes towards life having been shaped by his birth as a Polish nobleman's son and further refined by life at sea where a rigid hierarchy was the order of the day. Despite Conrad's early years at sea, or perhaps because of them, once he settled into his writing career he ceased to be a physically active man. His many illnesses, especially gout, prevented him from undertaking strenuous physical activity, and though he chose to live in the country, he did not engage in typical country pastimes such as riding or hunting. His temperament meant that his friends frequently had to deal with his mood swings, and most of his friends found his wife Jessie difficult. Conrad's autocratic nature thus contrasted sharply with Pinker's friendly demeanour, but despite their different temperaments, the two men became firm friends, developing bonds that were as close as one might find between brothers. This familial relationship was sorely tested over the years, but at the end of the day, one can safely say that Pinker was one of the most important figures in Conrad's life.

Frederick Karl offers a compelling analysis of their relationship that may well explain not only its longevity and closeness, but also its centrality to Conrad's life:

> Pinker was as welcome in the Conrad home as Garnett and Graham earlier. In their association we have only Conrad's side of the correspondence, but we can remark that in the relationship, if Conrad was a conscious martyr, Pinker was a saint; if Conrad was the artist seeking fulfillment in the only way he knew, Pinker was parental and sustaining. For the writer who needed support at every turn, Pinker was as supportive in the middle and later years as Conrad's uncle Tadeusz had been in the earlier.[57]

The key here is that Pinker provided both the financial and emotional support that Conrad had accepted as his due from his uncle. Just as he fought with Uncle Tadeusz over money and life choices when he was a teenager, so he fought with Pinker over money and literary choices later in life. Like any two family members, each knew how to lash out and hurt the other deeply. For instance, their major estrangement came about not solely because of their incessant wrangle over money but also because of a remark Pinker made that wounded Conrad deeply.

Conrad travelled to London in January 1910 to deliver the long-overdue *Under Western Eyes* to Pinker. Evidently they quarrelled; during the argument, Pinker apparently told Conrad he 'did not speak English.'[58] This remark hit Conrad very deeply, as Pinker must have known it would, given Conrad's sensitivity to his difficulties with spoken English. When Conrad collapsed three days later, Jessie Conrad wired Pinker that 'The doctor says it is a complete nervous breakdown and that it has been coming on for months.'[59] What she did not tell him at this point is that in the early stages of his severe illness Conrad was raving, mostly in Polish, apart from 'a few fierce sentences against poor J.B. Pinker.'[60] Conrad himself wrote a cold letter to Pinker in May that demonstrated the anger he still nurtured towards Pinker and the reason for it. Addressing him as 'Dear Sir' instead of the customary 'my dear Pinker,' he says, 'As it can't have escaped your recollection that the last time we met you told me that I "did not speak English" to you I have asked Robert Garnett to be my mouth-piece – at any rate till my speech improves sufficiently to be acceptable.'[61] As is the case in most family quarrels, the coldness gradually thawed, and by March 1912, Conrad was once again addressing his letters to 'my dear Pinker.'[62]

Conrad needed Pinker, not just for financial support, but also for the emotional security he provided. Pinker's unwavering belief in Conrad's ability formed the bedrock of that emotional support. Yet Conrad's attitude towards Pinker's literary judgment was, as usual, contradictory. Some comments he made to his friends indicate that he did not think highly of Pinker's literary taste. He wrote to Ford Madox Ford in reference to Pinker's opinion about *Romance* that 'Now if *he* isn't an average reader I want to know who is?'[63] The condescension and sneering tone can hardly be missed. At other points, though, he defended Pinker, using terms that demonstrate not only a faith in Pinker's literary acumen, but also the depth of his emotional dependence on his agent. For instance, he rose to defend Pinker from a nasty attack on his ethics launched by William Heinemann in which Heinemann accused Pinker of deliberately impoverishing Conrad. Conrad wrote to his friend Edmund Gosse in August 1904, advising him not to believe the charges and asking him to stop spreading such malicious gossip:

> my good friend Pinker – tho' he does not advertise himself by a volume of nauseous adulation from 'men of letters!' – is neither stupid nor a man without a conscience ... He has known me for six years. He has stepped gallantly into the breach left open by the collapse of my bank; and not only gallantly, but successfully as well. He has treated not only my moods but even my fancies with great consideration. I would not dream of wearying you with details and figures; but his action, distinctly, has not been of a mercenary character. He can not take away the weariness of mind which at the end of ten years strain has come upon me; but he has done his utmost to help me overcome it by relieving the immediate material pressure – and the even more disabling pressure of human stupidity. But let that pass! How much can he expect in return for these services? I don't know. But I fear I am not a 'profitable man' in anybody's speculation.[64]

The first part of the quotation contains a not-too-subtle dig at A.P. Watt. The latter portion of the letter illustrates Conrad's already growing emotional attachment to Pinker. Conrad makes clear to Gosse that the services Pinker renders go beyond mere business matters and that he, Conrad, finds them indispensable. For the next eighteen years, despite the ups and downs, Conrad relied heavily on Pinker's emotional support, to '[relieve] the immediate material pressure – and the even more disabling pressure of human stupidity.'

It is relatively easy to see why Conrad's bond with Pinker would go so deep: he depended on his agent for money, for emotional support, and for all kinds of practical services. Indeed, Pinker frequently paid household and personal bills for Conrad, arranged for housing, made travel arrangements, and looked after innumerable other tasks that went well beyond the agent's usual responsibilities. What is less easy to see is why Pinker would maintain his business relationship and his friendship with Conrad given the manner in which Conrad habitually treated him. That is a subject I will turn to shortly.

Conrad, Pinker, and Modernism

Chapter 5 looked briefly at Pinker's role as a patron of literary modernists such as D.H. Lawrence and James Joyce in order to highlight the ways in which Pinker altered A.P. Watt's standard agenting practices. I want to conclude this discussion of Conrad and Pinker by expanding on the discussion of Pinker as a patron of literary modernism. Before embarking on that topic, however, it is necessary to place Conrad firmly within the boundaries of literary modernism in order to give the argument about Pinker's central role in Conrad's success as a *modernist* writer a stable foundation.

Conrad began his writing career in the 1890s, during which time he produced fiction that could be, and sometimes is, classified as genre literature. His early stories – such as *Almayer's Folly* (1895), which might be labelled an imperial romance given its treatment of the Dutch trader Almayer's life with the inhabitants of a remote Bornean outpost, and *The Nigger of the Narcissus* (1897), which, given its maritime setting and the uprising of the ship's crew, could be read as an adventure story – fitted well into the popular demand for stories set in exotic locales that dealt with topical concerns such as imperialism, forbidden romance, and Englishmen's adventures among native populations. He continued to write such stories well into the twentieth century, with *Lord Jim* (1900) continuing his tales of adventure in the South Seas; *Heart of Darkness* (1902) exploring in depth the clash of an imperial culture with an indigenous one; and *The Secret Agent* (1907) adding espionage fiction to his repertoire. One could be forgiven for concluding from this brief account of Conrad's work that he should be grouped with writers such as Rudyard Kipling and Rider Haggard, who also produced adventure tales, spy stories, and imperial romances. Certainly, during his lifetime, Conrad would have been pleased to be associated with Kipling and Haggard, but at the same time, he also would have stressed his difference from them, a difference that would place him at the heart of literary modernism. Two factors set him apart from Kipling, Haggard, and others working on similar topics and in similar genres: Conrad's literary aesthetics and his conception of authorship.

Conrad's aesthetics are most famously expressed in his 'Preface' to the *Nigger of the Narcissus*. The oft-quoted passage – 'My task which I am trying to achieve is, by the power of the written word, to make you hear, to make you feel – it is, above all, to make you see. That – and no more, and it is everything'[65] – provides a glimpse of what he was trying to achieve as a writer. Conrad used what might be called an impressionist style to create vivid landscapes, and in doing so he employed techniques such as symbolism, fragmented narratives, and unreliable narrators to disrupt the reader's ordinary perceptual experiences.[66] But Conrad's landscapes were as much interior as they were exterior. The exotic physical locales he used complemented his explorations of the interior spaces of the human psyche, so that when Marlow in *Heart of Darkness* speaks for the first time – '"And this also," said Marlow suddenly, "has been one of the dark places of the earth"'[67] – the reader knows, or will know by the end of the story, that Marlow is referring not only to the physical setting but also to human nature. Conrad's foregrounding of formal innovations and his emphasis on his characters' psychological makeup aligned him closely with literary modernism. So even though he continued to write stories that could be classified as genre fiction, the ways in which he told his tales placed him firmly inside the confines of modernism.

The second factor that aligns Conrad with literary modernism is his conception of authorship. Recent scholarship has explored what Kevin Dettmar and Stephen Watt, in their introduction to *Marketing Modernisms*, call 'the critically suppressed relationship between canonical modernists and the commercial marketplace.'[68] One of the more provocative explorations of this relationship is Joyce Wexler's *Who Paid for Modernism?* She suggests:

> Despite their aesthetic of impersonality, modernist authors' professional strategy depended on self-promotion. Their dilemma was rooted in an ideological contradiction between art and money that pervaded their culture, as it continues to dominate our own. This contradiction posed the Romantic ideal of the writer as genius who expressed an inviolable inner vision without regard for its rhetorical effect or market value against a newer definition of the author as professional who earned a living by writing. Moreover, each ideal generated cautionary counterparts. The specter of the artist who wrote for himself was the amateur who wrote for no one else; the underside of the professional was the hack who wrote only for money. The modernist writer had to steer a course between both figures of contempt.[69]

In negotiating these differing ideals, early twentieth-century writers consciously assumed positions that not only situated them in the print culture field, but also reflected their conception of authorship. One could choose the Romantic position, accepting that the readership of one's work would be select though the economic capital derived from the work would be commensurately small. One could choose the position of the professional, accepting that the economic capital derived from the work might well be larger, but that the cultural capital might be less. Yet, as Wexler notes, modernist writers found themselves in a double bind. For as much as they wished to signal to their fellow writers that they were a certain kind of author – a 'purist,' to use Peter McDonald's term again – they nonetheless wished to secure the kind of income that the professional writer was earning.[70] As Wexler's comments suggest, the difficulty faced by the modernist was to find a way to travel this middle road without sacrificing art for money or money for art.

Conrad explicitly adopted the position of the artist; indeed, his first major argument with Pinker arose because of Conrad's perception that Pinker did not accord him the treatment an artist deserves. To quote again from that 8 January 1902 letter:

> I had asked you for £40 I believe. To this demand in the given circumstances there was the reply of no – in business – or in friendly – terms. I was prepared for it. But what does the last par: of your letter mean? Who are the people I am to send to you? My tradesman? Or my banker who has known me for some years and does not talk to me of failure because my acct/ is overdrawn? This is the sort of thing one writes to a grub street

dipsomaniac to stop him bothering one – not to a man of my value ... I am no sort of airy R. L. Stevenson who considered his art a prostitute and the artists as no better than one. I dare say he was punctual – but I don't envy him.[71]

Yet Conrad also desired the rewards available to writers in the market-place. His attack on Stevenson may well have been motivated by his sense of the injustice of a print culture field that would see Stevenson earn large sums of money from his stories and Conrad fail, in 1902 at least, to earn a commensurate amount from his.

One of the strategies adopted by modernists to 'steer a course' between the aesthetic ideal and the commercial necessity was to consign business matters to a third party, thereby creating a buffer between the author and the marketplace. This in itself was not new, for, as we have seen, authors' friends had long performed such roles and literary agents had emerged to enable all writers to avail themselves of the services of a literary middleman. Modernists typically employed a variety of individuals in the third-party role. Among the most prominent unpaid middlemen was Ezra Pound, who brokered deals for a number of literary friends, most notably for T.S. Eliot, James Joyce, and H.D. Pinker served a similar function for his clients, though unlike Pound he expected to be paid for his services in the form of the commissions he earned from his clients' sales. As chapter 5 illustrated, employing Pinker, or other literary agents, meant that modernist writers could publicly eschew the marketplace, taking what Ian Willison has called the position of 'virtually contract[ing] out of an establishment literary market' that they believed was 'now openly hostile to [them]'[72] while nonetheless ensuring that their interests in the establishment marketplace were well looked after. Certainly this is the method that Conrad chose to allow him to 'steer the course' between the competing positions available to writers in the early twentieth century print culture field.

But Pinker's work for Conrad went well beyond the boundaries of the usual services provided by a literary agent; as we have seen, he supported Conrad financially and emotionally throughout their twenty-year association. Indeed, Frederick Karl equates Pinker's role with that of 'the patron to the artist which had existed prior to the eighteenth century, before commercial success was possible.'[73] The fact that he had to wait more than a decade to see any return on his considerable financial investment tends to support Karl's construction of Pinker as an old-fashioned literary patron. But Karl gets it only partly right because

Pinker was not the disinterested literary patron of days gone by who was content to supply the writer with money in return for a glowing dedication in the next published book. As a businessman, he would have been expecting some return on his investments of money and time. The nub of the situation – what prompted Pinker to continue to support Conrad for as long as he did – is what makes him a fascinating figure in this period. For Pinker was a new kind of literary patron, one who measured his patronage on two scales – in the accumulation of both economic and cultural capital. In the case of Conrad, he initially earned a greater amount of cultural capital because he was supporting a writer whose work he, and others including many critics of the period, considered important. Over time, he also earned economic capital, sharing in Conrad's success from 1912 onwards. His work with Conrad, starting in 1900, set up a new mode of patronage, one that Pinker would practise with other writers, including D.H. Lawrence and James Joyce in the 1910s; Pinker's literary patronage would also prefigure changes that were occurring in the print culture field as literary modernism began to assume a more important place.

Scholars have long acknowledged the importance of patronage in literary modernism's development. For instance, Sylvia Beach's patronage of Joyce has been well documented.[74] More recently, critical reevaluations of literary modernism have included a reexamination of the role that patronage played. Paul Delany has argued that '[t]he direct source of money for much of early modernism was a regime of patronage.'[75] According to Delany, this patronage takes two basic forms: direct patronage in which wealthy individuals supplied writers with money so they could write what they wished without needing to take into account market pressures; and the emergence of a rentier culture to which many writers belonged. By rentier culture, Delany means that class that 'lived off financial wealth, which gave them a higher income than if they invested in land, and freed them from responsibility for an estate with its servants, laborers, and tenants.'[76] As noted in chapter 5, Lawrence Rainey also addresses the issue of patronage in literary modernism, suggesting that 'the patronage of literary modernism was rarely the pure or disinterested support that we typically associate with patronage.' Patronage had to be disguised in a number of ways for it 'not to seem too at odds with the modern world.'[77] Both men make convincing arguments for the central role this newly defined patronage played in literary modernism, but neither examines the role that literary agents like Pinker played in this rebirth of literary patronage.[78]

Conrad is something of an exception when it comes to modernists in that he told his friends about Pinker's significant role in his literary career. In 1916 Conrad wrote to John Quinn, himself a notable patron of literary modernism, about Pinker:

> Our relations are by no means those of client and agent. And I will tell you why. It is because those books which, people say, are an asset to English literature owe their existence to Mr Pinker as much as to me. For 15 years of my writing life he has seen me through periods of unproductiveness through illness through all sorts of troubles. I don't complain of not having had enough recognition. Indeed I had it in full measure. But the fact remains that P was the only man who backed his opinion with his money, and that in no grudging manner, to say the least of it ...
>
> And the fact is that P kept me going as much perhaps by his belief in me as with his money. And nobody can say it was mere business on his part. A publisher may finance a writer with a reasoned hope that should success come some day he will see his money back many times over. But P could have no such hope, since he could look to nothing more than his 10% comm. I can't enter into the detail of these 15 years but if I were to live a hundred years more I could not forget them. And that's why our relation is not business but of intimate friendship in the last instance.[79]

While Conrad's opinion appears unequivocal, Pinker has continued to be cast solely as Conrad's generous man of business whose literary taste was questionable, though his business sense was acute enough to spot emerging literary talent. Conrad's biographer Jocelyn Baines's comments are typical in this respect. Baines quotes from a portion of Conrad's 1916 letter to Quinn and then adds:

> Pinker was not a man of outstanding intellect and seems to have had no literary appreciation. But literary appreciation is often a handicap among publishers and agents and he had the qualities common to the most successful men in this sphere: a flare [sic] for sensing talent before it is generally recoginsed [sic], coupled with the courage to back his judgement financially. Thus, at his death he was one of the most important figures on the business side of the literary world.[80]

How one can lack literary appreciation and still sense talent before it is generally recognized is puzzling; certainly the glaring contradiction here does not seem to have been noticed by Baines or by most of

Conrad's subsequent biographers and critics.[81] Yet this stark contradiction is not surprising when one considers what modernist writers, and their subsequent critics, had at stake. Wexler writes that 'The opposition between "art" written for oneself and "hack work" written for an audience concealed the rhetorical aims and financial ambitions of modernists.'[82] To admit Pinker's part in their careers would require modernists to admit their financial ambitions. They would also have to admit that they wanted their work to reach a broader readership than the elite audience they, and their critics, had come to accept as the only one fit to judge their work.[83] However, by failing to acknowledge Pinker's role, modernists and their critics have failed to come clean about the construction and dissemination of modernist literature.

Conclusion

A.P. Watt died in 1914; J.B. Pinker in 1922. Their deaths marked the end of two eras in literary agenting, but they also coincided with two significant shifts in literary culture. It seems appropriate to conclude this discussion of the origins and rise of literary agency with some brief reflections on both of these points.

When A.P. Watt died on 3 November 1914, Europe was embroiled in the early days of the First World War. British papers were filled with war news from the continent and the home front. Accounts of battles taking place in previously obscure European locations; commentaries on government action, or inaction; and lists of men killed or missing in action occupied prominent places on the front pages. Watt's death merited little more than the standard obituary in the major papers. *The Times*, for instance, contained the following front-page notice on 4 and 5 November in the column headed 'Deaths':

Watt – On the 3rd inst., at his residence, Abinger House Abbey-road, N.W., Alexander Pollock Watt, in his 78th year. Funeral at Hampstead Cemetery, Fortune-green-road, West Hampstead, on Friday, at 11:30.

This simple announcement is situated beside and above the columns listing the names of those men who had been killed in action. Thus, the death of a man who had lived a long, productive, and successful life is ironically juxtaposed with the deaths of young men whose lives were cut short by war.

However, it is hard to ignore the inadvertent symbolism at work here. It is almost a cliché today to note that the First World War marked the death of a way of life, but like all clichés, there is a truth at play in its expression. The world did change dramatically after August 1914, for the First World War did cause enormous ruptures in virtually every facet of life in Europe and Britain. However, the onset of the war can be viewed as the culmination of actions that had begun years, perhaps decades, earlier. Various dates and events can be cited as starting points for the demise of European and British imperial cultures that led to the war, but the point here is not to establish when the demise began, but to acknowledge that August 1914 stands as the moment from which one can track the death throes of those imperial cultures. Indeed, the almost ritualistic listing of the names of those killed in action clearly signifies the passing of an old order. The simple, even stark, notice of Watt's death, in contrast, obscures the fact that it also signified the passing of an old order.

Though the changes in the print culture field were not as publicly significant as those in the political arena that prompted the First World War, they were nonetheless enormously important to those who wrote, published, and consumed printed material. During his lifetime, Watt had witnessed, and participated in, the rapid transformation of not only publishing practices, but also literary culture itself. For example, when he started out as a reader for his brother-in-law Alexander Strahan in 1871, it was common practice to exploit the copyright of texts by publishing them serially and in book form. For some texts, selling other outside rights could derive additional sources of income: dramatic rights, for example, often proved lucrative. When Watt began working as an agent in the late 1870s, he became an active participant, some would say an instigator, in the commercialization of literature that transformed the publishing world. Though Watt initially defined an agent's job as 'negotiat[ing] between authors and publishers (including proprietors of newspapers) for the efficient and advantageous publication of literary productions,'[1] agents' tasks quickly became much more broadly defined. Indeed, as the nineteenth century drew to a close, an agent's job became more and more the overseeing of literary properties and literary careers. Agents managed their clients' copyrights, exploiting an ever-growing number of outside rights that continued to emerge as the literary marketplace expanded and its dynamics altered.[2] They also managed their clients' public relations, arranging interviews and publicity tours, and even handling clients' fan mail. Watt's death, overshadowed as it was by political events, nonetheless marked the passing of one of the key players in this transformation of literature. It also coincided with the end of one phase of the commercialization of literature.

Indeed, though the twentieth century was to witness a continued commercialization of literature – the advent of television or, later in the century, computer games, for instance, creating a whole range of new commercial opportunities for authors whose agents were quick to exploit them – the basic techniques for exploiting the commercial possibilities of literature were well established by 1914. And yet, even at his death, Watt's agency had begun to adapt to other changes that were occurring in both agenting and publishing.

By 1914 a new generation of authors was emerging; they explicitly contested the dominance of commercial literature in the print culture field. Manifestos produced by leading figures of this generation – Ezra Pound, T.S. Eliot, Virginia Woolf, Richard Aldington, John Middleton Murry, to name a few primarily British-based writers – poured scorn on those who wrote for the literary marketplace. Commercialization of literature, in their view, was akin to writers' prostitution of their talents. Though they consciously situated themselves outside the mainstream organs of publishing in 1914, the publishing world was beginning to take notice of them. A.P. Watt and Son was no exception. For the most part, the agency's business practices had remained the same as they had been for years; indeed, the bulk of the firm's client list continued to be authors whose work was aimed at the lower- and middle-class readerships that continued to dominate the literary marketplace. But the firm was already recognizing that a new generation of writers was bound to have an impact on the dynamics of the marketplace. Thus the Watt agency made moves to represent some writers whose work did not reflect the tastes of the firm's founder, representing August Strindberg, for example, whose plays certainly challenged A.P. Watt's sensibility. After A.P.'s death, the firm approached many of the rising modernist writers seeking to represent them. Though few of those that they approached signed on with the firm, the fact that the Watts approached them indicated a real shift in their sense of what constituted commercially viable literature. Watt did negotiate at least eight contracts for Vita Sackville-West, and the firm became the main agents for W.B. Yeats, who had already established himself as a leading figure of the new generation of writers. Indeed, Alec Watt took on Yeats personally, thereby signalling that his firm was interested in representing the leading writers of the next generation. However, by championing Yeats, who could be seen as something of an elder statesman of modernism, Alec was continuing the firm's practice of stepping in to represent established authors, rather than identifying and then building the careers of emerging writers.

Despite their courting of the more prominent modernists, A.P. Watt and Son remained the establishment's literary agency. Indeed, Watt's sons and grandsons continued to cement their place in the upper echelons of British political and social life. As David Finklestein has demonstrated, Alec Watt played an important role as the 'official conduit and mediator between authors, publishers, and government bureaus in the commission, production, and distribution of printed material for the highly secret propaganda war waged against Germany and Austria-Hungary at home and abroad, and in particular in the United States and Canada'[3] during the First World War. Finkelstein's conclusion about the impact of Watt's actions is correct: the firm did '[emerge] strengthened from the war as a permanent part of a changed literary marketplace, handling increasingly complex and diverse methods of marketing literary products.'[4] In fact, through behaviour that exemplifies Bourdieu's assertion of the dynamic nature of cultural fields, the firm proved remarkably adept at sustaining its central position in the twentieth-century print culture field, making necessary adjustments to business practices, shifting to meet new trends in the literary world, yet always adhering to the basic tenets established by the founder. The name Watt thus became synonymous with agenting throughout the twentieth century.

J.B. Pinker's death on 8 February 1922 rated more media coverage than had Watt's. In part this was due to the fact that Pinker's death did not have to compete with war news, and in part because he died abroad – his death from pneumonia brought on by influenza occurring shortly after he had arrived in New York on a business trip. His death merited full obituaries in the leading papers. *The Times*, for example, published two notices on 10 February 1922: a brief one on the front page in the column marked 'Deaths' and a longer one on page 10, headed 'DEATH OF MR. J.B. PINKER,' which included 'An Appreciation' of Pinker underneath the brief notice of his death in New York. The appreciation stated that his death was 'a very real and important loss to the whole kingdom and constitution of English literature.' Pinker's death at age fifty-eight was a shock to his family, the literary community, and especially to those writers whom he had championed before they were established and with whom he had built a long and successful relationship, such as Joseph Conrad and Arnold Bennett. In contrast to Watt, who had lived a long, full life, Pinker appeared to have been cut down in his prime, with business yet unfinished. All of this made his death newsworthy in a way that Watt's was not.

Yet there is as compelling a symbolism in the date of his death as there is in Watt's, for 1922 is often cited as the seminal year in literary modernism. As Michael North suggests, 'Anyone who writes about or teaches modern literature spends a good deal of time in 1922.'[5] Indeed, 1922 was the year that witnessed the publication of James Joyce's *Ulysses*, Virginia Woolf's *Jacob's Room*, and T.S. Eliot's *The Waste Land*. Clearly it was an extraordinary year, and not only in Britain, as key modernist works by Americans such as Wallace Stevens and William Carlos Williams were also published during this period.[6] Though the roots of modernist literature may be traced back to the previous century, and several important modernist works were published prior to 1922, it is reasonable to say that 1922 witnessed literary modernism's public coming of age.[7] Nevertheless, just as modernism seems to have arrived as a literary movement capable of contesting the dominant position of commercial literature, at least for prestige value or cultural capital, the print culture field shifts to accommodate the newcomers.

In fact, by 1922 the rebels of modernism were on the brink of entering the mainstream marketplace. As Lawrence Rainey has demonstrated, Eliot's quintessentially modernist poem *The Waste Land* was offered to the exemplary mainstream magazine *Vanity Fair*, which did not publish it in the end, but later published other Eliot works.[8] Indeed, *Vanity Fair* published many modernist writers besides Eliot – D.H. Lawrence, Gertrude Stein, Jean Cocteau, and André Gide, among others, all appeared in the magazine during the 1920s, for instance. By the mid-1920s, Virginia Woolf's journalism was appearing in the British version of *Vogue*, and the magazine routinely reviewed the works of leading modernist writers including both Woolf and Eliot. *Vogue* was certainly not the kind of magazine that the 1914 modernists would have considered an appropriate venue for their work, but by the 1920s, modernists were happy to have their work published, reviewed, or mentioned there. In fact, T.S. Eliot wrote to Richard Aldington about his review of Eliot's work in *Vogue*, 'It says just what I should like to be said!'[9] One could add that it says it in a forum that would attract more readers to his work than would have been reached by a review in Eliot's own *Criterion*. Clearly, modernism was going mainstream. Indeed, as Paul Delany notes, 'a salient feature of literary modernism is the speed with which it established itself in the literary marketplace that it professed to despise.'[10]

The point here is not to discuss in detail the field's absorption of modernism, nor is it to point out the fact that modernists were willing accomplices in this movement from the margins to the centre. Rather, the point is to explore the interesting parallel between the date of Pinker's death and modernism's movement into the mainstream. When he died in 1922, Pinker had already spent years working with leading modernist writers – Conrad, Joyce, Lawrence, Wyndham Lewis, and Katharine Mansfield, to name a few prominent clients. His management of their literary affairs was determined by the successful agenting practices established by Watt, which Pinker had adapted to serve his particular interest in 'tak[ing] up the unknown man, the youngster struggling for reputation and bread and butter, and help[ing] him to build his reputation.'[11] Pinker defined success as 'singling out a youngster from the crowd of unknowns and pushing him to the top.'[12] By the top, he meant an accumulation of both economic and cultural capital. Thus Pinker's modernist clients had to go mainstream because that was one of the guiding principles upon which he managed their careers. Pinker's successful management of their careers is also manifested in the way in which his serving of these twin impulses transformed the print culture field: modernist aesthetics infiltrated the literary mainstream, changing the way in which writers and readers alike defined literature.

Unlike A.P. Watt and Son, the J.B. Pinker Literary Agency did not long outlive its founder, nor was it ever to become part of the publishing establishment in the same way that the Watt agency did. Although Pinker's sons Eric and Ralph had joined him in the firm, he had not made them partners, preferring to retain sole financial and business control himself. Significantly, the firm's contracts – both with clients and with publishers – terminated upon J.B.'s death, making it difficult for his sons to carry on business as usual. The firm limped along for another decade, but by the mid-1930s, the Pinker agency had lost most of its major clients and was verging on bankruptcy.[13] J.B.'s apparent mistrust of his sons' abilities seems merited, at least in hindsight, as clearly neither was a good businessman, and both were less trustworthy than their father had been. Each served a jail term for fraud involving the embezzlement of monies from clients and the failure to pay income tax on behalf of clients and themselves. The final irony, then, is that while the literary outsiders that Pinker helped to bring into the mainstream continued to prosper after his death, his agency was denied the same fate.

The contrasting fates of the Watt and Pinker agencies provide the basis for a few final conclusions one can draw about the emergence and rise of literary agency as a force in print culture. A.P. Watt began his career as an agent faced with enormous opposition from the literary establishment, some of it merited; yet at the time of his death, few individuals were more closely aligned with the literary establishment than he was. His success can be measured by the achievements he made during his lifetime – not the least of which was the publishing world's gradual acceptance of literary agents – and by the legacy he left to that world – not the least of which was the continuing prosperity of the agency he founded. J.B. Pinker entered the publishing world intent on redefining the role of literary agents – making them the champions of young, unproven authors. His achievement of this goal is evident in the critical and financial success of his clients. His personal success was as noteworthy; at his death he had amassed a considerable personal fortune and his peers lauded him for his work with emerging writers. Yet neither his agency nor his practice of championing unknown writers lived after him for more than a few years. This is a central point of difference in the stories of these two pioneering agents.

Putting aside the considerable difference in the abilities of Watt's and Pinker's heirs, it is possible to pinpoint two reasons for the different fates of their agencies. First, Watt's agency always worked from within the accepted norms of the literary marketplace. While he was clearly innovative in his business practices, he was much less innovative in terms of the authors he represented. His sons and grandsons continued the practice of building the company around the twin principles of keeping ahead of the curve in terms of business practices – establishing a film division before other major agencies, for instance – but drawing the majority of their clients from already established writers. Second, Pinker's strategy of seeking out new authors depended on his ability to spot those whose work would find an audience and it also depended on his ability to anticipate literary trends and the emergence of new literary markets. In other words, Watt's strategy was to build on what existed and to expand into areas only when they were firmly established. Pinker's strategy was riskier, depending on correctly assessing future developments. The skills required to carry on his agency were not transferable in the same ways that the practices established by A.P. Watt were. When Pinker died, his agency, in essence, died with him because there was no one in the firm capable of working as he did.

It is also true that Pinker emerged at a different moment in literary history from Watt. Watt was every inch the man of commerce whose particular business was 'buying and selling copyrights.' William Heinemann was exactly right when he complained in 1893, 'This is the age of the middleman.'[14] Watt was the quintessential middleman in an age in which middlemen flourished. For Watt, the commercialization of literature was no more, and no less, than the extension of sound business practices to the book trade. Pinker's background and professional experience were more closely aligned with the generation of writers and publishers who emerged in the 1890s. He shared with the men and women who challenged the dominant figures in the field a desire to modify the norms and rules of the print culture field. However, like Watt, Pinker also functioned as a middleman, both in terms of carrying out the standard tasks of a literary agent, and in terms of his work with emerging writers. Indeed, in this latter function, he can be seen as a literary patron, working with literary modernism, assisting it in its transition from a position outside the mainstream to a position at the heart of the print culture field. In the process, Pinker participated in the wholesale transformation of literature that occurred in the early twentieth century.

While Heinemann was thus correct about the middleman role that agents played, and have continued to play, he was surely wrong when he claimed, '[An agent] is generally a parasite.' Parasites live off their hosts, taking what they need to survive and moving on to a new host when the current one can no longer sustain them. They provide little or nothing to their hosts in exchange for what they take from them. The mutual interdependence of authors, agents, and publishers that has become a common feature of literary culture since Watt first founded his agency contradicts Heinemann's claim. Far from being parasites, then, A.P. Watt and J.B. Pinker were powerful cultural mediators whose influence on the print culture field should no longer be dismissed or underestimated.

Notes

Introduction

1 William Heinemann, 'The Middleman As Viewed by a Publisher', 663. Heinemann's remarks are frequently used to introduce the topic of publishers' resistance to agents' entry into the book trade. For instance, both James Hepburn in *The Author's Empty Purse and the Rise of Literary Agent* and Peter Keating in *The Haunted Study* quote these same lines in their discussions of literary agents.

2 Heinemann, 'The Middleman As Viewed by a Publisher,' 663. Heinemann's comments were made in an ongoing discussion with Walter Besant, founder of the Society of Authors, that played out in the pages of the *Athenaeum* from late 1892 through at least 1896, with other correspondents joining in the discussion. Heinemann began in 1892 with an article entitled 'The Hardships of Publishing' in which he made the case for a publishers' union that would protect the interests of publishers in an era in which the conditions of the publishing business had drastically changed.

3 Quoted in Frederic Whyte, *William Heinemann*, 124. These are comments that Heinemann made in 1917, long after the agent had established a central place for himself in the publishing world. However, the comments do reflect Heinemann's long-standing animosity towards agents. In the end, as Whyte said, even Heinemann admitted the worth of some agents and was prepared to work with them when it served his interests. See Whyte, *William Heinemann*, 122–33 in particular on this point.

4 This figure is taken from Hepburn's *The Author's Empty Purse*, 98.

5 Anne Goldgar, *Impolite Learning*, 41. Her comments on literary agents are found principally on 35–53.

6 A.B. Bence-Jones, 'Lord Brougham on Literary Agents.'

7 Charles Johanningsmeier in *Fiction and the American Literary Marketplace* provides an excellent account of both the workings of newspaper syndicates and their impact on the American literary marketplace.

8 Johanningsmeier, *Fiction and the American Literary Marketplace*, 4.

9 For an excellent account of syndicators in Britain, see Graham Law, *Serializing Fiction in the Victorian Press*.

10 This information may be found on Samuel French London's web page at: http://www.samuelfrench-london.Companyuk/sf/Pages/feature/history.html. To date no authoritative historical account of the Samuel French Agency has been published.

11 See Jeanne Fahenstock's 'Geraldine Jewsbury: The Power of the Publisher's Reader' for an account of her career. I will discuss briefly the role that Garnett played in Joseph Conrad's life in chapter 7.

12 Hepburn, *The Author's Empty Purse*, 22.

13 Robert Patten in *Dickens and His Publishers* discusses Forster's relations with Dickens, pointing out that he 'served as Dickens's unofficial literary agent from the days of *Pickwick* onward.' (27) As Patten says, Forster also negotiated agreements on behalf of Tennyson, Thackeray, Thomas Carlyle, and Robert Browning.

14 Heinemann's comments on the state of the book trade can be found in several articles that he wrote in the 1890s, most notably in 'The Hardships of Publishing.'

15 The early agents were almost always men. I am aware that some women – Elizabeth Marbury, for example – were involved in agenting by 1900, but masculine pronouns will be used throughout this study to refer to agents unless I am talking specifically about one of the pioneering female agents.

16 Heinemann, 'The Middleman As Viewed by a Publisher,' 663.

17 Peter Keating states that by 1914 there were more than thirty agencies and syndicates advertising their services in the various publishing trade journals. (*The Haunted Study*, 71). As one specific example from the publications of the era, *The Literary Year-Book* for 1914 lists twenty-three entries for agents under the heading 'Authors' Assistants: British Agents.'

18 Some critics continue to refer to this field of study as 'book history,' but I prefer the term 'print culture' because it permits a broader and more inclusive approach. By print culture studies I mean the study of the production, dissemination, and consumption of printed materials that is situated within a context that emphasizes the social and material complexities in which these activities take place.

19 John O. Jordan and Robert L. Patten, eds., *Literature in the Marketplace*, 2.

20 Jordan and Patten, *Literature in the Marketplace*, 1.

21 I consulted a number of different archives in which these papers may be
found; however, four archives proved most useful. The A.P. Watt and
Company Records housed at the Library of the University of North Carolina
at Chapel Hill are invaluable sources of information about the functioning of
the Watt agency from its inception to well into the twentieth century. The collection is extensive, containing letters to and from the Watts and their clients
as well as contracts, though papers pertaining to several prominent clients
are less complete than one would wish and it appears that some of these may
either have been destroyed, likely at the request of the client, or else sold separately to collectors. The James B. Pinker Papers are housed at the McCormick Library of Special Collection, Northwestern University Library. The
letters, contracts, and postcards in the collection deal mostly with the business relations between the Pinkers and their clients though some personal
correspondence may be found; together the papers provide a wonderful
insight into the workings of the Pinker agency from its inception in 1896
until it closed its doors in 1939. As is the case with the Watt Records, there are
significant gaps in the collection, as it appears that some material was possibly
destroyed or lost or sold separately, and in some cases material related to the
Pinkers and their clients can now be found in other archives. The Berg Collection of English and American Literature, The New York Public Library,
Astor, Lenox, and Tilden Foundations, contains correspondence and contracts relating to a number of library agents and their clients, some of which
fill in gaps in the Watt and Pinker archives. Finally, the Somerville and Ross
Papers housed in the Old Library at Trinity College Dublin, containing letters to and from the Pinkers (both business and personal), contracts, and
other business related papers, provide a fascinating glimpse into the working
lives of these two Irish cousins.

22 This is not to say that previous critics have not had access to agents' papers
that are contained in archives housed primarily in libraries in Europe and
North America, but rather that the current study relies more extensively on
them than most previous studies. A few notable exceptions spring to mind,
however, including Joyce Wexler's book *Who Paid for Modernism?*, which
makes extensive use of the J.B. Pinker Papers at Northwestern, and David
Finkelstein's *The House of Blackwood*, which uses the Blackwood Papers at the
National Library of Scotland. Some of the archival material to which I have
had access has become available only in recent years; thus previous scholars,
such as Hepburn, did not have access to it.

23 Janet Wolff, *The Social Production of Art*, 1.

24 I mention these four scholars because their work has had significant influence on my own. Chartier and Darnton's various studies have provided

examples of the possibilities of scholarship of the sort advocated by Jordan and Patten. Cross's *The Common Writer* and Keating's *The Haunted Study* provided models of scholarship that proved invaluable early on in the research for this book.

25 Radway's *A Feeling for Books* provides a fascinating account of the structures, processes, and politics of the Book-of-the-Month Club. However, here I am drawing on earlier work Radway did on the Book-of-the-Month Club – her 1996 Adam Helms Lecture entitled *Books and Reading in the Age of Mass Production*, 22.

26 Radway, *Books and Reading in the Age of Mass Production*, 24.

27 Finkelstein, *The House of Blackwood*, 18.

28 Simon Eliot, *Some Patterns and Trends in British Publishing 1800–1919*, table C1, 127.

29 Eliot, *Some Patterns and Trends in British Publishing 1800–1919*, table C4, 128.

30 Eliot, *Some Patterns and Trends in British Publishing 1800–1919*, 43.

31 The work of Catherine Gallagher (*Nobody's Story*) and Janet Todd (*The Sign of Angellica*) strongly make this case for eighteenth-century women writers. Works by Gaye Tuchman (*Edging Women Out*), Jane Eldridge Miller (*Rebel Women*), Dorothy Mermin (*Godiva's Ride*), Lyn Pickett (*The 'Improper' Feminine*), and Deirdre David (*Intellectual Women and Victorian Patriarchy*) are among the many fine studies that have been published. They take their place alongside the pioneering work of Sandra M. Gilbert and Susan Gubar, *The Madwoman in the Attic*.

32 It is true that MacDonald's children's stories are highly regarded, but in his lifetime his reputation rested more on his other novels and his theological works. Equally true is the fact that some critics hold Somerville and Ross's early work in high esteem. But the work that draws their attention and praise is generally not the series of hunting short stories known as the R.M. stories, but the early novel *The Real Charlotte*, published in 1894.

33 Jordan and Patten, *Literature in the Marketplace*, 12.

34 Jordan and Patten, *Literature in the Marketplace*, 11.

35 Jordan and Patten, *Literature in the Marketplace*, 14.

1. Why Did the Professional Literary Agent Emerge in the 1880s?

1 F.W., 'An Interview with Mr. A.P. Watt,' 21.

2 The phrase 'taxes on knowledge' was widely used to describe the various taxes that were applied to printed material. In 1833, for instance, the taxes on paper, newspapers, and advertisements drove the prices of newspapers beyond the reach of the average working-class Briton. As Richard Altick

suggests, there were political as well as economic motivations for imposing
the taxes in the first place, and political and economic reasons for repealing
them. See his discussion of the drive to repeal or reduce these taxes that
began around the time of the first Reform Bill in 1832 and culminated in
their repeal in 1855 and 1861 (*The English Common Reader*, 331, 339–42,
348–57).

3 Elizabeth Eisenstein's book *The Printing Press as an Agent of Change* provides
the classic account of the impact of technological change on the publishing
trade. For an interesting take on the nineteenth century, see John Feather's
'Technology and the Book in the Nineteenth Century.'

4 Altick, *The English Common Reader*, 357.

5 F.O. Matthiessen and Kenneth B. Murdock, eds., *The Notebooks of Henry James*,
180.

6 Altick, *The English Common Reader*, 1.

7 Other scholars have taken up Altick's challenge to produce 'large-scale work
on the reading public as a social phrenomenon' (*The English Common Reader*
8). Indeed, the 1980s and 1990s have seen a remarkable increase in interest
in this area. The 1998 edition of Altick's *The English Common Reader* contains
a supplemental bibliography that demonstrates the range and number of
scholars working in it.

8 Altick rightly notes that increased leisure time is also an important factor in
the increased demand for reading material, but I do not think it is as important as increasing the pool of readers. Individuals who cannot read will find
other ways of filling their leisure time, and of spending their discretionary
income. It is through an increase in the numbers of readers that reading
becomes a choice among activities for leisure time pursuits.

9 While Altick and Rose provide excellent overviews of literacy issues in the
nineteenth century, David Vincent's *Literacy and Popular Culture* provides a
more comprehensive account and it remains the standard work on literacy
in England in this period.

10 Several good studies survey the different types of schools available for
nineteenth-century children. See, for example, R.D. Anderson, *Education
and Opportunity in Victorian Scotland*; W.B. Stephens, *Education, Literacy and
Society, 1830–1870*; and Mary Stuart, *The Education of the People*. Jonathan
Rose disputes some of the findings about working-class students' experience
of schools, but he agrees that, on the whole, 'These schools certainly were
dismal places in the early nineteenth century' (*The Intellectual Life of the
British Working Classes*, 148).

11 The standard test was the ability of the individual to sign his or her name in
the marriage register, but, as Altick notes, this tells us very little about

whether they could read or at what level they could read. Thus, he concludes, 'the Victorian literacy figures that come down to us are, for one reason or another, very unsatisfactory evidence of how many people were able to read' (*The English Common Reader*, 170). It would therefore be reasonable to assume that fewer people were functionally literate than the statistics tell us.

12 Altick, *The English Common Reader*, 166.

13 Altick, *The English Common Reader*, 170.

14 Altick suggests that the percentage increase in literacy rates was about the same in 1891 as it was in 1871. That is that the rate for males had increased by 11.3 per cent from 1851 to 1871 (from 69.3 to 80.6) and by 13.0 per cent in 1891 (from 80.6 to 93.6). A similar pattern held true for females (*The English Common Reader* 171). Altick also warns us to take these figures with a grain of salt, as the definition of literacy usually applied was not necessarily a reliable indicator of whether one could actually read. Nonetheless, most accounts of literacy rates in the nineteenth century indicate that there was a steady increase in the numbers who could read throughout the century, but that the 1870 Education Act did have an impact on functional literacy – that is, those who claimed to be literate post-1871 were often better able to read than those who claimed this status before universal elementary education was mandated.

15 Altick, *The English Common Reader*, 172.

16 Jonathan Rose notes, 'Between 1856 and 1859 roughly 3,800 state-aided primary schools ordered 902,926 reading lesson books and 163,512 arithmetic and math texts.' They also purchased '82,836 geography texts, plus 14,814 school atlases and 14,369 wall maps' (*The Intellectual Life of the British Working Classes* 347). His point here is to reveal how poorly served these schools were in areas like sciences and geography, and this is true. But my point is that even prior to the 1870 Acts, publishers sold a substantial number of school texts, the majority of which were devoted to reading. The material in the reading texts was usually English literature. The numbers of textbooks sold post-1870 steadily increased, though Simon Eliot notes that the dramatic increase in sales did not materialize as expected in the 1870s. There are several reasons for this, including the fact that it took at least a decade to phase in universal elementary education, and that statistics do not necessarily indicate the size of a print run. See *Some Patterns and Trends in British Publishing 1880–1919*, 47–8.

17 Nigel Cross makes the point about readership, stating that 'by the 1890s there was a general belief that the 1870 Education Act ... had trebled the reading population and created a monstrous half-educated audience avid for new, lighter, cheaper reading matter' (*The Common Writer*, 205). Cross goes on to

say that 'there is still some controversy about the input of the Board schools [established by the 1870 Act] on the numbers and tastes of new readers' (206). He suggests, rightly, that an 'increase in disposable income' also had a significant impact on the growth of popular journalism. However, as I stated in note 7 above, I think that increasing the numbers of readers through education is the more significant factor.

18 On the demise of Mudie's see Guinevere L. Griest's *Mudie's Circulating Library and the Victorian Novel.*

19 Although the category 'author' was not officially designated as a separate profession until the 1861 census, authors were included within a broader group of educated persons broken down by occupation in the 1841 census. Thus we can get a good idea of the growth in numbers of writers who self-identified as professionals by comparing the census data from 1841, 1861, 1881, and 1911. In 1841, 167 individuals were listed in the category 'Authors, editors, journalists'; in 1861 the number listed in the category 'Author' was 687; in 1881 the number in this category was 3434; and by 1911 the number had grown to 13,786 (W.J. Reader, *Professional Men*, 147, and appendix 1, p. 211, 'Increase of Professional Occupations 1841–81–1911').

20 Most commentators accept that the professionalization of authorship began in the eighteenth century, and as a consequence of this belief, there are many good studies of the subject in that century. General studies that include brief discussions of the eighteenth century are John Feather's *A History of British Publishing* and Victor Bonham-Carter's *Authors by Profession.* Good studies with a specific eighteenth-century focus include Anne Goldgar's *Impolite Learning*, Alvin Kernan's *Printing Technology, Letters and Samuel Johnson*, and Catherine Gallagher's *Nobody's Story.*

21 Reader, *Professional Men*, 9.

22 Feather, *A History of British Publishing*, 102. Feather's emphasis is on literary writers, but the situation was similar for authors working in other disciplines.

23 Cross, *The Common Writer*, 90.

24 Cross, *The Common Writer*, 91.

25 Cross, *The Common Writer*, 93.

26 *The Compact Edition of the Oxford English Dictionary*, 1427.

27 For a full account of the dates on which different groups were accorded status as a profession, see Reader's study *Professional Men*, particularly chapter 10, 'Professional Men Established,' 146–66.

28 Reader, *Professional Men*, 1.

29 Walter Besant, *The Pen and the Book*, 22. His argument is that by the time of his writing, 1899, literature has achieved this standing, but his discussion details the struggles that authors went through to get there.

30 Besant, *The Pen and the Book*, 20. Besant goes on to enumerate the ways in which authors have attained these three conditions; tellingly, he cites the founding and growth of the Society of Authors as central to the fact that 'literature is growing independent.' He also lists the various distinctions authors have been given (and declined) and he makes clear that by great prizes he means financial rewards and control of their literary property (20–3).

31 Reader, *Professional Men* 163. Such organizations are typically self-governing. They determine the qualifications necessary for entry into the profession and the means for obtaining them. They also develop methods of certifying and regulating membership, and act as the public voice for their members. The various features of professional organizations are discussed in Reader's book. Though the specifics vary according to the organizations, the functions named here are common to most nineteenth-century professional associations or societies. By extension, the social status of the members of an occupation also rises with the founding of a professional organization.

32 The Society for the Encouragement of Learning existed from 1736 to 1748 and the Society for British Authors from 1843 to 1849. The first group was formed in part to enable authors to issue books independent of booksellers or printers. The second group was formed principally to deal with the issue of copyright, particularly the issue of international copyright. For an account of both of these organizations, see Bonham-Carter, *Authors by Profession* vol. 1, especially 28–9 and 80–9.

33 Quoted in Bonham-Carter, *Authors by Profession*, 1: 89.

34 Bonham-Carter, *Authors by Profession*, 1: 119.

35 In all of these he succeeded: among the writers who accepted positions were Matthew Arnold for poetry; Thomas Huxley for science; Wilkie Collins and Charlotte Yonge for fiction; and Cardinal Manning for theology. His great coup was securing the Poet Laureate – Alfred Tennyson – as president. Bonham-Carter gives a good account of Besant's activities securing leading writers and ushering the Society into being. See *Authors by Profession*, 1: 119–25.

36 The constitution set out the terms of membership: full members of the Society had to have written at least one full-length work. Associate members were aspiring writers. Fees for memberships were set and the rules and regulations of the Society were spelled out in detail. Women were initially excluded from membership; though they were eventually admitted in 1889, they were not made as welcome as men. See Tuchman, *Edging Women Out*, 151, 173–4.

37 Besant, *The Pen and the Book*, 16–17. This phrase comes from Besant's how-to book on writing as a profession that provides wonderful insights into his views on authorship as a profession.

38 For a fine account of the history of copyright in Britain see John Feather, *Publishing, Piracy and Politics*. See also Benjamin Kaplan, *An Unhurried View of Copyright;* David Saunders, *Authorship and Copyright*; Martha Woodmansee and Peter Jaszi, *The Construction of Authorship*; Mark Rose, *Authors and Owners*; and Catherine Seville, *Literary Copyright Reform in Early Victorian England.*

39 Feather, *Publishing, Piracy and Politics*, 64.

40 Feather, *Publishing, Piracy and Politics*, 67.

41 Mark Rose's *Authors and Owners* provides an excellent account of not only the evolution of copyright law in the eighteenth century, but also the ramifications of the laws on the concepts of intellectual property and on the literary field itself. His account of the importance of this case is particularly good. See chapter 6, 'Literary Property Determined' (92–112).

42 Mark Rose, *Authors and Owners*, 111–12.

43 Quoted in Seville, *Literary Copyright Reform in Early Victorian England*, 154.

44 Feather's account of Wordsworth's involvement in the copyright debates of the late 1830s is excellent. See *Publishing, Piracy and Politics*, chapter 5, 'The Reform of the Law 1800–1842' (122–48).

45 But it also had far-reaching consequences, for, as Seville argues, 'The Act formed the basis of modern copyright law: it provided the groundwork for the domestic aspects of the 1911 Act' (*Literary Copyright Reform in Early Victorian England*, 6). Seville provides a fascinating account of the personages and tactics involved in the debates that surrounded the five long years it took to reach a compromise that permitted the 1842 Act to be passed.

46 Feather, *Publishing, Piracy and Politics*, 177.

47 Besant, 'The Author,' 1.

48 Feather, *Publishing, Piracy and Politics*, 203.

49 I do not mean to suggest that all writers, or even the majority of those who put pen to paper in an effort to become published authors, benefited equally because of these changes. My point here is that these changes made it possible for writers to have more control of their property, thereby enhancing the opportunities for them to earn decent livings from their work.

50 Besant, *The Pen and the Book*, vi–vii.

51 Eliot, *Some Patterns and Trends in British Publishing 1880–1919*, tables C3–C5 contain figures from the *Publishers' Circular* that itemize titles published by subject classification. Similar increases were noted in other subjects: 648 titles published in Geography, Travel, History, and Biography in 1880 and 960 in 1900; Poetry and Drama titles numbered 187 in 1880 and 370 in 1900. Some subjects saw a marked decrease –

Religion went from 975 in 1880 to 708 in 1900 – but most showed an upward trend over the last quarter of the century, albeit a small one in many cases. Table E3 contains the information on journals and magazines; table F6 contains the information on employment in the various trades. I have tried to compare these figures over the same twenty-year period – 1880–1900 – but the employment figures were provided on a slightly different time frame – the second year of each decade (starting from 1841 and then every ten years to 1921).

52 Altick, *The English Common Reader*, 395.

53 Altick, *The English Common Reader*, 394–6.

54 Paul Delany, *Literature, Money and the Market*, 98.

55 Altick, *The English Common Reader*, 315.

56 Jonathan Rose notes 'J.M. Dent's Everyman's Library, begun in 1906, would be the largest, most handsome, and most coherently edited series of cheap classics, though it was certainly not the first' (*The Intellectual Life of the British Working Classes*, 131). One of the predecessor he cites is W.T. Stead's Penny Poets and Penny Novels series, of which by 'October 1897,' as Rose says, 'there were sixty volumes of Penny Poets with 5,276,000 copies in print, and about 9 million copies of ninety Penny Novels' (131). These figures give a sense of the size of the demand for cheap reading material, a demand that did not come solely from working-class readers. For further details on the Everyman's Library series see J.M. Dent, *The House of Dent 1888–1938* and John R. Turner, 'The Camelot Series, Everyman's Library, and Ernest Rhys.' For a broader view of cheap reprint series, see Richard Altick, 'From Aldine to Everyman.' 1989.

57 Altick, *The English Common Reader*, 359.

58 Jonathan Rose, *The Intellectual Life of the British Working Classes*, 322–31. The *Gem* and the *Magnet* made their appearances in 1907 and 1908, respectively. The Amalgamated Press published them weekly and readers paid a penny for an issue.

59 I will go into this in greater depth in chapter 6.

60 Delany, *Literature, Money and the Market*, 98. Delany's largely positive account of the market changes are in contrast to N.N. Feltes, for example, whose Marxist account in *Literary Capital and the Late Victorian Novel* presents a very different, and less laudatory, version of what he terms the 'distinctively capitalist organization of book production' (xi) that prevailed in the British publishing world by 1900.

61 David Finkelstein, *The House of Blackwood*, 18. Finkelstein briefly discusses how the Blackwood firm managed this on 18 and 24ff.

2. A.P. Watt: Professional Literary Agent

1 Hilary Rubinstein, 'A.P. Watt: The First Hundred Years,' 2354. The date seems to me a bit arbitrary. It is unlikely that Watt was actually established as an agent before 1878; he himself comments in 1892 that he had been acting as an agent for some fourteen years (note the interview in the *Bookman*) and that would make 1878 the year he began as an agent, not 1875.

2 W. Robertson Nicoll, 'A.P. Watt: The Great Napoleon of the Realms of Print.'

3 The facts here are obscure and accounts often vary according to the commentator. For instance, James Hepburn claims that Watt moved from a bookseller's in Edinburgh to join Strahan (*The Author's Empty Purse*, 54). However, Patricia Thomas Srebrnik, in her biography of Strahan, suggests that Watt may still have lived in Glasgow immediately prior to joining Strahan in London (*Alexander Strahan*, 230n94). The important points, however, are not in dispute: that Watt's marriage to Strahan's sister gave him an entry into the London publishing world and that he arrived in London in 1871 as a reader for Strahan's.

4 An item in the 'Trade Changes' section of the *Publishers' Circular* for 15 April 1876 states, 'Mr A.P. Watt has now become a partner in the firm of Strahan and Co.' Srebrnik concurs with this date (see 159).

5 A notice under the heading 'Trade Changes' in the *Publishers' Circular* for 18 January 1881 states that Watt is now an advertising and literary agent.

6 F.W., 'An Interview with Mr. A.P. Watt,' 20.

7 See Hepburn, *The Author's Empty Purse*, 54.

8 F.W., 'An Interview with Mr. A.P. Watt,' 21.

9 This is a partial list of publishers with whom Watt did business. The lists of publishers in the various collections of letters to Watt are more extensive and demonstrate just how widespread Watt's contacts were.

10 Quoted in D.S. Higgins, *Rider Haggard*, 214.

11 David Finkelstein, *The House of Blackwood*, 131.

12 Ford Madox Ford, *Return to Yesterday*, 64.

13 Arnold Bennett, *The Truth about an Author*, 60.

14 Janet Wolff, *The Social Production of Art*, 45. It is also important to acknowledge the role played by publishers' readers such as Geraldine Jewsbury and George Meredith. They functioned as de facto agents for publishers, reading material as it came in and providing detailed advice to the publishers about the publication merits of texts. Their editorial advice was often relayed to authors and in some cases a relationship between reader and author existed in which the publisher's reader became editorial advisor to the author.

Edward Garnett performed this valuable service for many authors including Joseph Conrad, as I will discuss in chapter 7. See Jeanne Fahenstock's article 'Geraldine Jewsbury: The Power of the Publisher's Reader' for an interesting account of Jewsbury's career.

15 'Literary Agents,' *Author* 9. 10 (10 March 1899): 232.

16 Raymond Savage, 'The Authors' Agent' 6.

17 F.W., 'An Interview with Mr. A.P. Watt,' 21.

18 Albert Curtis Brown, '"The Commercialisation of Literature" and the Literary Agent,' 359.

19 Wells's letters to Watt in both the Berg Collection (New York Public Library) and the A.P. Watt Records, (University of North Carolina, Chapel Hill) are filled with such cautions and requests that the publisher's books be made available to him so that he could keep a close eye on the figures.

20 Heinemann, 'The Hardships of Publishing,' 779.

21 Spencer C. Blackett, 'The Middleman in Publishing.' Blackett's letter was written in response to William Heinemann's article 'The Middleman As Viewed by a Publisher,' which was published in the *Athenaeum* the same month and from which I quoted in the Introduction.

22 Marie Belloc Lowndes, 'The Author's Agent.'

23 Nicoll, 'A.P. Watt: The Great Napoleon of the Realms of Print,' 127.

24 On this point see Bonham-Carter, *Authors by Profession*, 1: 133, 169.

25 Henry Holt, 'The Commercialization of Literature,' 583.

26 Curtis Brown, '"The Commercialisation of Literature" and the Literary Agent,' 357.

27 Curtis Brown, '"The Commercialisation of Literature" and the Literary Agent,' 358.

28 We need to be careful when examining Watt's client lists as presented in his own advertising efforts because they are somewhat misleading. They name clients for whom he did minimal work – Hardy and Oliphant, for example – or who moved on to other agents – Bennett and Wells, for example – alongside those for whom he did a great deal of work – Collins and MacDonald, for example. The lists' obvious purpose was to convince writers and publishers of Watt's importance and prominence, and listing famous individuals, even if he did little work for them, enhanced his credibility. Interestingly, the AP Watt web site continues this practice of listing famous authors as clients, including Arnold Bennett, who moved to the Pinker Agency very early in his career and remained a loyal client of Pinker's well into the 1920s.

29 Harry Ricketts, *The Unforgiving Minute*, 150.

30 Martin Seymour-Smith, *Rudyard Kipling*, 124.

31 Seymour-Smith, *Rudyard Kipling*, 124. Prior to the meeting with Watt, Kipling had already published a substantial number of short stories, many of which appeared in the six volumes of stories that he published for the Indian Railway Library with A.G. Wheeler and Company. The stories that appeared in these volumes, according to Seymour-Smith, put 'Kipling on the international map' (91), thereby contributing to his status as a rising literary star.

32 Quoted in Ricketts, *The Unforgiving Minute*, 157.

33 James Hepburn says that Watt 'served as Besant's own agent from 1884 onwards' (*The Author's Empty Purse*, 43).

34 D.S. Higgins indicates in his biography of Haggard that in January of 1886 Watt's first major task as Haggard's agent was to untangle a contract between Haggard and J. and R. Maxwell that gave 'them the right to bring out cheap editions of all [Haggard's] books written within five years' (*Rider Haggard*, 89).

35 Peter McDonald notes that Doyle began using the Watt agency in late 1890, a fact borne out by the Watt-Doyle correspondence in both the Berg Collection in New York and the Watt Records at Chapel Hill (*Literary Culture and Publishing Practice, 1880–1914*, 138).

36 The Watt Records at Chapel Hill contain contracts and correspondence from the majority of Watt's clients during the period under scrutiny in this book. When one scrolls through the index to materials, Yeats and Strindberg are joined by other experimental writers such as T.S. Eliot, Henry James, and D.H. Lawrence, making it appear as if Watt did take an interest in a larger number of experimental writers than my argument suggests. But the amount of actual work his firm performed for these writers is limited – two contracts related to Eliot's edited volume of Kipling's verses; one contract for a volume of Henry James stories; and two contracts for Lawrence stories. In the cases of James and Lawrence, they were both represented for longer periods of time by Watt's younger rival, James B. Pinker, though Lawrence eventually parted company with Pinker on acrimonious terms.

37 Despite their protestations about the deleterious effects of agents' growing influence, by 1910 most publishers used agents extensively to procure new material, and if the agent had a reputation for supplying material that sold well, his clients were at a distinct advantage when compared to an unknown author making a direct submission.

3. Establishing the Agency Model: George MacDonald and Watt

1 More detailed accounts of his early years may be found in the various biographies that have been written about MacDonald. See particularly the books

by Kathy Triggs (*The Stars and the Stillness*) and Richard H. Reis (*George MacDonald*). The biography written by MacDonald's son Greville, *George MacDonald and His Wife*, is also a very useful source of information, since in it Greville often quotes from his father's letters, thereby providing his father's thoughts in his own words.

2 Kathy Triggs notes that his education was interrupted for a year in 1842–3, likely because his family's financial difficulties made it impossible for them to send him even a small amount of financial support – in the form of oatmeal and potatoes which would provide his food while at university – and possibly because he needed to work to help support his family during this bleak period (*The Stars and the Stillness*, 17–19).

3 The poem was written in 1851, but not published until 1855 when Longmans agreed to take it.

4 Triggs, *The Stars and the Stillness*, 58.

5 Triggs, *The Stars and the Stillness*, 58. Money, or to be more precise the lack of it, was a recurring theme throughout the MacDonalds' life together.

6 Triggs quotes the reviewer from the *Athenaeum* who complained that the tale was 'a confusedly furnished, second-hand symbol shop' (*The Stars and the Stillness*, 73). Other reviews were more positive.

7 MacDonald remained a professor until 1867, when he resigned his post because of the introduction of external examinations, a practice that went against his belief that the examinations would foster competition and that competition was inimical to the development of each individual's talents.

8 Triggs says that MacDonald could earn a half-guinea per lecture (*The Stars and the Stillness*, 77).

9 Greville MacDonald, *George MacDonald and His Wife*, 313.

10 The variety of MacDonald's output not only during this period, but throughout his lifetime, has frequently prompted his critics to group together similar works for ease of discussion. We have his children's tales ('The Light Princess,' *The Princess and Curdie*, and *The Princess and the Goblin*, for example), his Scottish stories (*David Elginblood*, *Alec Forbes*, and *Robert Falconer*, for example), and his English novels (*Guild Court* and *Paul Faber, Surgeon*, for example).

11 In fact, this was the second novel that Smith, Elder rejected; the first was called *Seekers and Finders*, which MacDonald destroyed after it was rejected.

12 This collection contains the story 'The Little Princess,' which is still in print today. It is one of the stories that justifies MacDonald's reputation as a writer of excellent children's literature.

13 Patricia Srebrnik, in her admirable cultural biography *Alexander Strahan*, cites MacDonald's first appearance in a Strahan publication as 1866, when

MacDonald's *Annals of a Quiet Neighbourhood* were serialized in the *Sunday Magazine*. See 69. Macdonald continued to place works with other publishing houses, most notably Hurst and Blackett, who published *Annals of a Quiet Neighbourhood* in 1866, *Guild Court* and *Robert Falconer* in 1868, and a number of other novels throughout the 1870s, including *Wilfrid Cumbermeade* (1872), *The Marquis of Lossie* (1877), and *Sir Gibbie* (1879).

14 MacDonald was initially to be paid £600 a year for this post, but he agreed to continue in it in 1871 without a salary. The journal was renamed *Good Things for the Young* in 1872 and MacDonald stayed on as unpaid editor of the journal until 1873.

15 From the early 1870s onwards, Strahan encountered various difficulties as a publisher. He endured enforced retirement from Strahan and Company in 1872, and though he managed to hold on to some of his copyrights when he left the firm, and though some clients, including MacDonald, continued to publish with Strahan, his fortunes declined throughout the 1870s and 1880s and from 1884 onwards he published very little of note. On the later stage of Strahan's career, see Srebrnik, *Alexander Strahan: Victorian Publisher*, 110ff.

16 James Hepburn, *The Author's Empty Purse*, 52.

17 Greville MacDonald's biography of his parents outlines the circumstances of George MacDonald's move to Italy in 1877 and his settling in Bordighera. See *George MacDonald and His Wife*, 474ff.

18 See Greville MacDonald, *George MacDonald and His Wife*, 506ff. on this.

19 There is uncertainty over the exact starting date of their business arrangements – the Watt firm dates it as 1875, Hepburn at about 1878, MacDonald's letters as 1882. The 1882 date comes from a postscript to a letter MacDonald sent Messrs A.M. Black on 18 July 1882. MacDonald says: 'My friend Mr. Watt, who manages all my publishing business, has already written to you' (Glenn Edward Sadler, ed., *An Expression of Character: The Letters of George MacDonald*, 306).

20 Hepburn, in *The Author's Empty Purse*, 52, mentions this article, though he slightly mistranscribes it. This quotation is in *Bookman* 1 (October 1891–March 1892):20.

21 MacDonald accepted the money offered because he was in desperate financial straits again and because he had already had difficulty placing this novel, with even Strahan initially turning it down. See Triggs, *The Stars and the Stillness*, 132.

22 The only reference to the sale of *Paul Faber* to Hurst and Blackett that I have unearthed is a casual reference in a letter MacDonald wrote to a Mr Ireland on 20 July 1878. In the letter he refers to 'a book coming out in October,' which is clearly *Paul Faber*, and a few lines later he mentions that 'Hurst and

Blackett gave [him] £50 more' than he would have otherwise received because it hadn't been serialized in a magazine before publication in book form. See Sadler, *An Expression of Character*, 285.

23 Over the almost thirty years that Watt represented MacDonald, he placed two volumes of sermons, at least ten novels, a couple of volumes of poetry, several children's stories, and a great number of articles and literary criticism. From 1879 onwards, MacDonald in fact published some twenty-seven different works in book form, all of which flowed through Watt's office. This doesn't include the collected works that Watt and Greville MacDonald arranged in 1903.

24 One measure of proof for this assertion is the fact that while religious writing had made up 20.3 per cent of titles published between 1814 and 1846, by 1890 it accounted for only 9.5 per cent of titles published. With less demand, it is probable that the sums commanded by religious writing in the 1880s and 1890s also fell. See Simon Eliot, *Some Patterns and Trends in British Publishing 1800–1919*, table C4, 128.

25 Greville MacDonald, *George MacDonald and His Wife*, 185. This quotation comes from a longer letter in which MacDonald makes clear his belief in Christ and his desire to live a life that would be worthy of the sacrifice that Christ made.

26 Trustworthiness was a quality in short supply in other budding agents like A.M. Burroughs, who eventually served a jail term for fraud. Hepburn briefly outlines Burroughs's career as an agent, including his trial for fraud in 1912. Burroughs's son was also tried and found guilty of mishandling a client's property (*The Author's Empty Purse*, 50–1).

27 Typed letter dated 27 October 1884. A.P. Watt agency to George MacDonald. A.P. Watt Records, Chapel Hill.

28 Handwritten letter dated 22 October 1884. C.J. Longman to A.P. Watt. A.P. Watt Records, Chapel Hill.

29 Catherine Peters in her biography of Wilkie Collins says that Watt became Collins's literary agent in 1881, taking the place of Collins's close friend and financial advisor Charles Ward, who died that year (*The King of Inventors*, 393). Watt became Besant's agent in 1884.

30 Eliot, *Some Patterns and Trends in British Publishing 1880–1919*, 14.

31 Reis, *George MacDonald*, 17.

32 Triggs writes that 'Since the early 1860s MacDonald had taken no money for his preaching' (*The Stars and the Stillness*, 124). Thus, a potential source of income went completely untapped, though the effort and time that it took MacDonald to write and deliver a sermon clearly stole time from work that might be sold.

33 Greville MacDonald, *George MacDonald and His Wife*, 1.

34 Reis, *George MacDonald*, 17.

35 Greville MacDonald, *George MacDonald and His Wife*, 428.

36 Greville tells us: 'My father's repertory included *Hamlet, Tom Hood*, the *Lyrics of Tennyson, King Lear, Macbeth* and *Milton*; but the favourite subject with American audiences was Robert Burns' (*George MacDonald and His Wife*, 425). There is a lingering conception among his readership that MacDonald was otherworldly. David Robb notes, 'not only did MacDonald tend to view the mundane world, which is what we are principally aware of, as insubstantial, transitory and dreamlike ... but he also regarded it as lifeless and dull.' But Robb cautions, 'it is possible to exaggerate MacDonald's other-worldliness.' (*George MacDonald*, 22).

37 Greville MacDonald, *George MacDonald and His Wife*, 419.

38 Greville MacDonald, *George MacDonald and His Wife*, 425.

39 There does not seem to be a complete bibliography of George Mac-Donald's works. For dating of his works, therefore, I have relied on *George MacDonald, a Bibliographical Catalog and Record*, which was compiled by Mary Nance Jordan. It contains a reprint of a centennial bibliography of George MacDonald by John Malcolm Bulloch. Jordan's work was privately published in Fairfax, Virginia for the Marion E. Wade Collection, Wheaton College, Wheaton, Illinois, 1984. It is based on the collections of bound volumes in three special libraries: the Marion E. Wade Collection, Wheaton College, Wheaton, Illinois, the Beinecke Rare Book and Manuscript Library, Yale University, and the Houghton Library, Harvard University.

40 Handwritten Memorandum of Agreement dated November 1889. Berg Collection. Interestingly, as Catherine Peters has noted, Collins had from the mid-1850s insisted on retaining ownership of his copyrights, starting with the publication of *Hide and Seek* in 1854, so it is ironic that Watt, as his literary executor, would sell his copyrights in order to generate immediate income for Collins's heirs (*The King of Inventors*, 140).

41 This story is based on MacDonald's experience of the Italian earthquake that rocked his home in 1887.

42 Handwritten letter dated 16 January 1889. Blackie and Son to A.P. Watt. A.P. Watt Records, Chapel Hill.

43 Handwritten letter dated 20 May 1889. L.T. Meade, editor of *Atalanta* magazine, to A.P. Watt. A.P. Watt Records, Chapel Hill.

44 Handwritten undated Memorandum of Agreement between Earl Lytton and Macmillan and Company. Berg Collection.

45 Lytton had originally published the work under the name Owen Meredith in 1863.

46 From its first issue, the *Author*'s editorial stance on copyright was unwavering: it had to be reserved to the writer of the work. Any other handling of copyright was considered tantamount to theft of property. See, for example, 'Objects of the Society' in the first issue of the *Author*, in which two of the three objects dealt directly with copyright:
2. The consolidation and amendment of the laws of Domestic Copyright.
3. The promotion of international copyright. (*Author* 1. 1 [15 May 1891]:24).

47 Typed Memorandum of Agreement dated 30 April 1895 between Robert Morley and Henry and Company. A.P. Watt Records, Chapel Hill.

48 Typed Memorandum of Agreement dated 6 February 1896 between Roberts and J. Mentz and Company. Berg Collection.

49 Typed Memorandum of Agreement dated 29 July 1896 between MacDonald and Longmans, Green. A.P. Watt Records, Chapel Hill.

50 Typed Memorandum of Agreement dated 31 March 1897 between MacDonald and Hurst and Blackett. A.P. Watt Records, Chapel Hill.

51 The Chace Act's benefits to British writers were not as extensive as hoped. As James West shows, it 'did end the worst forms of international piracy, but it was a source of irritation to many British and American publishers' ('The Chace Act and Anglo-American Literary Relations' 311) who were required to ensure that British texts that were likely to sell in the American market were identified early enough to allow American versions to be printed in America (and deposited for copyright) at the same time as British editions in order to safeguard their claim to American copyright. As West further notes, the Act really only benefited established authors whose track record made it likely that new works would sell in sufficient numbers to warrant a separate American edition published in compliance with Chace Act requirements.

52 Collected works of various Victorian writers fitted nicely into this category. Thomas Hardy, for instance, retained most of his copyrights and was thus able to benefit directly in the form of royalties from later publications of his collected works.

53 Handwritten letter dated 1 June 1894. Cassell to A.P. Watt. A.P. Watt Records, Chapel Hill.

54 Typed Memorandum of Agreement dated 8 April 1895 between George MacDonald and Wells Gardner, Darton and Company. A.P. Watt Records, Chapel Hill.

55 Typed Memorandum of Agreement dated 17 February 1903 between Dr Greville MacDonald and Chatto and Windus. A.P. Watt Records, Chapel Hill.

56 Typed letter dated 12 November 1897. George MacDonald to A.P. Watt. A.P. Watt Records, Chapel Hill.

57 Typed Memorandum of Agreement dated 8 October 1890 between W. Clark Russell and Messrs Trischler and Company. Berg Collection.

58 Typed Memorandum of Agreement dated 8 April 1895 between George MacDonald and Wells Gardner, Darton and Company. A.P. Watt Records, Chapel Hill.

59 Handwritten letter dated 11 May 1887. H. Rider Haggard to A.P. Watt. Berg Collection.

60 It is evident from reading Wells's correspondence with Watt and other agents that his relations with all of his publishers went through difficult patches. Matthew Skelton's 'H.G. Wells, Kipps, and the House of Macmillan' presents an interesting account of Wells's relations with the Macmillans.

61 Peter D. McDonald, *British Literary Culture and Publishing Practice 1880–1914*, 2.

62 McDonald, *British Literary Culture and Publishing Practice 1880–1914*, 6. McDonald's book provides a subtle and sophisticated analysis of the print culture field of the 1890s and much of his argument I find persuasive. However, I am more interested in the gray areas that existed between the two poles that McDonald explores – the positions occupied by what he calls the purists and the profiteers – and how the agent worked between the two poles as well as in these gray areas than I am in staking out positions in the way that McDonald does.

63 Brenda Silver's work on Virginia Woolf as a twentieth-century literary icon is instructive here, as it makes a convincing case for the appropriation of a literary figure by a public which has likely never read the work produced by the author. See *Virginia Woolf: Icon.*

64 Cross, *The Common Writer*, 208.

65 Triggs says that during MacDonald's last lecture tour in 1891 he gave 'forty-eight lectures in fifty-eight days' (*The Stars and the Stillness*, 152).

66 I borrow the term from Triggs's account of this family activity (*The Stars and the Stillness*, 130).

67 Sadler, *An Expression of Character*, 312.

68 Sadler, *An Expression of Character*, 355.

69 Typed notes of a conversation with Mr and Mrs Kipling and A.S. Watt, 24 January 1929. Berg Collection.

70 Handwritten letter dated 11 December 1906. Marie Corelli to A.P. Watt. Berg Collection.

71 Handwritten letter dated 31 December 1906. Marie Corelli to A.P. Watt. Berg Collection.

72 Quoted in Finkelstein, *The House of Blackwood*, 131.

73 For example, he provided information to his friend Robertson Nicoll for the article on the literary agent that appeared in the 'London Letter' published in the American version of the *Bookman*.

74 Walter Besant, letter dated 7 March 1887 in *Letters to A.P. Watt*, 4.

4. Testing the Agency Model: 'Lucas Malet' and Watt

1 I will refer to Mary Harrison as Lucas Malet, the nom-de-plume she used throughout her writing career.

2 Patricia Srebrnik, 'The Re-subjection of "Lucas Malet,"' 194–5.

3 Susan Chitty, *The Beast and the Monk*, 269.

4 Perhaps the most significant public act of rebellion was her conversion to Roman Catholicism in 1902. Such an act would have outraged her father, who was a strong opponent of the Church of Rome.

5 Srebrnik, 'The Re-subjection of "Lucas Malet,"' 195.

6 Srebrnik says, 'Mary came increasingly to treat herself as an invalid, a role which entailed frequent trips to the Continent without her husband. William Harrison's stipend was insufficient to pay for these journeys, and so, ostensibly for the sole purpose of supplementing their income, his wife began to write fiction' ('The Re-subjection of "Lucas Malet,"' 195).

7 Srebrnik, 'The Re-subjection of "Lucas Malet,"' 198. Srebrnik does point out Malet's ambivalence 'concerning those "literary mothers" … in the fact that she searched for them in the paternal rather than maternal line.' The link to her father is thus covert, but nonetheless evident.

8 C.E. Oldham, 'Two Novelists on One Theme,' quoted in Srebrnik, The Re-subjection of "Lucas Malet,"' 198. It should be noted that other reviews were somewhat less positive, with the *Spectator*'s reviewer, for example, remarking, 'hardly a great book, but within a somewhat narrow boundary, the writer's workmanship is so intellectually effective, that if anyone were to speak of the novel as great, we should know what was meant, and should agree with the meaning' ('Recent Novels'). This review is also quoted by Patricia Lorimer Lundberg in her biography of Malet, '*An Inward Necessity*,' (146). Lundberg's biography is an invaluable source of information and I am indebted to it and to Lundberg for generously sharing information about Malet with me prior to its publication.

9 Lundberg states that Malet 'concluded the deal with Sonnenschein on August 16 for 550 copies of a three-volume edition paying her £150, to be followed by a one-volume six-schilling edition paying 20% and a two-schilling edition paying 10% royalties' ('*An Inward Necessity*,' 137).

10 Janet E. Courtney, 'A Novelist of the 'Nineties,' 231. I am grateful to Talia Schaffer for pointing out this article and for her generosity in sharing her own work on Malet.

11 *The History of Sir Richard Calmady*, her most famous work, is available on the World Wide Web through the University of Indiana's Victorian Women Writers Project, at http://www.indiana.edu/~letrs/vwwp/malet/calmady.html. Furthermore, Birmingham University Press published a new edition of this novel, edited by Talia Schaffer, in 2003.

12 Since both A.P. Watt and his son Alexander Strahan Watt handled Malet's career, I will look at both men's interactions with Malet.

13 Srebrnik, 'Lucas Malet,' 179.

14 Srebrnik, 'Lucas Malet,' 180.

15 The Dorset County Museum Thomas Hardy Collection contains five handwritten letters from Malet to Hardy, including what appears to be the first letter she wrote to him, which is dated 22 February 1989. None of these letters comments about her difficulties with Kegan Paul. However, it is clear from the letters that Hardy visited Malet in London in April of 1892, indicating that a friendship existed which would have prompted Hardy to offer Malet advice.

16 Richard Little Purdy and Michael Millgate, eds., *The Collected Letters of Thomas Hardy*, 7:120.

17 Hardy wrote to Watt on 10 January 1892: 'I enclose herewith the receipt, and have to thank you for saving me a considerable deal of trouble in arranging for the simultaneous publication of the story ["On the Western Circuit"] here and abroad. By your management the pecuniary result is bettered, without mulcting any one' (Purdy and Millgate, *The Collected Letters of Thomas Hardy*, 1: 251).

18 Malet writes to Hardy, 'I remember, when I had the great pleasure of seeing you in London this spring, you mentioned Mr. Watt – the literary agent – to me, and told me that I should do well to put my books with his hands. Would you kindly let me have his address – a note of introduction to him should, of course, be invaluable, but I hardly like to ask you to write it.' Handwritten letter dated 19 September 1892. Mary St Leger Harrison to Thomas Hardy Thomas Hardy Collection, Dorset County Museum.

19 Typed letter dated 24 November 1896. Marked copy. A.P. Watt to P. Wigram of Swan Sonnenschein and Company. A.P. Watt Records, Chapel Hill.

20 Handwritten letter dated 25 November 1896. Swan Sonnenschein and Company. Ltd. to A.P. Watt. A.P. Watt Records, Chapel Hill.

21 Handwritten contract dated 5 February 1885. A.P. Watt Records, Chapel Hill.

22 Typed contract dated 5 June 1899. A.P. Watt Records, Chapel Hill.

23 Typed contract dated 5 June 1899. A.P. Watt Records, Chapel Hill. A second contract dated 8 January apparently supersedes this one, but the copyright

implications of these clauses remain essentially unchanged, though the
financial terms spelled out in clause 1 do change considerably.

24　Typed letter dated 16 March 1906. Marked copy. A.S. Watt to A.M.S.
Methuen. A.P. Watt Records, Chapel Hill.

25　Typed letter dated 20 February 1900. A.P. Watt to A.M.S. Methuen. A.P. Watt
Records, Chapel Hill.

26　Typed letter dated 14 March 1900. A.P. Watt to A.M.S Methuen. A.P. Watt
Records, Chapel Hill.

27　Typed letter 15 July 1910. Copy for file. Unsigned, but from Watt Agency
[likely Alec Watt] to Mrs Harrison. A.P. Watt Records, Chapel Hill.

28　The contracts for her other books that are in the Watt Records at Chapel
Hill bear out Watt's consistent protection of her ownership of her own copyrights, with only a few exceptions.

29　As a measure of the revenue Malet garnered from her novels early in
her career, Lundberg notes that 'Watt paid Mrs Harrison £7,659 for 1896'
largely from royalties from *The Wages of Sin* and *The Carissima,* and
at several points in her biography of Malet states that '£10,000 [was what]
the family believed Malet earned on *Calmady*' ('*An Inward Necessity,*' 184,
247).

30　Lundberg, '*An Inward Necessity,*' 297.

31　The fact that Hutchinson had contracted to publish *Damaris* in 1902 is noted
in a 14 March 1902 letter from A.P. Watt to Malet, in which Watt points out
that Hutchinson had contracted for a book of 'about the same length as "Sir
Richard."' Typed letter dated 14 March 1902. A.P. Watt to Mrs Harrison
[Mary St Leger Harrison]. A.P. Watt Records, Chapel Hill.

32　Malet complained about Methuen's treatment of her work, particularly
about what she saw as his failure to advertise it properly. For instance, she
wrote Watt in 1902 that 'The advertising of the Gateless Barrier, and, since
the beginning of December, that of the Calmady book, has been so
unsatisfactory, that we certainly cannot contemplate future [struck out,
replaced by undecipherable handwritten emendation, likely the word
further] worry under that head.' Typed letter dated 11 February 1902.
Marked copy. Mary St Leger Harrison to A.P. Watt. A.P. Watt Records,
Chapel Hill.

33　Typed letter dated 14 February 1906. A.S. Watt to Mrs Harrison. A.P. Watt
Records, Chapel Hill.

34　Typed letter dated 19 February 1906. M. St Leger Harrison to A.S. Watt. A.P.
Watt Records, Chapel Hill.

35　Typed letter dated 2 April 1906. A.M.S. Methuen to A.S. Watt. A.P. Watt
Records, Chapel Hill.

36 The correspondence in the Malet-Watt Records at Chapel Hill attests to the complexity involved in this task, but there is nothing in this correspondence to explain why Newnes chose to publish only *Richard Calmady*.

37 Contracts for each of these may be found in the Malet-Watt Records. See contract dated 15 November 1907 between Mrs Mary St Leger Harrison and Messrs Thomas Nelson and Sons for publication of *The Wages of Sin*; contract dated 15 November 1907 between Mrs Mary St Leger Harrison and Messrs Thomas Nelson and Sons for *The Gateless Barrier*; contract dated 23 March 1908 between Mrs Harrison and the Joint Committee of Henry Frowde and Hodder and Stoughton for the publication of *Little Peter*.

38 Her royalty for *Colonel Enderby's Wife* was only 12½ per cent with thirteen copies being counted as twelve – a far cry from the royalties she had been earning on other works, even when price and format are taken into consideration. For instance, she received 'a royalty of 30% for the first 20,000 copies, [and] 33⅓% above 20,000 copies' from John Murray in 1909 for *The Score* (Lundberg, '*An Inward Necessity*,' 314).

39 These were *A Counsel of Perfection*, which appeared in *Murray's Magazine* (January–June 1888), and *The Wages of Sin*, which was serialized in the *Universal Review* (September 1889–December 1890). Two later novels were also serialized: *The Tutor's Story* (1916) appeared in the *Cornhill* (January–November 1916), and her 1920 novel *A Tall Villa* appeared in the *Times Weekly Edition* (25 July to 26 September 1919) (Lundberg, '*An Inward Necessity*,' 470–1).

40 As throughout this study, I use the term 'serial' here in a broad sense. It refers both to the more traditional type of serial publication pioneered in Britain in the early nineteenth century, which saw reprints of works for specific audiences (such as *Robinson Crusoe* in its many formats), and to the newer type of serial publication made possible in the late nineteenth century by the proliferation of syndicates such as Tillotson and Sons in England or S.S. McClure in America, which placed a variety of material – articles, short stories, novels by instalments – in newspapers and magazines located throughout the country and abroad. Watt was quick to exploit opportunities afforded to his clients by syndicates. Graham Law's *Serializing Fiction in the Victorian Press* provides an interesting insight into how syndicates worked in Britain at this time; chapters 3 and 4 deal specifically with Tillotson and its rivals. For an excellent account of syndication in America during this period, see Charles Johanningsmeier's *Fiction and the American Literary Marketplace*.

41 The contract is dated 7 July 1899 and it seems likely that the novel she ought to have given them was *The Gateless Barrier*.

42 Typed letter dated 13 May 1915. Marked copy. A.S. Watt to Mrs Harrison.
A.P. Watt Records, Chapel Hill. Malet was to have received £800 for the two
stories, and in the end did receive £400 for the one story she did submit,
though the magazine did not publish it.

43 Typed letter dated 14 May 1915. Marked copy. Mary St Leger Harrison to
A.S. Watt. A.P. Watt Records, Chapel Hill. Lundberg notes that the contract
was to have paid Malet £800 for the two stories and that she received £400
for 'Da Silva's Widow' despite the magazine's failure to publish it. ('*An
Inward Necessity*,' 358).

44 According to the bibliography of Malet's writing included by Lundberg in
her biography of Malet, it appears that Malet wrote fourteen short stories,
with only seven of them appearing in magazines. The others appeared in
one of her two collections of short stories – *Da Silva's Widow* (which contained nine stories) and *The Score* (which contained two stories). One story is
listed as a 'lost manuscript – which presumably means the story was not published – and two stories only appeared in magazine form (Lundberg, '*An
Inward Necessity*' 496).

45 Malet entered into an agreement with H.H. Kennedy to dramatize *The Wages
of Sin*, but the contract in the Malet-Watt records at Chapel Hill has 'cancelled' handwritten across it. Typed contract dated 15 November 1901
between Mrs Mary St Leger Harrison ('Lucas Malet') and H.A. Kennedy for
the dramatization of *The Wages of Sin*. A.P. Watt Records, Chapel Hill.

46 Typed contract dated 1 August 1926. A.P. Watt Records, Chapel Hill.
Lundberg details the events surrounding what she terms 'The sad tale of the
aborted drama.' In her narration of the complex sequence of events that
unfolded over a two-year period she illustrates the investment – in time and
emotions – that Malet put into it at the expense of her other work ('*An
Inward Necessity*,' 428–30).

47 The A.P. Watt Records, Chapel Hill contain correspondence and contracts
pertaining to these transactions. For example, in 1916, the Marchese Guido
Skrra Di Cassano contracted with Malet the 'exclusive license to produce a
novel written by [Malet] entitled "THE WAGES OF SIN" in moving picture
films, and to exhibit the said films and to lease the said films … in the
United Kingdom of Great Britain and Ireland and to lease or sell the said
films in the Colonies and Dependencies of the said United Kingdom
and all foreign countries in which cinematographic rights in the said work
are now existing.' Typed contract dated 29 March 1916. A.P. Watt Records,
Chapel Hill.

48 The A.P. Watt Records, Chapel Hill contain correspondence and
contracts pertaining to the translations of several of Malet's novels.

49 Typed letter dated 11 February 1902. Marked copy. Mary St Leger Harrison to A.P. Watt. A.P. Watt Records, Chapel Hill.

50 Typed letter dated 12 March 1902. Marked copy. Mary St Leger Harrison to Alec Watt. A.P. Watt Records, Chapel Hill.

51 Typed letter dated 16 March 1902. Marked copy. Mary St Leger Harrison to A.P. Watt. A.P. Watt Records, Chapel Hill.

52 A signed agreement, dated 31 July 1909, between Malet and the Watt agency can be found in the A.P. Watt Records, Chapel Hill. It is the standard agency contract, containing four clauses that spell out the business arrangements between Malet and A.P. Watt and Son.

53 The sad tale of Malet's finances is well told by Lundberg. It is clear that Malet's financial decisions – sinking the earnings from *Richard Calmady* into her country home The Orchard, holding the mortgage on her sister's home The Keys, supporting her cousin/adopted daughter Gabriel/Lillian Vallings during her training for a career as an opera singer, and so on – were ill advised at best and tragic at worst. Lundberg charts this downward spiral from chapter 11 onwards in the biography.

54 Lundberg, '*An Inward Necessity*,' 313–14.

55 Lundberg states that Malet's death certificate '"relates to the person described in policy of the Law Union and Rock Ins. Co dated 21 May 1915 as Mary St Leger Harrison, The Orchard, Eversley, Hampshire, Widow, aged 62." Her lawyers had insisted on it to cover advances they made her during the war' ('*An Inward Necessity*,' 444).

56 Typed letter dated 9 July 1915. Field, Roscoe and Company to A.S. Watt A.P. Watt Records, Chapel Hill.

57 As Hilary Rubinstein points out, A.P. Watt and Son was a family business right up to the 1960s, with Alec, Hansard, and W.P. (William), the sons of A.P. Watt, joining the firm, and then A.P.'s grandsons, Ronald (son of Alec) and Peter (son of W.P.). See 'A.P. Watt: The First Hundred Years,' 23–54.

58 Typed letter dated 26 April 1922. Field, Roscoe and Company to W.P. Watt. A.P. Watt Records, Chapel Hill.

59 I take this price from Lundberg, who notes that it might have been '£2040 or £2170, depending on how one interprets the Roscoe Fields ledger spanning from 1914 to 1924' ('*An Inward Necessity*,' 388).

60 Lundberg, '*An Inward Necessity*,' 388.

61 Typed letter dated 10 January 1924. Marked excerpt. Mrs Harrison to W.P. Watt. A.P. Watt Records, Chapel Hill.

62 Typed letter dated 10 January 1924. Mr Emery of Field, Roscoe to A.S. Watt. A.P. Watt Records, Chapel Hill.

63 Lundberg notes that Malet arranged with Watt to pay her £3 per thousand words delivered by her to Watt and that the money was to be counted against the publisher's advance. This is likely the weekly allowance that Watt provided her ('*An Inward Necessity*,' 413).

64 Srebrnik, 'Lucas Malet,' 184.

65 Lundberg notes that in Malet's application for a grant in 1927, she asked that Alec Watt be consulted as to her financial state, and when Gabrielle Vallings made an application to the fund on her own behalf in 1932, Lundberg says, 'Once again the Royal Literary Fund found itself in receipt of letters from Watt' and others ('*An Inward Necessity*,' 430, 454).

66 Srebrnik, 'Lucas Malet,' 184.

67 Schaffer and Srebrnik make persuasive arguments about other reasons for Malet's marginal status, relating it to the critical reception of her work, in particular the resistance to women writing about the subjects that Malet did; they also argue that Malet's fiction was marginalized by subsequent critics who failed to acknowledge her affinity with aestheticism and modernism and who saw her instead as a woman author who wrote middlebrow texts for women readers. See Schaffer's 'Connoisseurship and Concealment in *Sir Richard Calmady*: Lucas Malet's Strategic Aestheticism' and 'Malet the Obscure'; and Srebrnik's 'The Re-subjection of "Lucas Malet"' and 'Lucas Malet.'

68 For example, her first novel, *Mrs Lorimer: A Sketch in Black and White*, published in 1882, was reprinted in December 1882 and March 1883, and its publisher Macmillan brought out new editions in one volume in 1883, 1884, 1886, 1891, and 1910. *The Wages of Sin* had excellent sales, with almost the entire first run of a thousand copies selling out in the first month, prompting Swan Sonnenschein to reprint the novel. In fact, sales continued well, with the novel 'soar[ing] to first place in book sales' and passing the three-thousand-copies-sold mark by early 1892 (Lundberg, '*An Inward Necessity*,' 92, 156).

69 There is one short stretch – from the publication of a volume of short stories, *The Score* (1909), to the novel *Adrian Savage: A Novel* (1911) – where she did manage the book-a-year pace, but apart from this there were usually gaps of at least a year and usually longer between the appearance of new works.

70 One measure of the book's success is the fact that by early 1902 it had already gone through five editions. In a letter to Watt dated 11 February 1902, Malet remarks on the fact that 'the Calmady book continues to go fairly well' and asks Watt to 'Insist upon a reasonable amount of advertising when the 6th edition is announced.' Typed letter dated 11 February 1902. Marked copy. Mary St Leger Harrison to A.P. Watt. A.P. Watt Records, Chapel Hill.

71 Typed letter dated 11 February 1902. Marked copy. Mary St Leger Harrison
    to A.P. Watt. A.P. Watt Records, Chapel Hill.
72 Typed letter dated 12 March 1902. Marked copy. Mary St Leger Harrison to
    A.S. Watt. A.P. Watt Records, Chapel Hill.
73 Typed letter dated 16 March 1902. Marked copy. Mary St Leger Harrison to
    A.P. Watt. A.P. Watt Records, Chapel Hill.
74 She was willing to make editorial changes to work that had been accepted
    for publication, though very reluctantly. For example, when they were
    preparing the cheap edition of *The History of Sir Richard Calmady* for the
    American market, Dodd, Mead wrote to Watt: 'Since this special edition is to
    be sold at a very low price and be widely distributed among old and young, it
    will be necessary to make some few alterations in the text. This is a condition
    of the sale.' Typed letter dated 11 October 1905. Dodd, Mead and Company
    to A.P. Watt. A.P. Watt Records, Chapel Hill. Initially Malet refused to alter
    the text, writing to Watt: 'I regret to say I absolutely refuse to permit the
    Calmady book to be altered in any respect. If Messrs. Dodd Mead made it
    worth my while to do so I might be willing to cut out certain chapters and so
    shorten it.' Quoted in letter dated 7 November 1906. A.P. Watt to Dodd
    Mead. Letter marked copy b.3. A.P. Watt Records, Chapel Hill. Eventually,
    the specific alterations requested by the publisher were made, though obvi-
    ously Malet would have preferred to avoid them.
75 Srebrnik, 'Lucas Malet,' 178.
76 Srebrnik, 'Lucas Malet,' 179.
77 Lundberg, '*An Inward Necessity*,' 184, 185.
78 Lundberg, '*An Inward Necessity*,' 186.
79 Lundberg, '*An Inward Necessity*,' 204.
80 Quoted in Margaret Beetham, *A Magazine of Her Own?* 89.
81 Beetham, *A Magazine of Her Own?* 89–90.
82 Typed letter dated 1 July 1904. A.P. Watt to Percy Cox. A.P. Watt Records,
    Chapel Hill.
83 Stephen Gwynn, 'Sir Richard Calmady,' 480.
84 Gwynn, 'Sir Richard Calmady,' 483.
85 Gwynn, 'Sir Richard Calmady,' 487.
86 Srebrnik, 'Lucas Malet,' 182.
87 Schaffer, 'Malet the Obscure,' 242–3.
88 Schaffer, 'Malet the Obscure,' 199. I find Schaffer's argument compelling.
    Malet is not included in most of the recently published work on women writ-
    ers of the 1880s and 1890s, and Schaffer's argument effectively explains why.
    Malet was by turns a social commentator along the lines of New Woman writ-
    ers, without the politics being explicit; she was a female aesthete, without the

critics acknowledging that such a seeming oxymoron was possible; and her work was consciously modernist in areas such as viewpoint, narration, and depiction of sexuality, without being overtly avant-garde in the manner of May Sinclair or Virginia Woolf.

89 Schaffer, "Malet the Obscure,' 200.

90 This list of techniques is found in the introduction to Schaffer and Psomiades *Women and British Aestheticism*, 16. However, it is fairly generic in terms of the features that are customarily applied to modernist writers such as James Joyce, T.S. Eliot, and Virginia Woolf. The obvious difference is that here they are applied to Malet, a writer whose work is not included in the modernist canon.

91 Schaffer, 'Malet the Obscure,' 243.

92 Elisabeth Jay, *Mrs. Oliphant*, 245.

93 McDonald uses this term to refer to the younger generation of writers emerging in the 1890s, who coalesced initially around the Rhymers' Club and sought to contest the entrenched literary establishment by trying, 'as Yeats puts it, to "purify poetry of all that is not poetry,"' and who also stood against 'the seduction of money or social prestige' which they saw as the root of the demise of literature at the end of the nineteenth century (*British Literary Culture and Publishing Practice 1880–1914*, 16). McDonald provides a nicely nuanced argument that explores not only the positions the purists took on aesthetic and commercial matters, but also the contradictions within these positions.

94 It is true that some women were admitted to 'clubland,' but few enough, when one considers the number of women writers of the period, to make evident that gender was a consideration in determining whose work was acceptable and whose was not. One of the magazines that was a much sought after venue for publication by the 'purists' was *Blackwood's Magazine* (known by insiders and aspirants alike as *Maga*). Mrs Oliphant's long association with the magazine is well known, which makes it particularly ironic that her fiction was so lightly regarded by the very men who wished to have their work join hers in *Maga*'s pages.

95 Peter Keating, *The Haunted Study*, 175.

96 Dorothy Mermin, *Godiva's Ride*, xv. Though Mermin's book deals specifically with women's writing in the period 1830–80, her reason for using 1880 as a cut-off date reflects a strongly held critical view that women's writing was of lesser stature in the 1880s and 1890s.

97 There are a number of fine studies that argue for the central role of women writers, especially fiction writers, in the eighteenth and through the nineteenth century. In addition to Mermin, see especially Catherine Gallagher, *Nobody's Story*; Janet Todd, *The Sign of Angellica*; and Deirdre David, *Intellectual Women and Victorian Patriarchy*.

98 Stubbs's comments – 'The eighteen eighties and 'nineties saw the beginnings of a major revision in thinking about women and about sex, a process in which literature played an important part. Novelists in particular were moving towards new and radical images of women' – are echoed in various ways in the other studies and make clear the fact that women writers were challenging cultural norms of the period in their fiction. See Patricia Stubbs, *Women and Fiction*; Carolyn Christensen Nelson, *British Women Fiction Writers of the 1890s*; Ann L. Ardis, *New Women, New Novels*; Lyn Pickett, *The 'Improper' Feminine*; and Jane Eldridge Miller, *Rebel Women*.

99 Gaye Tuchman, *Edging Women Out*, 8. While I agree with this point of their argument, I am less inclined to accept other conclusions because of the small sample on which they base their generalizations.

100 Murray's judgment of the novel's 'painful subject' – 'it is very gruesome, and the details of the murder are especially so' – gives one the sense that he did not really approve of the subject matter, though the fact that he published it indicates that he thought there was a market for such subjects. Typed letter dated 25 March 1909. John Murray to A.P. Watt A.P. Watt Records, Chapel Hill.

101 Apart from the *Queen* magazine, Watt also placed or attempted to place her work with magazines such as the *Metropolitan* in New York, whose original audience had been New York's theatre-goers, though it underwent several format changes, including a phase in which it hired John Reed as a political reporter.

102 Malet's work continued to be reviewed in major publications such as the *Spectator*, the *Times Literary Supplement*, and the *Bookman*, to name but three, but it is noteworthy that her work did not appear in, nor was it reviewed by, leading modernist journals such as the *Egoist*, in whose pages the literary canon of modernism was being presented and debated.

103 Schaffer, 'Malet the Obscure' 199.

5. The Second Wave of Agenting: J.B. Pinker

1 It is not possible to provide an accurate count of the number of agents working in Britain during this period, since the profession was unregulated, many individuals called themselves agents who were not agents in the way that Watt established the office, and many who performed agenting services did not call themselves agents. Examination of entries in various trade publications (*Author, Publishers' Circular, Publisher & Bookseller*) reveals upwards of two dozen individuals calling themselves agents working during the 1890s.

2 From volume 3, number 8 onwards of the *Author*, one of the warnings at the beginning of each volume was about use of agents. The warning read: 'LITERARY AGENTS – Be very careful. You cannot be too careful as to the person whom you appoint as your agent. You place property almost unreservedly in his hands. Your only safety is in consulting the society, or some friend who has had personal experience of the agent.' This warning eventually became item 4 in the series of fourteen items published at the front of each number of the journal.

3 Besant's admiration for Watt is evident in his letter published in *Letters to A.P. Watt*. Besant writes in 1892: 'It is not enough to say that you have been my agent. I must also say that during these years I have never had any anxiety at all about my affairs' (*Letters to A.P. Watt* [1894] 6).

4 Among the more prominent agents I will not be discussing are William Morris Colles, who began the Authors' Syndicate in about 1889, J. Eveleigh Nash, who became an agent in 1898, and Elisabeth Marbury, the first female agent, who was an American specializing in drama.

5 He had been Sunday editor for the newspaper from 1894 to 1898 (Hepburn, *The Author's Empty Purse*, 65). Curtis Brown alludes to this briefly in his memoir *Contacts*, when he says that he 'arrived in London, as correspondent of the old 'New York Press'(1).

6 Brown, *Contacts*, 2.

7 Brown, *Contacts*, 1.

8 This story is told by Brown in *Contacts*, 1–2. Hepburn also repeats a variation of it in *The Author's Empty Purse*, 65.

9 For further information on Curtis Brown's career, see *Contacts*. His son Spencer joined the firm in 1927 to run the Play Department. He became manager of the firm in 1936 and eventually inherited it from his father. I am grateful to Stephanie Thwaites of Curtis Brown (London) for supplying me with this information.

10 Unlike Brown and Watt, Pinker did not open a North American office during his lifetime, preferring to deal with New York agents such as Elisabeth Marbury and Paul Reynolds. His sons opened a New York office in 1926.

11 Pinker's success in the management of these writers' careers varied. Henry James left Watt for Pinker, finding in Pinker a more satisfactory agent, one who recognized, in the words of James's biographer Leon Edel, that 'his wares required special handling.' Edel goes on to say, 'Wise, shrewd, tactful, friendly [Pinker] reviewed James's confused copyrights, a heavy accumulation of literary properties representing thirty-five years of continuous toil; he found new publishers; he reopened old relations. James spoke of "the germs of a new career" as Pinker began to place his work' (*Henry James* 4: 337).

Pinker was able to arrange for the publication of the collected works of Henry James, thereby accomplishing a long-cherished goal of James as well as bringing the writer a substantial sum of money. However, others, including Joyce and Lawrence, complained to friends about what they saw as Pinker's failures to handle their work as well as they wished.

12 Some scholars believe that J.B. Pinker was, like Watt, a Scot. This is a line taken by Frederick Karl, who refers to Pinker as a Scotsmen in several places, notably in his introduction and the listing of Conrad's correspondents in volume 2 of *The Collected Letters of Joseph Conrad*, xxiii, xxxiii. Jeffrey Meyers, in his biography of Conrad, also makes the assertion that Pinker was born in Scotland. See *Joseph Conrad: A Biography*, 204. Elsewhere, Karl refers to Pinker as being Jewish. There appears to be no foundation for this assertion. Indeed, in my correspondence with two of the children of Pinker's daughter Mary Oenone, both stated that family history revealed no evidence of the Pinkers as being Jewish, and they stated that in fact their mother had told them that their family roots were Welsh, though there was no documentary evidence in their possession to support that claim. I am particularly grateful to J.B. Pinker's granddaughter, Valerie Pinker, for information about her grandfather's early years. Her account of his background contradicts the line taken by previous scholars, but given her access to family records and lore, it is likely more accurate than some of the previous speculations.

13 James Hepburn, ed., *Letters of Arnold Bennett*, vol. 1 'Letters to J.B. Pinker,' 22. Hepburn's claim that Pinker worked as a clerk is corroborated by information Valerie Pinker obtained from the Librarian at the Museum in Docklands which states that 'JB was appointed as Supernumerary on 1st May, 1886, in the Engineer's Dept.' of the East and West India Dock Company. Typed Letter Valerie Pinker to Mary Ann Gillies dated 20 December 2006.

14 E-mail correspondence with Valerie Pinker, 28 February 2003.

15 In *The Author's Empty Purse* Hepburn does not name the publishing firm and I have been unable to unearth its name.

16 Hepburn, *Letters of Arnold Bennett* 1: 23.

17 Quoted in Hepburn, *The Author's Empty Purse*, 94.

18 Handwritten letter dated 15 November 1912. Alice Williamson to J.B. Pinker. Berg Collection, New York Public Library.

19 Handwritten letter dated 1 November 1904. Alan Milne to J.B. Pinker. Berg Collection, New York Public Library. The substantial Pinker archive at Northwestern University and the extensive Pinker material in the Berg Collection contain many examples of clients' solicitations for and reactions to Pinker's opinions about their work.

20 A.D., 'An Interview with Mr. J.B. Pinker' 9.
21 A.D., 'An Interview with Mr. J.B. Pinker' 9–10.
22 A.D., 'An Interview with Mr. J.B. Pinker' 10.
23 A.D., 'An Interview with Mr. J.B. Pinker' 10.
24 This comes from the section of the journal entitled 'Agents,' which contains the names of many agents active in London. There is no indication of whether these were paid advertisements, but it is likely that agents paid the journal for their listing and also submitted the notices themselves (*The Literary Yearbook and Bookman's Directory*, 118).
25 *The Literary Yearbook and Bookman's Directory*, 119.
26 In time, Watt pursued each of these writers. H.G. Wells went to Watt for a period and then returned to Pinker, though he never really settled on one agent. Bennett, like many of Pinker's clients who eventually became successful, chose to stay with Pinker principally because he found his services so useful, but also because he had established a friendly relationship with Pinker.
27 The earliest letter from Bennett to Pinker that James Hepburn was able to uncover is dated 5 January 1901. See Hepburn, *Letters of Arnold Bennett*, 1: 31.
28 Peter McDonald, *Literary Culture and Publishing Practice 1880–1914*, 115. McDonald's account of Bennett's deliberate manipulation of the print culture field for his own benefit is perceptive and convincing. However, it is not his intention to examine how Pinker's assistance enabled Bennett to accomplish his aims: thus despite Bennett's clear acknowledgment of Pinker's importance to his career, Pinker features very little in McDonald's chapter on Bennett.
29 McDonald, *Literary Culture and Publishing Practice 1880–1914*, 88.
30 James Hepburn notes that Pinker subsidized Bennett for nine years, 'during several of those years lending him £50 a month irrespective of Bennett's income. He charged him five per cent. interest on a debt that stood above £1000 at one time or another' (*Letters of Arnold Bennett*, 1: 25).
31 For a fuller account of the Bennett-Pinker relationship, see Mary Ann Gillies, 'The Literary Agent and the Sequel.'
32 See his letter to Pinker in Hepburn, *Letters of Arnold Bennett*, 1: 31.
33 *Anna* had been refused by a number of publishers, in Britain and America, according to James Hepburn (*Letters of Arnold Bennett*, 1: 31n2). As Hepburn notes about the American publication, *Anna* 'was issued by McClure, Phillips in 1903' (*Letters of Arnold Bennett*, 1: 33n4). Hepburn does not provide the financial details for the transaction, nor have I been able to discover them from other sources.
34 Bennett states that 'Tillotson is already paying me £3/3/– a thousand for short stories' in a February 1904 letter written to Pinker (Hepburn, *Letters of*

Arnold Bennett, 1: 44). The stories were published in the following periodicals: 'The Lion's Share' in *Pall Mall Magazine* 39 (June 1907): 739–45; 'The Baby's Bath' in *Windsor* 25 (June 1907): 321–8; 'The Silent Brothers' in *Windsor* 26 (July 1907): 231–40.

35 The stories which had appeared in print are 'The Lion's Share'; 'The Baby's Bath'; 'The Silent Brothers'; 'Vera's First Christmas Adventure,' which had appeared as 'The Christmas Present' in *Black and White* (Christmas 1906): 28–32; 'Vera's Second Christmas Adventure,' which had appeared as 'The Christmas Dream' in *Bystander* 12 (5 December 1906): 504–8, 511; 'The Burglary' in *Novel* 6 (December 1907): 377–82 and previously published as 'The Christmas Eve Burglary' in *Strand* 32 (December 1906): 745–52. The publication dates and places are taken from Anita Miller's *Arnold Bennett: An Annotated Bibliography 1887–1932.* It is likely that several other stories in the collection also appeared in print prior to the volume's publication, but they are not listed in Miller's admirable bibliography, and James Hepburn's edition of Bennett's letters to Pinker contains no publication information on these stories, other than a mention of one, 'The Beginning of the New Year,' which was originally entitled 'A Five Towns Xmas' and 'whose periodical publication is unknown,' according to Hepburn (*Letters of Arnold Bennett,* 1: 84).

36 Hepburn, *Letters of Arnold Bennett,* 1: 83.

37 According to Miller's bibliography, two stories from this volume were placed with *McClure's* magazine in 1910 – 'The Nineteenth Hat' in *McClure's* 35 (May 1910): 51–6 and 'From One Generation to Another' in *McClure's* 35 (July 1910): 249–54. Bennett wrote to Pinker about *McClure's* publication of 'The Nineteenth Hat,' indicating that he had only a 'vague' recollection that the editor had told him they were going to publish it and suggesting to Pinker that Pinker would 'doubtless be able to convey to them that if they want to keep on intimate terms with their latest darling discovery they will pay £10 or 3¾d' for the story (Hepburn, *Letters of Arnold Bennett,* 1: 134).

38 According to Miller's bibliography, the seven stories that were republished were 'The Baby's Bath,' 'The Death of Simon Fuge,' 'The Lion's Share,' 'The Silent Brothers,' 'Beginning in the New Year,' 'From One Generation to Another,' and 'The Murder of the Mandarin.'

39 Hepburn, *Letters of Arnold Bennett,* 1: 50.

40 Hepburn, *Letters of Arnold Bennett,* 1: 50–1.

41 Hepburn, *Letters of Arnold Bennett,* 1: 33.

42 The *Windsor Magazine* was a rival to the leading periodicals of the day, including the *Strand, Pall Mall Magazine,* and *Pearson's Magazine,* and as such was the kind of publication in which Bennett was hoping that Pinker could

place his story. At £3/3 a thousand words, this story would have earned around £20.

43 Hepburn, *Letters of Arnold Bennett*, 1: 37.

44 Hepburn, *Letters of Arnold Bennett*, 1: 55.

45 In 1913, Bennett wrote to Pinker about the 'some little difficulty with the Income Tax people' over 'the enormous discrepancy between my present income and my income three or four years ago.' He declined to agree to their request that he give Pinker authority to disclose his transactions, opting to have Pinker send him 'a list of the net sums' which Pinker had 'received on my behalf from English sources during the years 1906, 1907, 1908, and 1909' (Hepburn, *Letters of Arnold Bennett*, 1: 194–5). On another occasion, Bennett asked Pinker to sublet a room to him for Miss Nerney's use in April 1918. See Hepburn, *Letters of Arnold Bennett*, 1: 263. The Bennett-Pinker letters are filled with comments about how to deal with publishers, so rather than selecting one or two for comment, I direct the reader to that collection.

46 The sum is deceptively modest, since Bennett spent much of his income and thus did not leave as large an estate as he might have, given his earnings in the latter part of his career.

47 Hepburn, *Letters of Arnold Bennett*, 1: 3.

48 Hepburn, *Letters of Arnold Bennett*, 1: 303.

49 Baroness Emmuska Orczy was a prolific author whose famous novel *The Scarlet Pimpernel* was a runaway bestseller and a highly popular stage drama and later a film. She also wrote detective fiction, creating several different series of detective stories. Orczy used both Watt's and Pinker's services. Pinker certainly was happy to place her commercial literature, having little difficulty finding a market for her detective fiction. Marie Belloc Lowndes was the sister of Hillaire Belloc. Her first story was published when she was only sixteen. Her most famous work, *The Lodger*, was a fictionalized account of Jack the Ripper. It, too, was a bestseller, with sales of over one million copies, and it was made into a popular film. She also published short stories, novels, and essays. She was one of the first members of the Woman Writers Suffrage League and was active in the movement to obtain suffrage for women.

50 '"*The Bookman*" Gallery: Mr. and Mrs Williamson,' 114.

51 '"*The Bookman*" Gallery: Mr. and Mrs Williamson,' 115.

52 West's biographers do not mention when she became Pinker's client, so I have based this date on the letters in the Berg Collection which begin in 1916.

53 Handwritten letter, no date (in folder marked 1918). Rebecca West to J.B. Pinker. Berg Collection.

54 Handwritten letter dated [n.d.] February 1922. Rebecca West to Mr Pinker (likely Ralph, who worked in the London office). Berg Collection.

55 West's biographers do not provide a chronology for her movement from Pinker to Peters, though in the *Selected Letters of Rebecca West* the biographical sketch of Peters indicates that she made this move (Bonnie Kime Scott, ed., *Selected Letters of Rebecca West*, xlii).

56 Correspondence between Pinker and Mansfield/Murry, and between Pinker and Richardson, shows that he carried out the same tasks for them as he did for his other modernist clients, though with little success in Richardson's case. Both the Berg Collection and the Pinker Papers at Northwestern University contain many letters dealing with Mansfield/Murry business, while the Berg contains five letters pertaining to Richardson's business.

57 Egerton's association with the Bodley Head press was important to her not only for the income it provided, but also for the status of being associated with one of the most important new presses of the 1890s. A good discussion of Egerton's relationship with John Lane and the Bodley Head can be found in Margaret D. Stetz's '*Keynotes*: A New Woman, Her Publisher, and Her Material.'

58 As some critics have noted, Egerton's work is often seen as helping to shape the concept of the 'New Woman.' See, for example, Margaret D. Stetz's 'Turning Points.'

59 Henry James produced a cruel caricature of Egerton in his 'The Death of the Lion,' for instance. This is mentioned by, among others, Ann L. Ardis in *New Women, New Novel*, 47.

60 Ardis, *New Women, New Novels*, 3.

61 Ardis, *New Women, New Novels*, 100.

62 'A.D. 'An Interview with Mr. J.B. Pinker,' 10.

63 Lawrence Rainey, *Institutions of Modernism*, 39.

64 Rainey, *Institutions of Modernism*, 74.

65 A.D., 'An Interview with Mr. J.B. Pinker,' 10.

66 The story of Lawrence's anger over what he perceived as Pinker's deceit in saying he had submitted *Women in Love* to American publishers, including B.W. Huebsch, when he had not sent the typescript to any American publishers has been told many times, and is repeated again in John Worthen's latest biography of Lawrence (*D.H. Lawrence: The Life of an Outsider*, 209–10). This account may not be accurate, as I will suggest later in the chapter.

67 Quoted in Joyce Wexler, *Who Paid for Modernism?* 95; and in Hepburn, *The Author's Empty Purse*, 57.

68 Letter to Edward Garnett 19 November 1912 (Boulton and Robertson, eds., *The Letters of D.H. Lawrence*, 1: 478).

69 Boulton and Robertson, *The Letters of D.H. Lawrence*, 2: 174.

70 Boulton and Robertson, *The Letters of D.H. Lawrence*, 2: 189.
71 Lawrence's letters reveal the work undertaken by Pinker on his behalf with respect to this novel, which was extensive. It appears that G.H. Doran had agreed to publish *The Rainbow* in America, but got cold feet and allowed the book to go to Huebsch, for instance. This situation strained relations between Doran and Pinker, with Doran writing to Pinker, 'I cannot but regret that you felt it necessary to write me your letter of October twenty eighth ... Had I published the Lawrence book it would have put me out of the running for many other authors and would have brought a reproach to our name that would not have been good for me or for you or for the authors represented by you to me.' Typed letter dated 12 November 1915. G.H. Doran to J.B. Pinker. Berg Collection. For an interesting account of the censorship of *The Rainbow* see Adam Parkes, *Modernism and the Theater of Censorship*.
72 Boulton and Robertson, *The Letters of D.H. Lawrence*, 2: 331.
73 Boulton and Robertson, *The Letters of D.H. Lawrence*, 2: 334.
74 Boulton and Robertson, *The Letters of D.H. Lawrence*, 3: 466.
75 Typed letter dated 11 July 1917. Little Brown and Company to J.B Pinker. Berg Collection.
76 Boulton and Robertson, *The Letters of D.H. Lawrence*, 3: 136.
77 Boulton and Robertson, *The Letters of D.H. Lawrence*, 3: 439.
78 For information on Pinker's actions on behalf of publication of *The Rainbow* see Boulton and Robertson, *The Letters of D.H. Lawrence*, 2: 464.
79 Wexler, *Who Paid for Modernism?* 93.
80 Boulton and Robertson, *The Letters of D.H. Lawrence*, 4: 220.
81 Rainey, *Institutions of Modernism* 74.
82 John Worthen, 'Lawrence and the "Expensive Edition Business,"' 113.
83 Worthen, 'Lawrence and the "Expensive Edition Business,"' 113.
84 Wexler, *Who Paid for Modernism?* 49–50.
85 Quoted in John Firth, 'James Pinker to James Joyce, 1915–1920,' 206. This is also the letter referred to by Joyce's biographer, Richard Ellmann, when he says 'Joyce followed Wells' advice by signing an agreement with Pinker' (*James Joyce*, 395).
86 Stuart Gilbert, ed., *Letters of James Joyce*, 1: 77.
87 The publishing history of *Dubliners* is complex, but the story is well known. Joyce had completed the collection of short stories in late 1905, and Richards had announced the publication of the collection in 'his *First Catalogue of Books Published by Grant Richards* ... [March] 1906,' but a dispute over deletions of passages from the text resulted in Richards's refusal to publish the book. As a result, Joyce sought, unsuccessfully, to place the book with another publisher – both Elkin Mathews and Maunsel and Company came

close to publishing it – but finally, Richards did publish it in 1914. A concise account of *Dubliners'* publishing history may be found in John J. Slocum and Herbert Cahoon, *A Bibliography of James Joyce*. The quotation above is from page 13.

88 As Richards noted in his 28 July 1917 letter to Pinker, his contract with Joyce for the publication of *Dubliners* gave him the 'option on his work for a period of years.' Pinker did attempt to renegotiate the terms, but the letters indicate that Richards held fast to the terms of the original agreement, though he permitted *A Portrait* to be published in England by the Egoist Press. Typed letter dated 28 July 1917. Grant Richards to J.B. Pinker. Berg Collection. Joyce comments on this agreement in a July 1917 letter to Harriet Weaver in which he explains why he has had to offer *Exiles* to Richards, who will publish it in the autumn of 1917. Stuart Gilbert, ed., *Letters of James Joyce*, 1: 106–7.

89 Stuart Gilbert, ed., *Letters of James Joyce*, 1: 87.

90 Stuart Gilbert, ed., *Letters of James Joyce*, 1: 87.

91 Stuart Gilbert, ed., *Letters of James Joyce*, 1: 89.

92 Stuart Gilbert, ed., *Letters of James Joyce*, 1: 91.

93 For instance, Pinker was also involved in arranging the publication of *Ulysses*, receiving instructions from Joyce in November of 1919 that Huebsch could have *Ulysses* 'for America on any terms he likes provided [the] text be not tampered with' (Stuart Gilbert, ed., *Letters of James Joyce*, vol. 1: 130). However, Huebsch did not in the end publish the novel and Pinker arranged the contract between Joyce and Harriet Weaver for its publication by the Egoist Press.

94 Rainey, *Institutions of Modernism*, 99. Rainey makes an interesting and convincing argument about the modernist strategy of using these three separate markets to consolidate both economic and cultural capital. Rainey's discussion of Sylvia Beach's three editions of *Ulysses* touches on this argument, though he most fully documents the strategy in the case of T.S. Eliot's *The Waste Land*. For Rainey's discussion of *Ulysses*, see chapter 2; for his discussion of *The Waste Land*, see chapter 3.

95 For details of the earlier editions of *Pomes Penyeach* see Slocum and Cahoon, *A Bibliography of James Joyce*, 35–40.

96 In 1932, Paul Leon wrote to Ralph Pinker, remarking that 'As regards the filming of *Ulysses* ... Would you please try and find out, definitely from your brother how the matter stands legally ... if these rights are really Mr Joyce's [Eric Pinker] could begin negotiations.' Joyce was not in favour of the proposal, so Leon promised 'to prevail upon Mr Joyce to alter his present attitude which is principally due to the fact that he cannot see how the idea can be realized' (Stuart Gilbert, ed., *Letters of James Joyce*, 1: 326).

97 Typed letter dated 24 May 1933. Unsigned, on company letterhead, to
Ralph Pinker. Berg Collection.

98 Scholars have usually dismissed Pinker's role in Joyce's career, with Richard
Ellmann's comments being typical: the arrangement 'did not work out very
well, for the agent was to have little luck in marketing such peculiar mer-
chandise; he did, however, serve Joyce as the amiable recipient of the innumerable letters about small matters which Joyce soon began painstakingly
to send him.' (*James Joyce* 395). John Firth offers a dissenting view: 'It is a
credit to Pinker's reputation as a literary agent, in view of Joyce's frustration
at not seeing his work quickly in print and in spite of the complexity of
Joyce's maneuverings among many minor publishers, both continental and
British, that he remained dedicated to his client's long-range interests, preferring to wait upon established houses and insisting on decent contracts
between author and publisher' ('James Pinker to James Joyce, 1915–1920,'
205). However, Ellmann's view is still more widely known and accepted
than Firth's.

99 'Literary Agents,' *Author* 2.11 (1892): 348.

100 May Sinclair, "Letter to the Editor.'

6. The Agent and 'Popular' Literature: Somerville and Ross and Pinker

1 Violet Martin assumed the pen name of Martin Ross – in part to honour her
family's heritage as the Martins of Ross. Throughout this chapter, the
women will be referred to by the names they used for their writing (Edith
Somerville as Somerville and Violet Martin as Ross) when they are being
discussed as writers. For the other facets of their lives, Somerville will be
referred to as Edith, and Martin as Martin, since that is the name that she
preferred her family and friends to use.

2 John Cronin, one of their biographers, notes that 'Edith had published a
short story in the *Argosy* and Violet had had an article on Poor Relief published in the *Irish Times*' (*Somerville and Ross*, 25). The other biographers
also note the two women's early forays into print as individuals. For example, Hilary Robinson notes, while detailing Somerville's early art training,
'In 1885 she had an illustrated essay on art studios accepted by *Cassell's Magazine of Art*' (*Somerville and Ross: A Critical Appreciation*, 13). Violet Powell, in
her biography, writes that Ross's *Irish Times* piece 'was followed by a series in
The World, signed "Martin Ross"' (*Irish Cousins*, 16). Maurice Collis claims
that the cousins' 'first collaboration was an article for the *Graphic* on palmis-
try dated 11 October 1886' (*Somerville and Ross*, 38).

3 Ann Owens Weekes, *Irish Women Writers*, 60.

4 Declan Kiberd, *Inventing Ireland*, 69.

5 These diary entries are quoted in Collis, *Somerville and Ross*, 45.

6 Collis, *Somerville and Ross*, 63.

7 Gifford Lewis, *Somerville and Ross: The World of the Irish R.M.*, 78.

8 Lewis, *Somerville and Ross: The World of the Irish R.M.*, 79.

9 They sold all rights to the novel to the Rev. Frederick Longbridge, a friend who had requested they write the story, for £35 (Collis, *Somerville and Ross*, 73).

10 Their journalism at this time consisted principally of illustrated travelogues, including one of the wine country of Bordeaux undertaken for the *Lady's Pictorial* in 1891 (Collis, *Somerville and Ross*, 93).

11 Collis, *Somerville and Ross*, 98.

12 Gifford Lewis claims that 'Financial solvency for them both depended on publicity – and publicity was what Martin, string-puller supreme, gave to the partnership' (*Somerville and Ross: The World of the Irish R.M.*, 76).

13 Collis, *Somerville and Ross*, 19.

14 Robinson, *Somerville and Ross: A Critical Appreciation*, 16.

15 Collis, *Somerville and Ross*, 120. Aylmer was Edith's brother; Egerton was her sister Hildegard's husband. He succeeded his father, Sir Joscelyn Coghill, becoming the 5th Baronet in 1905.

16 Collis, *Somerville and Ross*, 123.

17 Gifford Lewis, ed., *The Selected Letters of Somerville and Ross*, 164.

18 Lewis, *The Selected Letters of Somerville and Ross*, 203.

19 Handwritten letter dated 7 March 1893. Richard Bentley Publishers to Edith Somerville. Somerville and Ross Papers, Trinity College Library, Dublin.

20 Proof of this is found in the later correspondence about *Charlotte* they had with Pinker. Edith wrote to Pinker on 8 July 1899 about the possibility of a new edition of the novel being brought out. She says 'We sold *all* rights in it, & have often regretted having given it to such bad people. They only paid at the point of the bayonet the £250, and they never pushed it in the least.' Handwritten letter dated 8 July 1899. Edith Somerville to James B. Pinker. Somerville and Ross Papers, Trinity College Library, Dublin.

21 Robert Martin moved to London, where he earned a living as a journalist, songwriter, and singer. He earned the nickname "Ballyhooly" from the title of his most successful song. Martin visited her brother in London, and it is likely that he would have proved a well-placed contact for the women.

22 Lewis, *The Selected Letters of Somerville and Ross*, 93.

23 Lewis, *The Selected Letters of Somerville and Ross*, 138.

24 Edith knew Wilde's family and he met some of the Martin girls when they lived in Dublin, so Edith felt relatively at ease in calling on him about her

writing. Added to this, the *Woman's World* had published an article by the cousins in September of 1887 (Collis, *Somerville and Ross*, 48).

25 Quoted in Collis, *Somerville and Ross*, 48. The quotations come from a letter Edith wrote to Martin the day after her visit to Wilde.

26 Collis, *Somerville and Ross*, 49.

27 For instance, Mrs Braddon, who would have been known to them through Yates and the *World*, was a long-standing client of Watt. Others whom they had met also dealt with Watt, including W.B. Yeats and Lady Gregory, Thomas Hardy, and Andrew Lang.

28 Lewis, *The Selected Letters of Somerville and Ross*, 220. Martin much enjoyed Lang's treatment of her as an important writer, and took him with her on a visit to Blackwood's Edinburgh office, where she discussed the publication of *Beggars on Horseback*. See Lewis, *The Selected Letters of Somerville and Ross*, 219–20.

29 *Black and White* commissioned *Beggars on Horseback*, about a riding tour of North Wales, but cancelled the series, as Robinson notes, 'when one of the articles was lost in the post' It was eventually published in *Blackwood's Magazine*. The cousins also were commissioned by the *Lady's Pictorial* for a series of travelogues – Connemara in 1891, Bordeaux in 1892, and Denmark in 1893. See Robinson, *Somerville and Ross: A Critical Appreciation*, 73–84 for a discussion of these travel narratives.

30 Lewis, *The Selected Letters of Somerville and Ross*, 224.

31 Lewis, *The Selected Letters of Somerville and Ross*, 242–4.

32 Handwritten letter dated 9 August 1904. J.B. Pinker to Violet Martin. Somerville and Ross Papers, Trinity College Library, Dublin.

33 Handwritten letter dated 11 October 1899. Edith Somerville to J.B. Pinker. Somerville and Ross Papers, Trinity College Library, Dublin.

34 Handwritten letter dated 1 January 1904. Aylmer Somerville to J.B. Pinker. Somerville and Ross Papers, Trinity College Library, Dublin.

35 Handwritten letter dated 5 August 1902. Edith Somerville to J.B. Pinker. Somerville and Ross Papers, Trinity College Library, Dublin.

36 Handwritten letter dated 20 February 1903. Violet Martin to J.B. Pinker. Handwritten letter dated 23 March 1903. Violet Martin to J.B. Pinker. Somerville and Ross Papers, Trinity College Library, Dublin.

37 Cronin, *Somerville and Ross*, 68.

38 E. OE. Somerville and Martin Ross, 'Étaples,' 69–70.

39 Somerville and Ross, 'Étaples,' 72–3.

40 Handwritten letter dated 28 December 1915. Edith Somerville to J.B. Pinker. Somerville and Ross Papers, Trinity College Library, Dublin. Further indication of their strong friendship and loyalty to Pinker is provided by the fact that, as Collis notes, 'When it was reported to [the cousins] that Watson, the

editor of the *Badminton* who had published so many of their stories, had been "drunkenly impudent to Pinker, we ceased to write for him'" (Collis, *Somerville and Ross*, 132).

41 E. OE. Somerville and Martin Ross, *Irish Memories*, 238.

42 Boyd was a nationalist literary critic, and when he first published *Ireland's Literary Renaissance* one of his goals was to establish a new Irish literary canon that would be dominated by nationalists. His book was, and to some extents still is, highly influential in just the way he intended it to be.

43 Boyd, *Ireland's Literary Renaissance*, 385–6.

44 Kiberd, *Inventing Ireland*, 72.

45 Kiberd, *Inventing Ireland*, 77.

46 Somerville and Ross, *Irish Memories*, 236.

47 See handwritten letter dated 8 July 1899. Edith Somerville to J.B. Pinker. Somerville and Ross Papers, Trinity College Library Dublin. Edith writes: 'Do you know anything of Ward and Downey, the people who pubd our book "*The Real Charlotte*"? They were very slack about it, and tho' the book is still in demand they have not brought out any further editions or pushed the sale in any way. I have often been asked where it can be bought and I believe a cheap edition wld sell well – all the 3 vol. and the 6/– editions sold out. Do you think it wld be worth while seeing what they wld sell the copyright for and trying another edition.'

48 James H. Cahalan, *Double Visions*, 68.

49 Claire Denelle Cowert, 'Edith Somerville and Martin Ross,' 338.

50 Cahalan, *Double Visions*, 84.

51 Cahalan, *Double Visions*, 67.

52 Cahalan, *Double Visions*, 70–1.

53 Robinson, *Somerville and Ross: A Critical Appreciation*, 46.

54 Robinson, *Somerville and Ross: A Critical Appreciation*, 136.

55 Handwritten letter dated 8 March 1899. J.B. Pinker to Edith Somerville. Somerville and Ross Papers, Trinity College Library, Dublin.

56 Powell, *Irish Cousins*, 65.

57 Robinson, *Somerville and Ross: A Critical Appreciation*, 87.

58 For instance, in 1913, Longmans published a book 'By the brown bag' (a pseudonym) which apparently poached their territory, presenting not only plot devices and characters similar to the R.M. stories, but even taking chunks of text from their stories. They wrote to Longmans, 'It is nearly fourteen years since you published the "Experiences of an Irish R.M.", and we understand that you have sold nearly 40,000 copies of it. We should therefore have thought that those who read for your firm would have had ample opportunity of being acquainted with our work, and of recognising an

imitation so patent; and we should also have hoped that you, who have been so long our publisher and friend, would have hesitated to place before the public a book so hurtful to us personally, and detrimental to our interests, especially at a moment when we are engaged upon another volume of "R.M." stories for your firm.' Handwritten letter dated 7 June 1913. Edith Somerville and Violet Martin to Mr Longman. Somerville and Ross Papers, Trinity College Library, Dublin. The women also corresponded frequently and at length with Pinker over this imitation, taking his advice that they ask the Society of Authors about possibly seeking legal action against the writer of the stories on the basis of copyright infringement. Typical of their correspondence on this matter is this exchange: 'We now send you a further and amended list of identical and similar passages and hope that you will place them before the Counsel of the Society of Authors … and will draw to his attention the following facts.' It concluded, 'We feel we can safely leave it to you to point out the nature of the injury done to us. The jading of the public taste and the consequent depreciation of the market value of our books & c & c.' Handwritten letter dated 11 June 1913. Edith Somerville to J.B. Pinker. Somerville and Ross Papers, Trinity College Library, Dublin.

59 Handwritten letter dated 3 June 1908. Edith Somerville to J.B. Pinker. Somerville and Ross Papers, Trinity College Library, Dublin.

60 Cronin, *Somerville and Ross*, 68–9, 104.

61 Lewis, *The Selected Letters of Somerville and Ross*, 285.

62 Cahalan, *Double Visions*, 75.

63 Somerville and Ross, *Irish Memories*, 288. Cahalan also quotes from this passage (*Double Visions*, 69).

64 Handwritten postcard dated 3 September 1913. Edith Somerville to J.B. Pinker. Somerville and Ross Papers, Trinity College Library, Dublin.

65 Somerville and Ross, *Irish Memories*, 1–2.

66 Edith wrote to Pinker in 1900, delighted that the King and Queen had accepted a copy of *Some Experiences of an Irish R.M.* as a gift to read while they were resident in Ireland. Handwritten letter dated 16 April 1900. Edith Somerville to J.B. Pinker. Somerville and Ross Papers, Trinity College Library, Dublin.

67 Handwritten letter dated 13 November 1902. Edith Somerville to J.B. Pinker. Somerville and Ross Papers, Trinity College Library, Dublin.

68 Handwritten letter dated 1 February 1918. Edith Somerville to J.B. Pinker. Somerville and Ross Papers, Trinity College Library, Dublin.

69 Lewis, *The Selected Letters of Somerville and Ross*, 277. The reference to Miss Woolf is not to Virginia Woolf, who did not marry Leonard until 1912, and thus was still Virginia Stephen in 1905.

70 Lewis, *The Selected Letters of Somerville and Ross*, 278.
71 Handwritten letter dated 11 October 1906. J.B. Pinker to Violet Martin.
    Somerville and Ross Papers, Trinity College Library, Dublin.
72 There are some notable exceptions – Bennett springs to mind, for instance.
    But even such commercial authors as Marie Corelli, who was a frequent vic-
    tim of nasty press attacks, embraced this authorial paradox.

7. Building a Career: Joseph Conrad and Pinker

1 Joyce Wexler, *Who Paid for Modernism?* xii.
2 Peter McDonald's chapter on Conrad in *British Literary Culture and Publishing
   Practice 1880–1914* situates him within the framework of McDonald's central
   discussion about the purist vs profiteer positions available to writers in the
   1890s. I want to complicate the portrait McDonald provides by asserting that
   Conrad was as interested in the economic rewards he could obtain for his
   work as he was in the cultural capital it would bring him. As this chapter will
   demonstrate, Conrad was able to use Pinker to obtain the economic rewards
   and thus was free to claim lack of interest in becoming a popular author
   when in fact he desired to be one.
3 The major biographies – by Jocelyn Baines, Zdzislaw Nadjer, Frederick R.
   Karl, and Jeffrey Meyers – and literary studies of Conrad's work usually mention the Pinker-Conrad relationship briefly. However, there are a few studies
   that focus specifically on it. See, for example, Keith Carabine, 'Conrad,
   Pinker, and *Under Western Eyes: A Novel*'; Emily Dalgarno, 'Conrad, Pinker
   and the Writing of *The Secret Agent*'; Frederick R. Karl, 'Conrad and Pinker';
   and David Farmer, 'The Bibliographical Potential of a 20th Century Literary
   Agent's Archives: The Pinker Papers.'
4 Frederick R. Karl, *Joseph Conrad: The Three Lives*, 866.
5 Jeffrey Meyers, *Joseph Conrad: A Biography*, 206.
6 This letter is quoted in many of Conrad's biographies. See, for example,
   Karl, *Joseph Conrad: The Three Lives* 867; and Meyers, *Joseph Conrad: A
   Biography*, 346.
7 Conrad also transferred to him the role of father figure, which had been
   filled by his uncle Tadeusz Bobrowski up until his death in February 1894.
   This was a pattern that Conrad followed with his other literary mentors,
   including Pinker.
8 Karl discusses this briefly in his biography of Conrad. See Karl, *Joseph Conrad:
   The Three Lives*, 383.
9 Frederick R. Karl, ed., *The Collected Letters of Joseph Conrad*, 1: 312.
10 Karl, *The Collected Letters of Joseph Conrad*, 2: 195.

11 Karl, *The Collected Letters of Joseph Conrad*, 2: 294.

12 He published the first two with T. Fisher Unwin. *Almayer's Folly* was issued on 29 April 1895 with a first print run of two thousand copies, and it was sold at six shillings; *An Outcast of the Islands* was issued on 16 March 1896, with a first print run of three thousand copies, and it was sold at six shillings. *The Nigger of the Narcissus* was published by William Heinemann first in a limited edition pamphlet in 1897 (likely to protect copyright) and then issued on 2 December 1897, with a print run of fifteen hundred copies, and the price was six shillings. See Thomas J. Wise, *A Bibliography of the Writings of Joseph Conrad*, 5–10.

13 The volume consisted of five stories. Their places of first publication were: 'Karain' in *Blackwood's Magazine* (1897); 'The Idiots' in *Savoy* (1896); 'An Outpost of Progress' in *Cosmopolis* (1897); 'The Return' (not previously published); and 'The Lagoon' in *Cornhill* (1897) (Wise, *A Bibliography of the Writings of Joseph Conrad*, 16).

14 His article on Daudet appeared in the *Outlook* on 9 April 1898 and 'Tales of the Sea' was published in the 4 June 1898 edition of the *Outlook*. 'An Observer in Malaya' was published in the *Academy* on 23 April 1898 (Wise, *A Bibliography of the Writings of Joseph Conrad*, 106–7).

15 Ford Madox Heuffer changed his name to Ford Madox Ford in 1919. I will follow convention and refer to him as Ford Madox Ford.

16 Details of Blackwood's arrangements with Conrad can be found in the exchange of letters between Conrad and William Blackwood III that took place on 14 December and 18 December 1900. See William Blackburn, ed., *Joseph Conrad: Letters to William Blackwood and David S. Meldrum*, 119, 121. David Finkelstein, in *The House of Blackwood*, also discusses Conrad's relations with Blackwood and Pinker's role in them. See especially 145–9.

17 Meyers, *Joseph Conrad: A Biography*, 203.

18 Karl, *The Collected Letters of Joseph Conrad*, 2: 11.

19 Edward Garnett, ed., *Letters from Joseph Conrad: 1895–1924*, 69.

20 Karl, *The Collected Letters of Joseph Conrad*, 2: 295.

21 Conrad described 'Lord Jim' in a 14 February letter to William Blackwood as a 'story ... half-written or one-third written (10,000 words) which is intended for the volume' (Karl, *The Collected Letters of Joseph Conrad*, 2: 166). It was eventually to grow into a novel, thus causing Conrad and Blackwood to renegotiate their contract for this volume of stories.

22 Karl, *The Collected Letters of Joseph Conrad*, 2: 169–70.

23 Karl, *The Collected Letters of Joseph Conrad*, 2: 190.

24 Conrad had broached the subject of a second volume of short stories in a letter to Meldrum on 14 February 1899. Meldrum replied to Conrad's

overture positively on 27 February, saying that he should be 'glad to have them for Maga.' The contract that Conrad returned to him on 31 July is evidently the formalizing of Conrad's informal offer and Meldrum's equally informal acceptance. See Blackburn, *Joseph Conrad: Letters to William Blackwood and David S. Meldrum*, 56–7.

25 Karl, *The Collected Letters of Joseph Conrad*, 2: 237.

26 Karl, *The Collected Letters of Joseph Conrad*, 2: 271–3.

27 The details surrounding the renegotiations of these contracts may be found in Conrad's correspondence with Blackwood. See Blackburn, *Joseph Conrad: Letters to William Blackwood and David S. Meldrum*, 93–103.

28 Karl, *The Collected Letters of Joseph Conrad*, 2: 304.

29 Karl, *The Collected Letters of Joseph Conrad*, 2: 318.

30 The *Pall Mall Magazine* was founded in 1893 by the American William Waldorf Astor. Its target audience was the upper middle class, and its first editors were Lord Frederick Hamilton and Sir Douglas Straight. Despite the fact that many prominent writers appeared in *PMM*, including Rider Haggard and Robert Louis Stevenson, Conrad, and others in his circle, rated it less highly than *Blackwood's Magazine*.

31 Karl, *The Collected Letters of Joseph Conrad*, 2: 318.

32 Karl, *The Collected Letters of Joseph Conrad*, 2: 70–1.

33 For instance, Conrad sold the copyright of *Almayer's Folly* outright to Fisher Unwin for £20 and the French translation rights. His second novel, *An Outcast of the Islands*, was also sold to Unwin, but this time he retained the copyright, settling for '12 ½% royalty and £50, plus half serial and American rights.' (Karl, *Joseph Conrad: The Three Lives*, 354). His third book, *Nigger of the Narcissus*, was serialized in the *New Review* and then published in volume form by Heinemann. Conrad says to Ted Sanderson that he would ask Sydney Pawling, Heinemann's editor, for '£100 for the serial and book rights,' from which I infer that he sold them the copyrights for those particular publishing venues. (See Karl, *The Collected Letters of Joseph Conrad*, 1: 319.) It is not clear in the letters if he got that amount, but he does say in a later letter that Pawling gave him a 15 per cent royalty progressing to a 20 per cent royalty depending on sales with the translation rights. (See Karl, *The Collected Letters of Joseph Conrad*, 1: 432.)

34 Karl, *The Collected Letters of Joseph Conrad*, 2: 376–7.

35 Karl, *The Collected Letters of Joseph Conrad*, 2: 381.

36 Karl, *The Collected Letters of Joseph Conrad*, 2: 382–3.

37 Karl, *The Collected Letters of Joseph Conrad*, 2: 385.

38 Karl, *The Collected Letters of Joseph Conrad*, 2: 455.

39 See Karl's account of this in his biography, *Joseph Conrad: The Three Lives*, especially 518–19.

40 Karl, *Joseph Conrad: The Three Lives*, 526.
41 This phrase occurs in a letter Conrad wrote to Edward Garnett on
    7 June 1895. See Garnett, *Letters from Joseph Conrad: 1895–1924*, 37.
42 Karl, *The Collected Letters of Joseph Conrad*, 2: 370.
43 Karl, *The Collected Letters of Joseph Conrad*, 2: 370.
44 Karl, *The Collected Letters of Joseph Conrad*, 3: 464.
45 Karl, *The Collected Letters of Joseph Conrad*, 4: 92. The letter is written on
    Pinker's letterhead and it appears that Conrad had written it in Pinker's
    office, where he had hoped to meet Pinker, who was not in. A letter to John
    Galsworthy later in the week outlines the circumstances of this letter. See
    Karl, *The Collected Letters of Joseph Conrad*, 3: 93.
46 Karl, *The Collected Letters of Joseph Conrad*, 4: xxxi.
47 McDonald, *British Literary Culture and Publishing Practice 1880–1914*, 24.
48 McDonald, *British Literary Culture and Publishing Practice 1880–1914*, 23–4.
49 Karl, *The Collected Letters of Joseph Conrad*, 2: 368.
50 Karl, *The Collected Letters of Joseph* Conrad, 3: 112.
51 Conrad notes to Pinker in a 22 October 1905 letter of complaint that the
    Standard has edited the article he wrote for them, that 'it has been *asked for*
    3 times and that they were at liberty to decline it' (Karl, *The Collected Letters of
    Joseph Conrad*, 3: 291). This suggests that Pinker's message to the literary
    community that Conrad was willing to publish his work in mainstream
    organs like the *Standard* had been effective.
52 Conrad says this in a 3 March 1900 letter to R.B. Cunninghame-Graham
    (Karl, *The Collected Letters of Joseph Conrad*, 2: 254).
53 Karl, *The Collected Letters of Joseph Conrad*, 2: 457. Ironically, Conrad offered Pinker
    a photograph of himself to hang in his office, writing to him in November of
    1908, 'herewith the photograph of which I spoke. If you don't like it throw it on
    the fire, but I think it is more characteristic of me than the horrible faked portrait
    over your office-mantelpiece' (Karl, *The Collected Letters of Joseph Conrad*, 4: 152).
54 Karl, *Joseph Conrad: The Three Lives*, 720.
55 Karl, *The Collected Letters of Joseph Conrad*, 4: 110.
56 Quoted in Karl, *Joseph Conrad: The Three Lives*, 3.
57 Karl, *Joseph Conrad: The Three Lives*, 853.
58 Karl, *The Collected Letters of Joseph Conrad*, 4: 334.
59 Karl, *The Collected Letters of Joseph Conrad*, 4: 321n1.
60 Karl, *Joseph Conrad: The Three Lives*, 680.
61 Karl, *The Collected Letters of Joseph Conrad*, 4: 334.
62 Karl, *The Collected Letters of Joseph Conrad*, 5: 40.
63 Karl, *The Collected Letters of Joseph Conrad*, 2: 387.
64 Karl, *The Collected Letters of Joseph Conrad*, 3: 154.

65 Joseph Conrad, *The Niger of the 'Narcissus'/Typhoon and Other Stories*, 13.

66 Jesse Matz provides a compelling account of Conrad's impressionist style and its relation to literary modernism in his important study *Literary Impressionism and Modernist Aesthetics*.

67 Joseph Conrad, Heart of Darkness, 18.

68 Kevin J.H. Dettmar and Stephen Watt, eds., *Marketing Modernisms*, 3.

69 Wexler, *Who Paid for Modernism?* xii.

70 McDonald's *British Literary Culture and Publishing Practice 1880–1914* provides an excellent account of the way in which Conrad negotiated this difficult middle ground in the early years of his career. See especially 22–32.

71 Karl, *The Collected Letters of Joseph Conrad*, 2: 371.

72 Ian Willison, Warwick Gould, and Warren Chernaik, eds., *Modernist Writers and the Marketplace*, xiv. It is interesting to note that even Pound eventually employed a literary agent, using Curtis Brown. W.B. Yeats was one of the few modernists to employ A.P. Watt.

73 Karl, *Joseph Conrad: The Three Lives*, 526.

74 Much discussion has taken place about Pound's and Beach's respective roles. Reassessments of their actions have also formed part of the recent surge in materialist critiques of the traditional account of modernism. For a study outlining the conventional view of Pound, see Hugh Kenner, *The Pound Era*. For a study outlining the traditional view of Beach, see Shari Benstock, *Women of the Left Bank*. For a more recent account of the third-party role played by figures such as Pound, see Lawrence Rainey, 'The Price of Modernism: Reconsidering the Publication of *The Waste Land*.'

75 Paul Delany, *Literature, Money and the Market*, 147.

76 Delany, *Literature, Money and the Market*, 125.

77 Lawrence Rainey, *Institutions of Modernism*, 74.

78 Delany does discuss literary agents, and Pinker specifically, briefly in his book, but he does not accord the same sort of status to Pinker and other agents that I believe is warranted.

79 Karl, *The Collected Letters of Joseph Conrad*, 5: 619–20.

80 Jocelyn Baines, *Joseph Conrad*, 427.

81 Although both Frederick Karl and Jeffrey Meyers treat Pinker's role more fully in their later biographies of Conrad, they, too, tend to dismiss Pinker's literary abilities, focusing more on the friendship and the business relations.

82 Wexler, *Who Paid for Modernism?* xxi.

83 Wexler's argument about the Flaubertian concept of an elite readership, which, as she points out, is also articulated by Bourdieu, is compelling. See especially xvii–xxi. She discusses Pinker's role more fully than previous critics, though she does not go as far in her discussion as I do in this chapter.

Conclusion

1 This is from a notice in the January 1881 *Publishers' Circular,* 44.1040 (January 1881): 6.
2 Michael Joseph, in *The Commercial Side of Literature,* notes that by 1925 some agents were making as many as twenty-five different sales for one piece of literature. Included among the sales were rights to playing-card and cigarette-packet pictures. See 92–3.
3 David Finkelstein, *The House of Blackwood,* 133–4. Finkelstein's article 'Literature, Propaganda, and the First World War' goes into greater detail on this topic.
4 Finkelstein, *The House of Blackwood,* 134.
5 Michael North, *Reading 1922,* v. To be fair to North, his project in this book is to look more broadly at the literature and culture of 1922, but his comment about the importance of the year 1922 to modernist studies is nonetheless widely embraced by scholars of the field.
6 North points out that 1922–3 was also a significant time frame for American modernists, with important works by Willa Cather and Jean Toomer as well as Stevens and Williams all being published.
7 This is a point made by several important modernist scholars, including Hugh Kenner in *The Pound Era,* Michael Levenson in *A Genealogy of Modernism,* and Sanford Schwartz in *The Matrix of Modernism.* This viewpoint has more recently been contested by, among others, Michael North, who argues for a broader definition of modernism that would 'shift the analytical emphasis from the production to the reception of literary modernism' (*Reading 1922,* 30). What remains constant, however, is the sense that 1922 was a watershed year.
8 Lawrence Rainey relates the publishing history of *The Waste Land* in 'The Price of Modernism: Reconsidering the Publication of *The Waste Land.*' He later revised and incorporated this article as chapter 3 in his *Institutions of Modernism.*
9 This comment comes from an unpublished letter Eliot wrote to Aldington that is quoted in the 'Introduction' to Kevin Dettmar and Stephen Watt, eds., *Marketing Modernisms,* 8.
10 Paul Delany, *Literature, Money and the* Market, 154.
11 A.D., 'An Interview with Mr. J.B. Pinker,' 9.
12 A.D., 'An Interview with Mr. J.B. Pinker,' 10.
13 In fact, J.B. Pinker's widow sold the estate that she had purchased shortly after his death as well as all her investments in an attempt to pay off the debts that the firm had incurred through her sons' mismanagement. Even with this sacrifice, the firm was unable to repay all its debts.
14 William Heinemann, 'The Middleman As Viewed by a Publisher.'

Works Cited

Archives

I quote throughout this book from archival materials – letters and contracts – that may be found in one of four archives. Rather than listing each item individually in the Works Cited, I have chosen to indicate in the endnote the archive in which individual items may be found. I list here the names of these archives.

J.B. Pinker Collection, The McCormick Library of Special Collections, Northwestern University Library, Evanston, Illinois (cited in the notes as J.B. Pinker Papers, Northwestern)

The Berg Collection of English and American Literature, The New York Public Library, Aster, Lennox and Tilden Foundations (cited in the notes as Berg Collection)

A.P. Watt and Company Records, Manuscripts Department, Library of the University of North Carolina at Chapel Hill (cited in the notes as A.P. Watt Records, Chapel Hill)

The Papers of Edith OE. Somerville and Martin Ross, Trinity College Library, Dublin (Cited in the notes as Somerville & Ross Papers, Trinity College Library, Dublin)

Printed Sources

A.D. 'An Interview with Mr. J.B. Pinker.' *Bookman* 14.79 (April 1898): 9–10.
'Agents – A.P. Watt.' In *The Literary Yearbook and Bookman's Directory*, ed. Herbert Morrah, 119. London: George Allen, 1901.
'Agents – James B. Pinker.' In *The Literary Yearbook and Bookman's Directory*, ed. Herbert Morrah, 118. London: George Allen, 1901.

Altick, Richard. *The English Common Reader: A Social History of the Mass Reading Public.* 2nd edition. Columbus: Ohio State University Press, 1998.

– 'From Aldine to Everyman: Cheap Reprint Series of the English Classics, 1830–1906.' In *Writers, Readers, and Occasions: Selected Essays on Victorian Literature and Life,* ed. Richard Altick. Columbus: Ohio State University Press, 1989.

Anderson, Nancy Fix. *Woman against Woman in Victorian England: A Life of Eliza Lynn Linton.* Bloomington: Indiana University Press, 1987.

Anderson, R.D. *Education and Opportunity in Victorian Scotland: Schools and Universities.* Oxford: Clarendon Press, 1983.

Ardis, Ann L. *New Women, New Novels: Feminism and Early Modernism.* New Brunswick, NJ: Rutgers University Press, 1990.

'Authors' Assistants: British Agents. *Literary Year-Book* (1914): 502–9.

Baines, Jocelyn. *Joseph Conrad.* London: Weidenfeld and Nicolson, 1960.

Beetham, Margaret. *A Magazine of Her Own? Domesticity and Desire in the Woman's Magazine, 1800–1914.* London: Routledge, 1996.

Belloc Lowndes, Marie. 'The Author's Agent: Is He the "Fifth Wheel on the Literary Coach"?' *Author* 42.4 (Summer 1932): 96.

Bence-Jones, A.B. 'Lord Brougham on Literary Agents.' *Athenaeum* no. 3020 (13 March 1897): 348.

Bennett, Arnold. *The Truth about an Author.* London: Methuen, 1914.

Bennett, Bryan, and Anthony Hamilton. *Edward Arnold: 100 Years of Publishing.* London: Edward Arnold, 1990.

Benstock, Shari. *Women of the Left Bank.* Austin: University of Texas Press, 1986.

Besant, Walter. 'Address to the Annual Meeting of the Society, Thursday, December 17, 1892.' Qtd in 'The English Society.' *Bulletin of the League of Authors* (New York) 2.2 (May 1914): 8.

– *The Art of Fiction.* London: Chatto and Windus, 1902.

– 'The Author' *Author* 1.1 (15 May 1890): 1.

– 'The Hardships of Publishing.' *Athenaeum* no. 3398 (10 December 1892): 819.

– 'Dear Mr. Watt.' In *Letters to A.P. Watt,* 4. London: A.P. Watt & Son, 1893.

– 'Dear Mr. Watt.' In *Letters to A.P. Watt,* 6. London: A.P. Watt & Son, 1894.

– 'The Literary Agent.' *Author* 4.1 (1 June 1893): 240.

– *The Pen and the Book.* London: Thomas Burleigh, 1899.

Blackburn, William, ed. *Joseph Conrad: Letters to William Blackwood and David S. Meldrum.* Durham, NC: Duke University Press, 1958.

Blackett, Spencer C. 'The Middleman in Publishing.' *Athenaeum* no. 3447 (18 November 1893): 699.

Bonham-Carter, Victor. *Authors by Profession.* 2 vols. London: Society of Authors, 1978.

The Bookman: An Illustrated Literary Journal (New York). Vol. 9 (March–August 1899): 206.

'"*The Bookman*" Gallery: Mr. and Mrs. Williamson.' *Bookman* (December 1906): 114–115.

Boulton, James T., and Andrew Robertson, eds. *The Letters of D.H. Lawrence*. 4 vols. Cambridge: Cambridge University Press, 1977–87.

Bourdieu, Pierre. *Distinction* London: Routledge & Kegan Paul, 1984.

– *The Field of Cultural Production*. Ed. and intro. Randal Johnson. New York: Columbia University Press, 1993.

– 'The Forms of Capital.' Trans. Richard Nice. In *Handbook of Theory and Research for the Sociology of Education*, ed. John G. Richardson, 241–58. New York: Greenwood Press, 1986.

– *In Other Words: Essays towards a Reflexive Sociology*. Trans. Matthew Adamson. Stanford: Stanford University Press, 1990.

– *Outline of a Theory of Practice*. Trans. Richard Nice. Cambridge: Cambridge University Press, 1977.

Boyd, Ernest. *Ireland's Literary Renaissance*. New York: Barnes and Noble, 1968.

Broomfield, Andrea L. 'Much More than an AntiFeminist: Eliza Lynn Linton's Contribution to the Rise of Victorian Popular Journalism.' *Victorian Literature and Culture* 29.2 (September 2001): 267–83.

Brown, Albert Curtis. '"The Commercialisation of Literature" and the Literary Agent.' *Fortnightly Review* 80 (1 August 1906): 355–63.

– *Contacts*. New York: Harper & Brothers, 1935.

Cahalan, James H. *Double Visions*. Syracuse: Syracuse University Press, 1999.

Carabine, Keith. 'Conrad, Pinker, and *Under Western Eyes: A Novel*.' *Conradian* 10.2 (November 1985): 144–53.

Casey, Ellen Miller. 'Edging Women Out?: Reviews of Women Novelists in the *Athenaeum*.' *Victorian Studies* 39.2 (Winter 1996): 151–72.

Chitty, Susan. *The Beast and the Monk*. London: Hodder and Stoughton, 1974.

Colby, Vineta. *The Singular Anomaly: Women Novelists of the Nineteenth Century*. New York: New York University Press, 1970.

Collis, Maurice. *Somerville and Ross*. London: Faber and Faber, 1968.

The Compact Edition of the Oxford English Dictionary. Oxford: Oxford University Press, 1971.

Conrad, Jessie. *Joseph Conrad and His Circle*. New York: E.P. Dutton and Co., 1935.

Conrad, Joseph. *Heart of Darkness*. London: Penguin Books, 1995.

– *The Nigger of the 'Narcissus'/Typhoon and Other Stories*. London: Penguin Books, 1987.

Courtney, Janet E. 'A Novelist of the 'Nineties' *Fortnightly Review* no. 137 (1932): 230–41.

Cowert, Claire. Denelle. 'Edith Somerville and Martin Ross.' In *Dictionary of Literary Biography*, vol. 135, 335–46. Detroit: Gale Research, 1994.

Cronin, John. *Somerville and Ross*. Lewisburg: Bucknell University Press, 1972.

Cross, Nigel. *The Common Writer*. Cambridge: Cambridge University Press, 1985.

Darnton, Robert. 'What Is the History of Books?' In *The Kiss of Lamourette*, 107–35. London: Faber and Faber, 1990.

Dalgarno, Emily. 'Conrad, Pinker and the Writing of *The Secret Agent*.' *Conradiana*. 9 (1977): 47–58.

David, Deirdre. *Intellectual Women and Victorian Patriarchy*. London: Macmillan, 1987.

'Death of Mr. J.B. Pinker.' *The Times* (London). 10 February 1922: 10.

'Deaths – Watt' *The Times* (London). 4 November 1914: 1.

Delany, Paul. *Literature, Money and the Market*. London: Palgrave, 2002.

Dent, J.M. *The House of Dent 1888–1938*. London: J.M. Dent and Sons, 1938.

Dettmar, Kevin J.H., and Stephen Watt, eds. *Marketing Modernisms*. Ann Arbor: University of Michigan Press, 1996.

Edel, Leon. *Henry James*. Vol. 4, New York: Lippincott, 1969.

Eisenstein, Elizabeth. *The Printing Press as an Agent of Change: Communications and Cultural Transformations in Early-Modern Europe*. Cambridge: Cambridge University Press, 1980.

Eliot, Simon. *Some Patterns and Trends in British Publishing 1880–1919*. London: Occasional Papers of Bibliographical Society no. 8 (1994).

Ellmann, Richard. *James Joyce*. New York: Oxford University Press, 1959.

Fahenstock, Jeanne. 'Geraldine Jewsbury: The Power of the Publisher's Reader.' *Nineteenth-Century Fiction* 28.3 (1973): 253–72.

Farmer, David. 'The Bibliographical Potential of a 20th Century Literary Agent's Archives: The Pinker Papers.' *Library Chronicle of the University of Texas* 21 (1968): 27–35.

Feather, John. *A History of British Publishing*. London: Croom Helm, 1988.

– *Publishing, Piracy and Politics: An Historical Study of Copyright in Britain*. London: Mansell, 1994.

– 'Technology and the Book in the Nineteenth Century.' *Critical Survey* 2, (1990): 5–13.

Federico, Annette R. '"Marie Corelli: Aestheticism in Suburbia."' In *Women and British Aestheticism*, ed. Talia Schaffer and Kathy Alexis Psomidades, 81–98. Charlottesville: University Press ot Virginia, 1999.

Feltes, N.N. *Literary Capital and the Late Victorian Novel*. Madison: University of Wisconsin Press, 1993.

Finkelstein, David. *The House of Blackwood*. State College: Pennsylvania State University Press, 2002.

– 'Literature, Propaganda and the First World War: The Case of *Blackwood's Magazine*.' In *Grub Street and the Ivory Tower: Essays on the Relations between Literary Journalism and Literary Scholarship*, Oxford: Oxford University Press, 1998.

Firth, John. 'James Pinker to James Joyce, 1915–1920.' *Studies in Bibliography: Papers of the Bibliographical Society of the University of Virginia* 21 (1968): 204–24.

Ford, Ford Madox. *Return to Yesterday.* London: Liveright, 1932.

F.W. 'An Interview with Mr. A.P. Watt.' *Bookman* 3.13 (October 1892): 20–2.

Gagnier, Regenia. *Idylls of the Marketplace: Oscar Wilde and the Victorian Public.* Stanford: Stanford University Press, 1986.

Gallagher, Catherine. *Nobody's Story: The Vanishing Acts of Women Writers in the Marketplace 1670–1820.* Berkeley: University of California Press, 1994.

Garnett, Edward, ed., with intro. and notes. *Letters from Joseph Conrad: 1895–1924.* Indianapolis: Bobbs-Merrill Company, 1928.

Gilbert, Sandra M., and Susan Gubar. *The Madwoman in the Attic: The Woman Writer and the Nineteenth-Century Literary Imagination.* New Haven: Yale University Press, 1979.

Gilbert, Stuart, ed. *Letters of James Joyce.* Vol. 1. New York: Viking Press, 1957.

Gillies, Mary Ann. 'The Literary Agent and the Sequel.' In *Part Two: Reflections on the Sequel*, ed. Paul Budra and Betty A. Schellenberg, 131–43. Toronto: University of Toronto Press, 1998.

Goldgar, Anne. *Impolite Learning.* New Haven: Yale University Press, 1995.

Griest, Guinevere L. *Mudie's Circulating Library and the Victorian Novel.* Bloomington: Indiana University Press, 1970.

Gwynn, Stephen. 'Sir Richard Calmady.' *New-Liberal Review* 2 (1901–2): 480–8.

Heinemann, William. 'The Middleman As Viewed by a Publisher.' *Athenaeum* no. 3446 (11 November 1893): 663.

– 'The Hardships of Publishing.' *Athenaeum* no. 3397 (3 December 1892): 779–80.

Hepburn, James. *The Author's Empty Purse and the Rise of the Literary Agent.* London: Oxford University Press, 1968.

Hepburn, James, ed. *Letters of Arnold Bennett.* Vol. 1. *Letters to J.B. Pinker.* London: Oxford University Press, 1966.

Higgins, D.S. *Rider Haggard: The Great Storyteller.* London: Cassell, 1981.

Hills, Richard L. *Papermaking in Britain, 1488–1988.* London: Athlone Press, 1988.

Holt, Henry. 'The Commercialization of Literature.' *Atlantic Monthly* 96.5 (November 1905): 576–600.

Howsam, Leslie. *Kegan Paul: A Victorian Imprint.* London: Kegan Paul, 1999.

Jay, Elisabeth. *Mrs. Oliphant: A Fiction to Herself.* Oxford: Clarendon Press, 1995.

Johanningsmeier, Charles. *Fiction and the American Literary Marketplace.* Cambridge: Cambridge University Press, 1997.

Jordan, J. O., and Robert L. Patten, eds. *Literature in the Marketplace.* Cambridge: Cambridge University Press, 1995.

Jordan, Mary Nance. *George MacDonald, a Bibliographical Catalog and Record.* Fairfax, Va: Wheaton College, 1984.

Joseph, Michael. *The Commercial Sale of Literature.* London: Hutchinson & Co., 1925.

Kaplan, Benjamin. *An Unhurried View of Copyright.* New York: Columbia University Press, 1967.

Karl, Frederick R. 'Conrad and Pinker: Some Aspects of the Correspondence.' *Journal of Modern Literature* 5 (1976): 59–78.

– *Joseph Conrad: The Three Lives.* New York: Farrar, Straus and Giroux, 1979.

Karl, Frederick R., gen. ed. *The Collected Letters of Joseph Conrad.* 5 vols. Cambridge: Cambridge University Press, 1983–96.

Keating, Peter. *The Haunted Study.* London: Secker and Warburg, 1989.

Kenner, Hugh. *The Pound Era.* Berkeley: University of California Press, 1973.

Kernan, Alvin. *Printing Technology, Letters and Samuel Johnson.* Princeton: Princeton University Press, 1987.

Kiberd, Declan. *Inventing Ireland.* Cambridge, Mass.: Harvard University Press, 1995.

Kingsford, R.J.L. *The Publishers' Association 1896–1945.* Cambridge: Cambridge University Press, 1970.

Law, Graham. *Serializing Fiction in the Victorian Press.* London: Palgrave, 2000.

Levenson, Michael. *A Genealogy of Modernism.* Cambridge: Cambridge University Press, 1984.

Lewis, Gifford. *Somerville and Ross: The World of the Irish R.M.* New York: Viking, 1985.

Lewis, Gifford, ed. *The Selected Letters of Somerville and Ross.* London: Faber and Faber, 1989.

'Literary Agents.' *Author* 2.11 (1892): 348.

'Literary Agents.' *Author* 3.8 (1893): 267.

'Literary Agents.' *Author* 9.10 (10 March 1899): 231–3.

The Literary Yearbook and Bookman's Directory. Ed. Herbert Morrah. London: George Allen, 1901.

Lundberg, Patricia Lorimer. *'An Inward Necessity': The Writer's Life of Lucas Malet.* New York: Peter Lang, 2003.

MacDonald, Greville. *George MacDonald and His Wife.* New York: Dial Press, 1923.

McDonald, Peter D. *British Literary Culture and Publishing Practice 1880–1914.* Cambridge: Cambridge University Press, 1997.

Masters, Brian. *Now Barabbas Was a Rotter.* London: Hamish Hamilton, 1978.

Matthiessen, F.O., and Kenneth B. Murdock. *The Notebooks of Henry James.* New York: Oxford University Press, 1947.

Matz, Jesse. *Literary Impressionism and Modernist Aesthetics.* Cambridge: Cambridge University Press, 2001.

Meem, Deborah T. 'Eliza Lynn Linton and the Rise of Lesbian Consciousness.' *Journal of the History of Sexuality* 7 (1997): 537–60.

Menand, Louis. *Discovering Modernism.* New York: Oxford University Press, 1987.

Mermin, Dorothy. *Godiva's Ride.* Bloomington: Indiana University Press, 1993.

Meyers, Jeffrey. *Joseph Conrad: A Biography.* New York: Charles Scribner's Sons, 1991.

Miller, Anita. *Arnold Bennett: An Annotated Bibliography 1887–1932.* London: Garland, 1977.

Miller, Jane Eldridge. *Rebel Women: Feminism, Modernism, and the Victorian Novel.* London: Virago, 1994.

Morgan, Charles. *The House of Macmillan 1843–1943.* London: Macmillan, 1943.

Najder, Zdzislaw. *Joseph Conrad.* New Brunswick, NJ: Rutgers University Press, 1983.

Nelson, Carolyn Christensen. *British Women Fiction Writers of the 1890s.* New York: Twayne Publishers, 1996.

Nicoll, W. Robertson. 'A.P. Watt: The Great Napoleon of the Realms of Print.' *British Weekly.* 12 November 1914: 127.

– 'London Letter.' *Bookman* (American version) 1.4 (February 1895–July 1895): 249–51.

Nicolson, Nigel, and Joanne Trautmann, eds. *The Letters of Virginia Woolf.* Vol. 6. 1936–1941. New York: Harcourt Brace Jovanovich, 1980.

North, Michael. *Reading 1922.* Oxford: Oxford University Press, 1999.

Nowell-Smith, Simon. *House of Cassell, 1848–1958.* London: Cassell, 1958.

Oldham, C.E. 'Two Novelists on One Theme.' *New House Magazine: A Monthly Review for Churchmen and Churchwomen* 7 (1892): 161–9.

Parkes, Adam. *Modernism and the Theater of Censorship.* New York: Oxford University Press, 1996.

Patten, Robert. *Dickens and His Publishers.* Santa Cruz: Dickens Project, 1991.

– 'The People Have Set Literature Free.' *Review* 9 (1987): 1–34.

Peters, Catherine. *The King of Inventors: A Life of Wilkie Collins.* London: Secker and Warburg, 1991.

Pickett, Lyn. *The 'Improper' Feminine: The Women's Sensation Novel and the New Woman Writing.* London: Routledge, 1992.

Powell, Violet. *Irish Cousins.* London: Heinemann, 1970.

Publishers' Circular 44.1040 (January 1881).

Purdy, Richard Little, and Micheal Millgate, eds. *The Collected Letters of Thomas Hardy.* Vols 1 and 7. Oxford: Clarendon Press, 1988.

Radway, Janice. *Books and Reading in the Age of Mass Production: The Adam Helms Lecture.* Stockholm: Stockholm University Library, 1996.

– *A Feeling for Books: The Book-of-the-Month Club, Literary Taste, and a Middle-Class Desire.* Chapel Hill: University of North Carolina Press, 1997.

Rainey, Lawrence. *Institutions of Modernism: Literary Elites and Public Culture.* New Haven: Yale University Press, 1998.

– 'The Price of Modernism: Reconsidering the Publication of *The Waste Land.*' *Yale Review* 78.2 (1989): 279–300.

Reader, W.J. *Professional Men: The Rise of the Professional Classes in Nineteenth-Century England.* London: Weidenfeld and Nicolson, 1966.

'Recent Novels [*The Wages of Sin*].' *Spectator* 66 (28 February 1891): 311.

Reis, Richard H. *George MacDonald.* New York: Twayne, 1972.

Ricketts, Harry. *The Unforgiving Minute: A Life of Rudyard Kipling.* London: Chatto & Windus, 1999.

Robb, David. *George MacDonald.* Edinburgh: Scottish Academic Press, 1987.

Robinson, Hilary. *Somerville and Ross: A Critical Appreciation.* New York: St Martin's Press, 1980.

Rogers, Pat. *Grub Street: Studies in a Sub-Culture.* London: Methuen, 1972.

Rose, Jonathan. *The Intellectual Life of the British Working Classes.* New Haven: Yale University Press, 2001.

Rose, Mark. *Authors and Owners: The Invention of Copyright.* Cambridge, Mass.: Harvard University Press, 1993.

Rubinstein, Hilary. 'A.P. Watt: The First Hundred Years' *Bookseller* (3 May 1975): 2354–8.

Sadler, Glenn Edward, ed. *An Expression of Character: The Letters of George MacDonald.* Grand Rapids: William B. Eerdmans Publishing Company, 1994.

Salmonson, Jessica Amanda. 'Marie Corelli and Her Occult Tales.' http://www.violetbooks.com/corelli.html.

Saunders, David. *Authorship and Copyright.* London: Routledge, 1992.

Savage, Raymond. 'The Authors' Agent.' *Author* 43.1 (Autumn 1932): 6–10.

Schaffer, Talia. 'Connoisseurship and Concealment in *Sir Richard Calmady*: Lucas Malet's Strategic Aestheticism.' In *Women and British Aestheticism,* ed. Talia Schaffer and Kathy Alexis Psomiades, 44–61. Charlottesville: University Press of Virginia, 1999.

'Malet the Obscure.' In *The Forgotten Female Aesthetes,* 197–243. Charlottesville: University Press of Virginia, 2000.

Schaffer, Talia, and Kathy Alexis Psomiades, eds. *Women and British Aestheticism.* Charlottesville: University Press of Virginia, 1999.

Schwartz, Sanford. '*The Matrix of Modernism.*' Princeton: Princeton University Press, 1985.

Scott, Bonnie Kime, ed. *Selected Letters of Rebecca West.* New Haven: Yale University Press, 2000.

Seville, Catherine. *Literary Copyright Reform in Early Victorian England.* Cambridge: Cambridge University Press, 1999.

Seymour-Smith, Martin. *Rudyard Kipling.* London: Queen Anne Press, 1989.

Shillingsburg, Peter. *Pegasus in Harness.* Charlottesville: University Press of Virginia, 1992.

Silver, Brenda. *Virginia Woolf: Icon.* Chicago: University of Chicago Press, 1999.

Sinclair, May. 'Letter to the Editor' *Author* 22.3 (October 1911–July 1912): 80–1.

Skelton, Matthew. 'H.G. Wells, Kipps, and the House of Macmillan.' *Publishing History* 49 (2001): 49–81.

Slocum, John J., and Herbert Cahoon. *A Bibliography of James Joyce.* New Haven: Yale University Press, 1953.

Somerville, E. OE., and Martin Ross 'Étaples.' *Happy Days.* London: Longmans, Green and Co, 1946. 65–76.

– *Irish Memories.* London: Longmans, Green and Co., 1918.

Srebrnik, Patricia Thomas. *Alexander Strahan: Victorian Publisher.* Ann Arbor: University of Michigan Press, 1986.

– 'Lucas Malet' In *Dictionary of Literary Biography* no. 153, 177–85. Detroit: Gale Research, 1995.

– 'The Re-subjection of "Lucas Malet": Charles Kingsley's Daughter and the Response to Muscular Christianity.' In *Muscular Christianity: Embodying the Victorian Age,* ed. Donald E. Hall, 194–214. Cambridge: Cambridge University Press, 1995.

Stephens, W.B. *Education, Literacy and Society, 1830–1870: The Geography of Diversity in Provincial England.* Manchester: Manchester University Press, 1987.

Stetz, Margaret D. '*Keynotes*: A New Woman, Her Publisher, and Her Material.' *Studies in the Literary Imagination* 30.1 (1 March 1997): 89–106.

– 'Turning Points: "George Egerton" (Mary Chavelita Dunne Bright).' *Turn-of-the-Century Women* 1 (1984): 2–8.

Stuart, Mary. *The Education of the People: A History of Primary Education in England and Wales in the Nineteenth Century.* London: Routledge and Kegan Paul, 1967.

Stubbs, Patricia. *Women and Fiction: Feminism and the Novel 1880–1920.* New York: Barnes & Noble, 1979.

Sutherland, John. *Victorian Fiction: Writers, Publishers, Readers.* London: Macmillan, 1995.

Todd, Janet. *The Sign of Angellica: Women, Writing and Fiction, 1660–1800.* London: Virago, 1989.

'Trade Changes.' *Publishers' Circular* 39.926 (15 April 1876): 296.

'Trade Changes.' *Publishers' Circular* 44.1040 (18 January 1881): 6.

Triggs, Kathy. *The Stars and the Stillness: A Portrait of George MacDonald.* Cambridge: Lutterworth Press, 1986.

Tromp, Marlene, Pamela K. Gilbert, and Aeron Haynie. *Beyond Sensation: Mary Elizabeth Braddon in Context.* Albany: State University of New York Press, 2000.

Tuchman, Gaye, with Nina E. Fortin. *Edging Women Out: Victoria Novelists, Publishers, and Social Charge.* New Haven: Yale University Press, 1989.

Turner, John R. 'The Camelot Series, Everyman's Library, and Ernest Rhys.' *Publishing History* 31 (1992): 27–46.

United Kingdom. 54 Geo III c. 156.

– 5 & 6 Victoria c. 54.

Vandenberghe, Frederic. 'The Sociological Ambition of Pierre Bourdieu.' *Radical Philosophy* no. 113 (May/June 2002): 7–9.

van Thal, Herbert. *Eliza Lynn Linton.* London: George Allen and Unwin, 1979.

Vincent, David. *Literacy and Popular Culture: England 1750–1914.* Cambridge: Cambridge University Press, 1989.

Watt, A.P. 'To Authors' *Author* 1.11 (18 May 1891): 307.

– *Letters to A.P. Watt.* London: A.P. Watt & Son, 1893, 1894.

Watt, Ian. *Conrad in the Nineteenth Century.* Berkeley: University of California Press, 1979.

Waugh, Arthur. *A Hundred Years of Publishing, Being the Story of Chapman and Hall, Ltd.* London: Chapman & Hall, 1930.

Weekes, Ann Owens. *Irish Women Writers: An Uncharted Tradition.* Lexington: University Press of Kentucky, 1990.

West, James L., III. 'The Chace Act and Anglo-American Literary Relations.' *Studies in Bibliography* 45 (1992): 303–11.

Wexler, Joyce. *Who Paid for Modernism?* Fayetteville: University of Arkansas Press, 1997.

Whyte, Frederic. *William Heinemann: A Memoir.* London: Jonathan Cape, 1928.

Willison, Ian, Warwick Gould, and Warren Chernaik, eds. *Modernist Writers and the Marketplace.* London: Macmillan, 1996.

Wise, Thomas J. *A Bibliography of the Writings of Joseph Conrad.* London: Dawsons of Pall Mall, 1964. Rpt of 1921 edition printed by Richard Clay and Sons.

Wolff, Janet. *The Social Production of Art.* 2nd edition. New York: New York University Press, 1993.

Woodmansee, Martha, and Peter Jaszi. *The Construction of Authorship.* Durham, NC: Duke University Press, 1994.

Worthen, John. *D.H. Lawrence: The Life of an Outsider.* London: Allen Lane, 2005.

– 'Lawrence and the "Expensive Edition Business"' In *Modernist Writers and the Marketplace*, ed. Ian Willison et al., 105–23. London: Macmillan, 1996.

Index

Novalis, 41
Novel, 205n35

Oldham, C.E., 66
Oliphant, Margaret, 81, 83, 184n28, 200n94
Orczy, Baroness, 97, 206n49; and Pinker, J.B., 206n49; and Watt, A.P., 206n49
Outcast of the Islands, An. See Conrad, Joseph, works
Outlook, 152, 216n14
outside rights, 29, 52–4. *See also* dramatic rights; film rights; translation rights

Pall Mall Magazine, 87, 152, 204–5n34, 205n42, 217n30
paper duty, 12
Parker, Louis Napoleon, 73
Parkes, Adam, 208n71
patronage, 99, 161, 162–3
Patten, Robert L., 6, 9–11, 51, 174n13
Paul Faber, Surgeon. See MacDonald, George, works
Pearson's Magazine, 89, 91, 205n42
Peek, Hedley, 118–21, 120, 127
Penny Poets and Penny Novels, 182n56
periodical press, 8. *See also individual periodicals*
Peters, Catherine, 188n29
Phantastes. See MacDonald, George, works
Phillpotts, Eden, 89
Pickett, Lyn, 84, 176n31, 201n98
Pinker, Eric, 107, 209n96; and Conrad, Joseph, 137
Pinker, James Brand, 7–8, 35, 39, 52, 87–110; advertising, 91; agenting

approach, 90–2, 118–22, 134–5; and American magazines, 95; as author's agent, 92–3; and *Black and White*, 89, 91, 117; and *Blackwood's Magazine*, 144; *Bookman* interview, 90–2, 98, 99–100; and Chapman and Hall, 95; and Chatto and Windus, 94–5; and copyright protection, 92; and cultural capital, 93, 99, 108, 162; daughter of, 203n12; death, 165, 168–9; and Doran, G.H., 95; and Duckworth, 105; and editorial advice, 92; and Egerton, George, 97; and Eliot, T.S., 88; employment, 88–9; end of agency, 108; establishment as agent, 90; finances, 89; and *Fortnightly Review*, 153; and *Harper's Magazine*, 153; and Heinemann, 105; and Hunt, Violet, 89; image, 91–2; influence of, 88; and international copyright laws, 88; and James, Henry, 88, 89, 202n11; and Joyce, James, 88, 103–8, 162, 170, 202–3n11, 210n98; and Lewis, Wyndham, 170; and literary modernism, 88, 137, 158–64, 172; and literary property, 92; and Little, Brown and Company, 102; and Lowndes, Belloc, 89, 97; and Madox Ford, Ford, 88; and Mansfield, Katherine, 88, 97–8, 170; and Marbury, Elisabeth, 202n10; marriage, 88; and Marshall, John, 106; and McClure, S.S., 94; and Milne, A.A., 90; and *Mirror, The*, 153; and modernist writers, 99–108; and Murry, John Middleton, 88, 98; and Orczy, Baroness, 97; and outside rights, 92; and *Pall Mall Magazine*, 144; as patron, 99–103, 158, 161–4, 172;

STUDIES IN BOOK AND PRINT CULTURE

General Editor: Leslie Howsam

Dean Irvine, *Editing Modernity: Women and Little-Magazine Cultures in Canada, 1916–1956*

Janet Friskney, *New Canadian Library: The Ross-McClelland Years, 1952–1978*

Benjamin C. Withers, *The Illustrated Old English Hexateuch, Cotton Ms. Claudius B.iv: The Frontier of Seeing and Reading in Anglo-Saxon England*

Mary Ann Gillies, *The Professional Literary Agent in Britain, 1880–1920*